Arsenal to Armenia

Dennis Loze

Order this book online at www.trafford.com/08-0172
or email orders@trafford.com

Most Trafford titles are also available at major online book retailers.

© Copyright 2008 Dennis Loze.

All rights reserved. No part of this publication may be reproduced, stored in a retrieval system, or transmitted, in any form or by any means, electronic, mechanical, photocopying, recording, or otherwise, without the written prior permission of the author.

Note for Librarians: A cataloguing record for this book is available from Library and Archives Canada at www.collectionscanada.ca/amicus/index-e.html

Printed in Victoria, BC, Canada.

ISBN: 978-1-4251-7076-9

We at Trafford believe that it is the responsibility of us all, as both individuals and corporations, to make choices that are environmentally and socially sound. You, in turn, are supporting this responsible conduct each time you purchase a Trafford book, or make use of our publishing services. To find out how you are helping, please visit www.trafford.com/responsiblepublishing.html

Our mission is to efficiently provide the world's finest, most comprehensive book publishing service, enabling every author to experience success. To find out how to publish your book, your way, and have it available worldwide, visit us online at www.trafford.com/10510

www.trafford.com

North America & international
toll-free: 1 888 232 4444 (USA & Canada)
phone: 250 383 6864 ♦ fax: 250 383 6804 ♦ email: info@trafford.com

The United Kingdom & Europe
phone: +44 (0)1865 487 395 ♦ local rate: 0845 230 9601
facsimile: +44 (0)1865 481 507 ♦ email: info.uk@trafford.com

10 9 8 7 6 5 4 3 2

INTRODUCTION

Before you say "Oh! Not another book on Football", let me put your mind at ease, well partly at ease.

The aim of this book is to show you, the life of a sportsman involved in various sports, but then through his medical qualifications and sporting knowledge, finds himself in the world of professional football, here in England and overseas.

That person is me, starting with my working career in the Royal Air Force as a Physical Training Instructor, and representing the RAF in Rugby and Athletics, selected to represent Wales at Athletics, before moving into the medical profession as a specialist in Rehabilitation, followed by a conversion course to be a Member of the Chartered Society of Physiotherapy.

Using that, combined with coaching and teaching qualifications, I moved into sports medicine. All sounds good but with some massive personal problems, a trail of disasters, then a change in my life which started to put things right and bring about a 180 degree change of direction. This led to spending 5 years working with Mission East in Armenia.

This is not a kiss and tell about other people but of my life and involvement in sport.

Bill Shankley once said that football was more important than life, but was he right or wrong?

Dennis Loze

ACKNOWLEDGEMENTS

With thanks to my family for their love and forgiveness.
To Jane for her continued love, and her red pen on proof reading.
Also remembering, the children of Armenia.

Just two days after finishing the last few words of this book, Jane's body could no longer withstand the great demand put upon it. She died peacefully. The only part of the book that she failed to read and to proof read are the last two chapters, these I have left uncorrected, in her memory.

All profits of this book will be donated to the Macmillan Cancer Support in England and to the Oncology Dept. in Alcoy, Spain.

Chapter One

"In the beginning"
GENESIS 1:1

Every story has to have a beginning and an end. This story doesn't actually start at Arsenal and end in Armenia, but episodes that happened during those years had and still do have a great influence in my life.

You tend to think that you are equipped to deal with whatever life throws at you, good or bad, but on this particular day nothing of my past had prepared me for this.

Standing in a consultant's office in Victoria Hospital, Blackpool with Jane my wife, a hospital that both of us had previously worked in, and also where our daughter Morgana was born. We felt unthreatened in that environment until the words of the consultant hit me like a rocket pinning me back to the wall that I was leaning against. "Mrs. Loze, I am sorry to say that the lump we found is a malignant growth" The rest was just a haze, but over the next 20 years we were to hear those same words being repeated, not just once but four more times.

How do you cope with news like that?

A few years previous to that incident, I wouldn't know how, but something had happened to me a few months previously, which gave me the answer to that question.

Dennis Loze

Sport had been and still is a large part of my life and sometimes I think too much! "Are there areas that I would change?" The answer would be a resounding yes! That is why I am writing this book 'Arsenal to Armenia.'

What led me to Arsenal:-

ARSENAL FACTS

Founded: 1886
Professional: 1891

Former Names:
1886	Dial Square
1886-91	Royal Arsenal
1891-1914	Woolwich Arsenal
1914-	Arsenal

Club Nickname:
The Gunners

Previous Grounds:
1886	Plumstead Common
1887	Sportsman Ground
1887	Manor Ground
1890-93	Invicta Ground
1893-1913	Manor Ground
1913-2006	Highbury
2006-	Emirates Stadium

Ground Capacity:
38,500 (Highbury)

Pitch Measurements: (Highbury)
110yd x 73yd

Record Attendance:
73,295 v Sunderland, League Division 1, 9th March 1935

Lowest Attendance
4,554 v Leeds United Division 1, 5th May 1966

Arsenal to Armenia

Record Transfer Paid:
£13,000,000 for Sylvain Wiltord from Bordeaux Aug 2000

Record Transfer Received:
£23.5m for Nicholas Anelka from Real Madrid, August 1999

Most Appearances
David O'Leary 558 League, 772 in all competitions

League Scoring Record:
Ted Drake 42 Division 1, 1934-35

Most Goals Scored in all Competitions
188 Teirry Henri

Arsenal was formed in 1886 as Dial Square before becoming Royal Arsenal, Woolwich Arsenal and finally Arsenal. They began playing in South London but eventually moved to Highbury in 1913, then the spectacular Emirates Stadium in 2006. Arsenal holds the record for unbroken years in the top division having been there since 1919.

The legendary Herbert Chapman brought the glory years to North London during the 1930s when the Gunners won the league championship 5 times and the FA Cup twice and although the 1940s brought more trophies, their finest hour didn't come until 1971 when they became only the fourth team to win the League and FA Cup double.

It was only when Arsene Wenger arrived that they began to be a force to be reckoned with again as the late 70's and 80's brought a mixed bag of results and difficulties. They won the League and Cup double again, both in 1998 and 2002, and retained the championship in 2004.

Managers

1996-	Arsene Wenger
1995-96	Bruce Rioch
1986-95	George Graham
1984-85	Don Howe
1976-83	Terry Neill
1966-76	Bertie Mee
1962-66	Billy Wright

1958-62   George Swindon
1956-58   Jack Crayston
1947-56   Tom Whittaker
1934-47   George Allison
1925-34   Herbert Chapman
1919-25   Leslie Knighton
1908-15   George Morrell
1904-08   Phil Kelso
1899-04   Harry Bradshaw
1898-99   George Elcoat
1897-98   Tom Mitchell
1894-97   Sam Hollis

Honours
  Premier Division
      Champions
       1997-98
       2001-02
       2003-04
      Runners-up
       1998-99
       1999-00
       2000-01
       2002-03

  Division 1
      Champions
       1930-31
       1932-33
       1933-34
       1934-35
       1937-38
       1947-48
       1952-53
       1970-71
       1988-89
       1990-91
      Runners-up
       1925-26
       1931-32
       1972-73

Division 2
>**Runners-up**
>1903-04

FA Cup
>**Winners**
>1930
>1936
>1971
>1979
>1993
>1998
>2002
>2003
>
>**Runners-up**
>1927
>1932
>1952
>1972
>1978
>1980
>2001

Charity Shield
>**Winners**
>1930
>1931
>1933
>1934
>1938
>1948
>1953
>1998
>2002
>2004

League Cup
>**Winners**
>1987
>1993
>**Runners-up**
>1968
>1969
>1988

European Cup-Winners' Cup
>**Winners**
>1993-94
>
>**Runners-up**
>1979-80
>1994-95

European Fairs Cup
>**Winners**
>1969-70

UEFA
>**Runners up**
>2002

So what led me from that to Armenia:-

I expect the first thing going through your mind is "Where or what is Armenia"? No need to worry that was my first reaction when I heard the name!

Please do not skip this introduction to Armenia, if you do you will miss the whole reason behind my going there, with Jane and our daughter Morgana (then aged 12)

The Republic of Armenia

I was eventually to locate Armenia in my atlas. Its position is the gateway to Asia, situated with its southern border sitting on top of Iran, to the west is Turkey, to the east, Azerbaijan, and to the north Georgia and Russia.

It would be wrong of me not to mention something about the history of Armenia as during the 5 years I was to spend there, Armenia entered my bloodstream. Their culture, history and heritage are of utmost national importance to every Armenian, therefore I must include a resume of Armenian history.

The history of Armenia is an endless narrative of rise and fall, of triumph and tragedy. Geography has undoubtedly had a decisive influence upon its course. Forming an important area of vantage and a highway of great value for trade and commerce between two continents, Armenia was, it seems destined to be constantly at grips with adversity. The land, with its untold riches and its strategic position of primary import, stirred the ambitions of many an invader before and subsequent to the advent of its Christian civilization.

Armenia prides itself on being the first nation to formally adopt Christianity (early 4th century). Despite periods of autonomy, over the centuries Armenia came under the sway of various empires including the Roman, Byzantine, Arab, Persian, and Ottoman. It was incorporated into Russia in 1828 and the USSR in 1920. Armenian leaders remain preoccupied with the long conflict with Muslim Azerbaijan over Nagorno-Karabakh, a primarily Armenian-populated region, assigned to Soviet Azerbaijan in the 1920s by Moscow. Armenia and Azerbaijan began fighting over the area in 1988; the struggle escalated after both countries attained independence from the Soviet Union in 1991. By May 1994, when a cease-fire took hold, Armenian forces held not only Nagorno-Karabakh but also a significant portion of Azerbaijan proper. The economies of both sides have been hurt by their inability to make substantial progress toward a peaceful resolution. Turkey imposed an economic blockade on Armenia and closed the common border because of the Armenian occupation of Nagorno-Karabakh and surrounding areas.

The Genocide of 1915

When the First World War broke out in the summer of 1914 there seemed to be no doubt that Turkey, virtually a German protectorate since the early eighties, would inevitably throw in her lot with Germany. In the event of an Allied victory, Russia would occupy the Armenian provinces, while England and France could not be suspected of great love for Turkey, argued the Turkish leaders. On the other hand, when the "invincible Kaiser" won the war, they could not only offset the Russian menace, but could also settle the Armenian Question with their scimitar and German blessing.

Dennis Loze

The final decision over the participation in the war pending, the Young Turks approached the leaders of the Armenian minority, and told them, without beating about the bush, that they expected them to incite their kinsmen in the Caucasus to organize an insurrection against the Tsar. It was explained to the Turks very plainly that the Armenians in Russia would fight for their Emperor as loyal citizens just as much as the Armenians in Turkey would fight for theirs. The Armenians did not visualize the horrifying consequences their manly repudiation of the Turkish offer would have for their future. Turkey entered the war on the side of Germany in October 1914. From then on the sinister shadow of an unprecedented cataclysm was hovering over the heads of the Armenians.

In 1915, while the civilised nations were engaged, on two fronts, in a bitter struggle against the enemies of freedom and justice, the Turks were attacking the Armenians ferociously.

The Turks uprooted the Armenians overnight from their homes, robbed them of their early possessions, drove them in endless caravans to the scorching deserts of Arabia, and subjected the Armenians to atrocities the magnitude of which even the barbarity of the Middle Ages pales.

The Turks obliterated all traces of Armenian culture; they razed to the ground 2,000 churches and more than 2,000 schools; they converted convents and monasteries into stables or military depots, and reduced to dust all architectural monuments.

After coming to power in Constantinople, the Young Turks made the policy of "No Armenians – no Armenian Question" their main priority. Taking advantage of the favourable political conditions created by the World War I, they began the "final resolution of the Armenian question" on April 24th, 1915, by executing hundreds of Armenian intellectuals of Constantinople without trial. In the Armenian province of Eastern Anatolia, all Armenian males aged 15-62 had been conscripted, disarmed and executed. Defenceless Armenian women, children and the elderly were deported to the Syrian, Desert Der-el-Zor; most of them were brutally murdered on the way by Turkish soldiers or Kurdish nomads, or died of starvation and exhaustion. More than one and half million Armenians, i.e. 80% of the Armenian population of Western Armenia, perished in this first Genocide of the twentieth century. Several hundred thousand survivors of the Genocide found refuge in neighbouring counties, laying the foundation of the worldwide Armenian Diaspora. By the year 1923 Western Armenia was completely de-Armenised and successfully incorporated into the newly formed Turkish Republic.

A New Era

The Armenian people in Soviet Armenia endured the hardships of survival under communism and especially under the despotic Stalin. Through it all they managed to build up the nation, providing for its population and emphasizing its cultural progress.

In February 1988, the popular demonstrations in Armenia for the liberation of Artsakh (Nagorno-Karabakh) began, heralding populist movements that would soon be sweeping throughout the communist world.

On December 7, 1988, at 1141 am. a magnitude 6.9 earthquake shook north eastern Armenia and was followed four minutes later by a 5.8 aftershock. Numerous aftershocks, some as large as 5.0 continued for months in and around the area of Spitak. The earthquakes hit an area of 80km in diameter comprising the towns of Leninakan (later to be renamed Gyumri), Spitak, Stephanavan, and Kirovakan.

Despite its moderate size, the deaths and damage that December earthquake caused was disasterous.

The town of Spitak (population 25,000) was totally raised to the ground, the city of Leninakan was 50% destroyed, damages also occurred to Stepapavan and Kirovakan and other smaller towns.

The actual figures of deaths were slightly confused due to the numbers released by Russia and also the unknown number of refugees from Azerbaijan and Nagorno Karabakh. Figures ranged from 25,000 to 45,000 dead, 15,000 seriously injured, and 517,000 people made homeless. For the first time, foreign aid was permitted to penetrate into the Soviet Union.

Two years later parliamentary elections took place with the formation of a national parliament and Levon Ter-Petrosyan, an activist for the Karabagh movement, was elected President of the Parliament. Armenia approved a process toward independence on August 23, 1990, and shortly thereafter the Tricolor and Mer Hayrenik were adopted as the official flag and anthem, respectively.

A national referendum on September 21, 1991, overwhelmingly approved independence and on October 16, 1991, the first free election took place with Levon Ter-Petrosyan elected president, ushering in a new era with new responsibilities and new challenges.

After his reelection in 1998, President Levon Ter-Petrosyan resigned and Robert Kocharian was elected as president of the Armenian Republic.

Dennis Loze

The 71 years of Soviet rule in Armenia were a period of relative security, of great economic development, and of cultural and educational achievements. During the same period, the government of Soviet Azerbaijan was conducting a systematic policy of removing the Armenians from Nakhidjevan, which today has no Armenian population whatsoever. The same policy was less effective in Nagorno-Karabakh, where Armenians remained the overwhelming majority. In February 1988 a peaceful, democratic movement for the reunification with Armenia began in Nagorno-Karabakh, and the regional Assembly of the Nagorno-Karabakh Autonomous Region adopted a resolution seeking transfer of Karabakh from Azerbaijan to Armenia, as a realization of the right of the peoples under alien domination to self-determination. The Azeri side responded by Armenian massacres in the Azeri cities of Sumgait, Kirovabad and Baku, transforming the peaceful movement into a violent conflict, and lately committing an act of military aggression against the Armenian population of Nagorno-Karabakh. The newly proclaimed Republic of Nagorno-Karabakh managed to defeat the invading Azeri forces and to create a security zone around its territory and a humanitarian corridor to Armenia. The negotiations on the future status of Nagorno-Karabakh are being conducted within the Organization for Security and Cooperation in Europe, through the so-called Minsk Group, co-chaired by USA, Russian Federation and France

Armenia restored its full independence on September 21, 1991, and became a member of the United Nations on March 2, 1992. On January 25, 2001, Armenia also became a member of the Council of Europe.

The climate in Armenia is markedly continental. Summers are dry and sunny, lasting from June to mid-September. The temperature fluctuates between 22° and 36°C. however; the low humidity level mitigates the effect of high temperatures. Evening breezes blowing down the mountains provide a welcome refreshing and cooling effect.

Spring is short, while autumn is long. The autumn is remarkable for the spectacularly colourful foliage.

Winters are quite cold with plenty of snow, with temperatures ranging between -5° and -20°C.

Lake Sevan nestled up in the Armenian highlands, is the second largest lake in the world relative to its altitude. Its bright turquoise water is 1,900 meters above sea level

So that lays the foundation of "Arsenal to Armenia."
But what first brought me to Arsenal?

Chapter Two

"It's just a job of work!"
FRED STREET
ARSENAL AND ENGLAND PHYSIOTHERAPIST

I remember so well my first ever visit to Highbury. A colleague and friend of mine, Cliff Speight, who was leaving the Army, to work in Saudi Arabia with Jeda FC, said that he was paying a visit to Arsenal to meet up with Fred Street, who was the Arsenal and England Physiotherapist, to discuss the types of injuries to be expected in Saudi. As Cliff, like me, was nearing the end of his forces commitment, our actual casework was reduced, so getting time off was easy and I joined him on his visit.

Fred had actually shared a similar background as me, being a former member of the Royal Air Force, teaching PE, and working in Joint Services Rehabilitation, a period of hospital work, before moving into the football world with Stoke before being approached by Arsenal. Not only was he approached, but Arsenal was actually paying Stoke a transfer fee!

Soon I was walking up the steps through the main double doors into the famous marble hall, with the bust of the legionary manager Herbert Chapman looking down at me. Then I thought of all the stars of Arsenal, besides other clubs who had walked up those steps and actually stood on the very spot where I was standing!

Bill Harper (January 1889 – April 1989) Bill was born in Tarbrax, Lanarkshire. He was a sporting natural, but this was put on hold because of World War 1. Bill joined the 5th Brigade of the Scots Guards and served on the Western Front. Not only did he play football, but was Guards heavyweight boxing champion and was captain of the Guards rugby team also.

After the war ended he joined Hibernians in 1921. He then spent 4 seasons making over 100 appearances, and also collected 9 Scottish caps.

In November 1925 he became one of Herbert Chapman's first signings, for a record for goalkeepers of £4,000. He became Arsenals first choice keeper, and gained a further 2 Scottish caps. During the following seasons things started to go wrong for him. Herbert Chapman blamed him for the 4-2 defeat against Tottenham and he was ruthlessly dropped. Young Welshman Dan Lewis was promoted to first choice and he also would keep goal in the ill fated 1-0 FA Cup final, losing to Cardiff City, later that season. Bill left at the end of that season and moved to the United States and played for Fall River in the American Soccer League.

In 1930 he returned to England and re-signed for Arsenal, and once again became the first choice keeper. But Chapman would never settle on a regular keeper and signed Frank Moss in Nov. 1931. Bill then was signed by Plymouth Argyle, after playing a total of 73 games for Arsenal.

Bill remained at Plymouth for the rest of his career, playing over 100 league games in the 8 years before the 2nd World War broke out. Bill continued to serve the club in all aspects of the game from groundsman to laundryman.

Bill died at the age of 91, in 1989. In his honour the club named their training ground Harper's Park.

I had the great honour of meeting and knowing Bill during my stay with Argyle, he was still working as steward in the Directors room, at the age of 80.

He will feature later on in the book.

Joe Mercer, OBE (August 9, 1914 - August 9, 1990) He was born in Ellesmere Port, Cheshire and at first played for Ellesmere Port F.C. Joe played at left-half. He was a powerful tackler and good at anticipating an opponent's moves. He joined Everton in September 1932 at the age of 18 and claimed a regular first team place in the 1935-36 season. He made

186 appearances for Everton, scoring two goals and a winning a League Championship medal in the 1938-39 season. While playing for Everton he gained five England caps.

Unfortunately, like many players of his generation, Joe lost out on seven seasons of football due to the Second World War. He became a sergeant-major but nevertheless played in 26 wartime internationals, many of them as captain. The Everton manager Theo Kelly accused him of not trying in an international against Scotland, but in reality he had sustained a severe cartilage injury. Even after consulting an orthopaedic specialist, the Everton management refused to believe him so he had to pay for the surgery himself (after 14 years with the club). Understandably upset, Joe moved in 1946 for £9,000 to Arsenal, although he commuted from Liverpool. Theo Kelly brought Joe's boots to the transfer negotiations to prevent him having a reason to go back to say goodbye to the other players at Everton.

At Arsenal, he quickly became captain, and won an FA Cup winner's medal in 1950 and League Championship medals in 1947-48 and 1952-53. He initially decided to retire in May 1953, but recanted and returned to Arsenal for 1953-54. However, he was forced to retire for good that season, after breaking his leg in two places in a match against Liverpool. He played 275 times for Arsenal in all, and was voted FWA Footballer of the Year in 1950.

On August 18, 1955, two days before the first game of the season against Newcastle United, he was appointed to replace Sheffield United manager Reg Freeman who had died during the closed season. As a manager he began inauspiciously. He lacked experience and his first season ended in relegation.

The rest of his time as manager was spent in the Second Division and in December 1958, wanting to move to a bigger club, he resigned and moved to Aston Villa who was bottom of the First Division. Although he led them to the FA Cup semi-finals he was relegated to Division Two for a second time.

He molded a talented young side at Villa and his team became known as the 'Mercer Minors'. He led Villa to victory in the inaugural League Cup in 1961 but was then sacked in 1964 on the grounds of ill health.

Despite this, his health improved and he went on to enjoy great success as a manager with Manchester City between 1965 and 1972. During his time there he won the First Division (1968), FA Cup (1969), League Cup (1970), and European Cup Winners' Cup (1970).

He had a spell as manager at Coventry City from 1972 to 1975, during which he was also caretaker manager of the English national football team for a brief period in 1974, after Sir Alf Ramsey's resignation. He served as a director of Coventry from 1975 to 1981.

He was made an Officer of the Order of the British Empire in 1976.

Edwin Raymond "Ray" Bowden (September 13, 1909 – 1998) Born in Looe, Cornwall, he played for local non-league side Looe; a prolific centre forward, despite his slight frame he scored over 100 goals in a season, including ten in a single match. He was spotted by Plymouth Argyle and signed for the Pilgrims as an amateur in 1926; he still worked as an auctioneer in his day job. By the start of the 1928-29 season, Ray had impressed enough to win a first-team place and was a regular goal scorer for the club for the next five seasons; Argyle were promoted in 1929-30 from the Third Division South to the Second Division. In all he scored 83 goals in 149 matches for Argyle, more than a goal every other game.

He signed for Herbert Chapman's Arsenal in March 1933 for £4,500. Although he did not play enough games to win a First Division winners' medal that season, he was a regular for the next two seasons, as Arsenal won two more titles on the trot. Playing now as an inside forward, behind Ted Drake, but he still scored many a goal, and was the club's joint-top goal scorer, with Cliff Bastin, in 1934-35. That season he also won his first cap for England, against Wales on September 29, 1934. Two months later, Ray was one of the seven Arsenal players who played for England against World Champions Italy in the "Battle of Highbury" match, which England won 3-2.

He won an FA Cup winners' medal in 1936, but by then his ankle was causing him problems, limiting his appearances for the club that season and the next. By the start of the 1937-38 season he had seemingly bounced back, playing ten matches in the first two months of the season, but he was sold to Second Division Newcastle United in November 1937 for £5,000. In all he played 138 matches for the Gunners, scoring 48 goals.

Ray was a regular for Newcastle for the next two years (although the club narrowly escaped relegation in his first season). With the outbreak of World War II, first-class football was suspended and the 30-year-old decided to call it quits. He returned to Plymouth, where he ran a sports shop with his brother. He died in 1998 aged 89.

Arsenal to Armenia

Raymond will appear later on in the book.

Alfred John "Jack" Kelsey (19 November, 1929 – 18 March 1992) Jack spent most of his career at Arsenal, after the club signed him from Welsh side Winch Wen in 1949. After two years in the reserves, he finally made his debut at Highbury against Charlton Athletic in February 1951 - his first start was not an auspicious one, as Arsenal lost 5-2. He stayed in the reserves for another year and a half after that. He returned to the side during the 1952-53 season, sharing goalkeeping duties with George Swindin, and made 29 appearances in a side that won the First Division.

With a rugged build and consistently solid catching, Jack was Arsenal's No. 1 for the next eight seasons; though he didn't win any major honours with Arsenal, he was a runner-up in the first Inter-Cities Fairs Cup (precursor of the UEFA Cup) final in 1958, playing for a London XI representative side against FC Barcelona. He became a regular for Wales as well, winning 41 caps. He was Wales's keeper in the 1958 World Cup, their only finals appearance to date, where they were eventually knocked out 1-0 by winners Brazil in the quarter-finals.

His career was cut short after he sustained a back injury playing for Wales in a friendly against Brazil in May 1962, whilst trying to save at the feet of Vavá; despite many attempts to rectify his injury, he was forced to retire a year later. In all he played 352 times for Arsenal, the second-highest number of appearances by a 'keeper for the club (bettered only by David Seaman). He later worked for Arsenal as the club's commercial manager. He died in 1992, at the age of 62.

Jack was the commercial manager at Highbury at the time of my visit.

Tommy Docherty Tommy is renowned as one of the most colourful characters in football – the man who often claims that he had more clubs than Jack Nicklaus!

The fast-talking, wisecracking Glaswegian is now a stalwart of the After Dinner circuit and is known throughout the country simply as The Doc.

As a player, he launched his career with Celtic, before moving to Preston North End in 1949. He played a total of 342 games for North

End before being transferred to Arsenal at the beginning of the 1958-59 season. At Arsenal he played a total of 83 games before moving on to Chelsea in 1961. He also represented Scotland a total of 25 times.

When his playing career was over, he turned to management, and lent his experience to a long list of clubs – Chelsea, Rotherham, Aston Villa, Oporto, Manchester United, Derby, Queens Park Rangers, (3 times), Sydney Olympic (twice), Preston North End and Wolves – with a varying degree of success.

It was under his guidance that Scotland qualified for the World Cup, but perhaps his most memorable success came at Old Trafford, where he created an exciting team which took Manchester United to the 2nd Division Championship in 1975 and F.A. Cup glory two years later.

Tommy will appear later on in the book.

William John Terence "Terry" Neill (born May 8, 1942) Born in Belfast, Terry played as a youth for Bangor, before moving in 1959 to Arsenal. He made his debut in December 1960 against Sheffield Wednesday, becoming an accomplished centre half (but also playing at full back). He became a regular in the Arsenal side of the 1960s, as well as the Northern Ireland national side, and went on to captain both club and country. In all he played 255 times for Arsenal and 59 times for Northern Ireland.

Towards the end of the 1960s, he became affected by injuries and a bout of jaundice, missing the 1969 League Cup final (which Arsenal lost). Although still only 28, he was signed by Hull City in July 1970 as player-manager, one of the youngest ever managers in the history of the game; he later became player-manager of his country as well. Terry retired from playing in 1973, and left Hull a year later to succeed Bill Nicholson as manager of Arsenal's fiercest rivals, Tottenham Hotspur. He managed Spurs for two seasons, nearly getting the club relegated in the process.

Despite his less than sterling record at Spurs, he was recruited by the Arsenal board to replace Bertie Mee in 1976, to become the youngest manager in the club's history. With new signings like Malcolm Macdonald and Pat Jennings, the club enjoyed a minor revival, reaching a trio of FA Cup finals between 1978 and 1980, though only winning the middle one of the three, and the 1980 final of the Cup Winners' Cup (which Arsenal lost on penalties to Valencia). However, Arsenal's success in the cups could not be matched in the league, and the departures of star players such as Liam Brady and Frank Stapleton only made things worse. A series of embarrassing cup defeats in the early 1980s made things worse; a League Cup loss at home to Walsall proved to be the final straw, and he was sacked in December 1983.

He retired from football, and has since opened sports bars in Hendon and Holborn, central London.

Terry was the Arsenal manager at the time of my visit.

Jonathon Charles "Jon" Sammels (born July 23, 1945) Born in Ipswich, Jon joined Arsenal, the club he supported as a boy, in 1961. He was a regular in the reserves and a successful youth international for England, before his first-team debut for the Gunners on April 27, 1963. However, he did not secure a place in the side until the departure of Geoff Strong, and later George Eastham. A skilful central midfielder with an accurate passing foot and a strong shot, he had become a regular by the 1966-67 season, and played in both of Arsenal's League Cup final defeats in 1968 and 1969, and the 1970 Inter-Cities Fairs Cup final, scoring Arsenal's winning goal in their 4-3 victory over RSC Anderlecht.

However, he lost his first team place in the 1970-71 season, thanks to an ankle injury and the emergence of George Graham. Although he played enough games to win a First Division winner's medal, he did not take part in the Gunners' FA Cup win that completed their Double-winning season. Jon submitted a transfer request, and he was duly sold to Leicester City. In all he played 270 matches for Arsenal, scoring 52 goals.

He was a regular in the Leicester side for the next seven seasons, playing 265 matches for the Foxes, scoring 25 goals. Under Jimmy Bloomfield, Leicester were a talented and exciting side, but the only trophy they won was the 1971 Charity Shield, and they never finished above seventh in the League. He left Leicester on a free transfer in 1978, and played for the Vancouver Whitecaps in the NASL for a single season. After that, he retired from the game and returned to the UK. He now works as a driving instructor in Leicester.

Jon will appear later on.

Alan Ball MBE (born Farnworth, Lancashire, May 12th 1945) A tireless, marauding midfield player who could operate centrally or on the right flank, Ballie came to prominence at Blackpool after falling foul of his headmaster over missing games for his school team due to a youth contract he had acquired with Wolverhampton Wanderers.

After leaving school, Wolves decided not to take him on, and he started training with Bolton Wanderers but they too decided not to give him a professional deal, saying he was too small. Blackpool then signed him up after his father, an ex-player himself, called in a favour with the coach, an old friend with whom he used to play. Ballie was given a trial and was immediately signed up.

He made his debut in 1962 and managed 116 League appearances. Despite being in an unglamorous and struggling team, his industry, stamina and distribution was noticed by England manager Alf Ramsey, who gave him his international debut in 1965 in a 1-1 draw with Yugoslavia, three days before he turned twenty.

Ramsey was preparing for the World Cup a year later, which England was to host and was developing a system whereby England could deploy midfielders with a defensive and industrious bent, something which was not wholly guaranteed from conventional wide men. As a result, Ballie became a useful tool for Ramsey to use - able to play conventionally wide or in the centre but still in possession of the energy to help out his defence when required.

Ballie was the youngest member of the squad of 22 selected by Ramsey for the tournament, aged only just 21. Though England as a team emerged collectively heroic from the tournament, he was one of many players regarded as an individual success, especially as he was one of the more inexperienced charges with no proven record at the very highest level. Indeed, he, Geoff Hurst and Martin Peters emerged with enormous credit and eternal acclaim from the competition - and all of them were still only in single figures for caps won by the time they were named in the team for the final against West Germany.

The 100,000 crowd at Wembley witnessed a magnificent personal performance from Ballie. Full of running, he continued to work and sprint and track back while team-mates and opponents alike were out on their feet. With fewer than 15 minutes to go, he won a corner on the right which he promptly took. Hurst hit a shot from the edge of the area which deflected into the air and down on to the instep of Peters, who rifled England 2-1 ahead.

The Germans equalised with seconds to go, meaning that the game went into extra time. Somehow, this instilled extra bounce into Ballie's play and the image of his continuous running round the Wembley pitch, socks round his ankles, is one of the most enduring of the occasion. It was his chase and low cross which set up Hurst's massively controversial second goal, and England's third; he was also sprinting upfield, unmarked and screaming for a pass, as Hurst took the ball forward to smash his historic hat-trick goal with the last kick of the game.

England's fans and media were thrilled with the achievement and Ballie was taken to the sport's bosom to the extent that the bids started coming in. It took a record offer of £110,000 from Everton later in 1966 before Blackpool let him go.

He settled into what became regarded as his generation's best midfield trio alongside Colin Harvey and Howard Kendall. Everton got to the 1968 FA Cup final but lost to West Bromwich Albion and were knocked out by Manchester City in the semi-finals the following year. He was instrumental in the team which won his first and only major domestic honour in the game as Everton took the 1970 Football League Championship title, seeing off a late challenge from Leeds United.

By now, Ballie was one of the first names on Ramsey's England team-sheet and he was in the squad which traveled as defending champions to the altitude of Mexico for the 1970 World Cup. Ballie famously hit the crossbar with a shot as England lost one of their group games 1-0 to Brazil, one of six strikingly prominent incidents from a fabulous game (the others being Jairzinho's goal; Jeff Astle's miss; Gordon Banks' save from Pelé; Bobby Moore's impeccable tackle on Jairzinho; and the sight of Pelé and Moore's mutual smiles of respect at the end as they exchanged shirts). England won their other group games and progressed to another showdown with West Germany in the quarter finals but the heat sapped Ballie's natural industry. England lost a 2-0 lead and their reign as world champions ended with a 3-2 reverse.

Back at club level, Everton again capitulated in the semi-finals of the FA Cup in 1971, with his opening goal overhauled by two strikes from Merseyside rivals Liverpool, who went on to lose the final to "double"-chasing Arsenal. He later picked up his 50th England cap in a match against Northern Ireland and at the end of 1971, Arsenal came up with a record offer of £220,000 to take him to Highbury.

It was a great move by Arsenal, with Ballie now 26 years of age and at his peak for both form and fitness. That said, Arsenal couldn't defend their League title in 1972 and also lost their grasp on the FA Cup when Leeds beat them 1-0 in the centenary final at Wembley. He again had to be content with a runners-up medal.

Dennis Loze

In 1973, he became only the second player to be sent off in a full international, reacting with fury to violent tactics by Poland in a qualifier for the 1974 World Cup in Warsaw. As a result, he missed the return game at Wembley which became one of the most notorious in England history - a 1-1 draw in which England were kept out almost entirely by Polish goalkeeper Jan Tomaszewski. England failed to qualify for the World Cup.

Ramsey was sacked as a result and Joe Mercer took over at a caretaker level, for whom Ballie never appeared due to injury. However, his relationship with his national side was enhanced and then infamously soured beyond repair when Don Revie was appointed as Ramsey's permanent replacement.

Ballie was given the captaincy after the abrupt dropping of Emlyn Hughes by Revie and he held it for six consecutive games of varying importance, none of which England lost. Yet even though his charges had just comprehensively beaten Scotland 5-1 in May 1975, Ballie was not called up at all, let alone retained as captain, when Revie announced his next squad for a game against Switzerland three months later. Ballie only found out when his wife took a call from a journalist asking for her reaction. Only just 30, Ballie's international career had ended suddenly and acrimoniously after 72 appearances and eight goals, when it had always seemed certain that he would get to 100 caps but for injury. His omission from the squad was one of a handful of PR calamities which raged through the Revie era at the helm of the England team.

Ballie continued with Arsenal until the end of 1976 when he was sold to Southampton. Here was completed a coincidental symmetry to the three transfers in his career - he had arrived at each club - Everton, Arsenal and Southampton - at the end of the calendar years of 1966, 1971 and 1976 respectively, when each were holders of the FA Cup. Yet he never won the Cup himself.

He helped Southampton back to the First Division in 1978 and picked up a League Cup runners-up medal in 1979 after they were beaten 3-2 by Nottingham Forest. Ballie then went to play in the North American Soccer League.

His first club, Blackpool, came calling and he returned to Bloomfield Road as player manager but this didn't last after he was tempted back to Southampton to play alongside fellow veterans and former England team-mates Mick Channon and Kevin Keegan.

Arsenal to Armenia

Ballie played for Southampton in the top flight until he was 37 before joining Bristol Rovers, where he ended his playing days. He played a huge 975 competitive matches in his career.

Bravely, Ballie went to Portsmouth to resume his management career and was a huge success, guiding them to the top flight in 1987 while not incurring too much wrath from Southampton fans in the process. He left Portsmouth in 1989 and had two years in charge at Stoke City and spells at Exeter City and on Graham Taylor's backroom team with England.

In 1994, he went back to Southampton as manager and despite initial success, was tempted away a year later to become Manchester City's manager under the ownership of ex-England team-mate Francis Lee. Ballie's tenure at Maine Road was controversial, in that many observers and supporters felt he was appointed for his name and friendship with the chairman rather than for any credentials as a coach (and pointed out that previous manager Brian Horton, whom Lee had inherited from the previous regime, had done no wrong), and City were relegated from the Premiership on the last day of Ballie's first full campaign. He quit three games into the following season.

He later had another spell at Portsmouth but has now been out of the coaching side of football for some years. In 2000, he and four other members of the World Cup winning team were awarded the MBE for their services to football, an award which many felt was long overdue. Ballie, along with Roger Hunt, Nobby Stiles, Ray Wilson and George Cohen, had to wait more than three decades for official recognition of their achievements.

In 2003 Ballie was inducted into the English Football Hall of Fame in recognition of his talents.

Always a distinctive figure thanks to his diminutive stature, his high-pitched voice and flame-red hair, He released his autobiography, *Playing Extra Time*, in 2004 and received much critical acclaim. Aside from his highs and lows in football, it also candidly detailed his private struggle as a family man after his wife and daughter were both diagnosed with cancer. His wife died later the same year.

In May 2005, Ballie, who has three grandchildren, put his World Cup winners' medal and commemorative tournament cap up for auction to raise money for his family. It was sold for £140,000.

Ballie will appear later on in the book.

Robert "Bob" McNab (born July 20, 1943) Born in Huddersfield, Yorkshire, Bob started out at his local club, Huddersfield Town. He was signed by Bertie Mee for Arsenal in October 1966, and immediately won a place in the Arsenal side. He was the Gunners' first-choice left back for the next nine seasons, reaching the 1968 and 1969 League Cup finals (both of which Arsenal lost).

He made his debut for England in 1968 against Romania; he made four appearances in all for England, but never became a regular. However, he certainly had success domestically, winning the 1970 Inter-Cities Fairs Cup and then the Double in 1971. Bob continued to play through much of the early 1970s for Arsenal, including the FA Cup final loss to Leeds United in 1972 and finishing second in the league a year later. However, the latter part of his career at Arsenal was blighted by injury and the emergence of Sammy Nelson meant Bob was no longer guaranteed a place in the first team.

He was released on a free transfer in the summer of 1975; and played first for Wolves before trying his luck in the NASL in the United States. He finished his playing career at Barnet, before moving to Canada to coach the Vancouver Whitecaps. He later emigrated to Los Angeles, California, where he still lives today, working as a property developer. He is the father of the actress Mercedes McNab.

Bob will appear later on in the book.

Robert "Bob" Primrose Wilson (born October 30, 1941 Chesterfield, England.) His unusual middle name has often been a source of amusement; it stems from a Scottish tradition of giving children their mother's maiden name as a middle name.

Bob started late as a professional player as his father would not let him sign papers with Manchester United. as he thought it wasn't a reasonable job while he was a youth and he then went on to Loughborough College for training as a teacher before signing for Arsenal in 1963. He had been playing non-league games for Wolves as an amateur and made his debut for Arsenal as an amateur, the last non professional to play in the top division, and the first amateur to have a transfer fee paid (around £6,500). Even then it was five years before he became the first choice keeper in 1968. In 1971 he was Arsenal's player of the year in their famous double winning season.

Arsenal to Armenia

He became eligible to play for Scotland when the rules were changed in the 1970s to allow players to play for their parent's country of origin if they had not already played for their own country. Bob was selected by Tommy Docherty for his two games but Tommy then left the position and the next manager preferred another English-born keeper: David Harvey of Leeds United.

As a student and teacher of goalkeeping, Bob has identified his own signature technique as diving at his opponents' feet to save goals. This has caused him a number of injuries throughout his career.

He also played goal without the use of goalkeeping gloves, something very rare at the time and completely unknown today.

He was goalkeeping coach for Arsenal during the period of Pat Jennings, John Lukic, and David Seaman.

After his football career he immediately became a football TV presenter working firstly for the BBC then for ITV until his retirement in 2002. During this period he was also immortalised in comic strip form when, despite a certain lack of plausibility due to his age, he spent a season playing for the fictional Melchester Rovers team in the Roy of the Rovers strip.

At this time, although full time in TV, still attended some of the training sessions as a specialist goal keeping coach at Highbury.

Don Howe Don is recognised as one of the finest coaches that England has ever produced. He started his football career at West Bromwich where he played a total of 342 games, between the seasons of 1955-63 before being transferred to Arsenal in 1964. He played a total of 70 games between 64-66 seasons.

Don was 1st team coach at this time.

Brian Kidd (Born 1949 in Collyhurst) "Kiddo" signed school boy forms with Manchester United in 1963 and made his 1st team debut in 1967. He played a total of 204 games and scored 52 goals between the seasons of 1966-74. He was transferred to Arsenal as Manchester United started to struggle to repeat the success of the 60's and found themselves in the 2nd Division. The time at Arsenal brought back his scoring touch with 44 goals in 68 games during the seasons 1974-76. It was soon the turn of Manchester light blues to capture this scoring machine and he didn't let them down, scoring a total of 44 goals in 68 appearances in the

Dennis Loze

seasons of 1976-79. It wasn't to finish there as Everton recognised their need, and signed Kiddo mid season of 1979, There he played a further 40 games and scored 11 goals before being transferred again this time to Bolton. The playing career came to an end at Bolton in 1981-82 season which included a short spell in the NASL with Fort Lauderdale and Minnesota Strikers, after he had played a further 43 games with a tally of 14 goals. Management was his next calling, after a successful spell at Barrow, but an unsuccessful spell at Preston North End with Tommy Booth, he joined up with Manchester United and Alex Ferguson.

After an extremely successful time at United, Blackburn Rovers came a calling but after an eleven month spell as manager, saw him move back to the coaching scene.

Kiddo will appear later in the book.

Plus all these past players (See Appendix A for full details of these players).

Edris Albert "Eddie" Hapgood (September 24, 1908 — April 20, 1973)

David Bone Nightingale Jack (April 3, 1899 - September 10, 1958)

Alexander Wilson James (September 14, 1901 – June 1, 1953)

Clifford Sydney Bastin (March 14, 1912 — December 4, 1991

Leslie Harry Compton (born Woodford, Essex September 12, 1912 - died Hendon, Middlesex 27 December 1984)

Edward Joseph "Ted" Drake (August 16, 1912 - May 30, 1995)

George Hedley Swindin (December 4, 1914 – October 27, 2005)

Lawrence "Laurie" Scott (April 23, 1917 – July 7, 1999)

James Tullis "Jimmy" Logie (November 23, 1919 – April 1984)

Wallace "Walley" Barnes (January 16, 1920 – September 4, 1975)

Denis Charles Scott Compton CBE (23 May 1918 - 23 April 1997)

David Lloyd "Dave" Bowen (June 7, 1928 – September 25, 1995)

David Herd (born April 15, 1934 in Hamilton)

George Edward Eastham OBE (born September 23, 1936)

Joe Baker (August 17, 1940 – October 6, 2003)

John Radford (born 22 February 1947 in Hemsworth, Yorkshire)

Peter Edwin Storey (born September 7, 1945)

Frederick Charles "Charlie" George (born October 10, 1950)
Ray Kennedy (born Northumberland, England, 28 July 1951)

Also the past mangers:-
Herbert Chapman (1925-34)
Tom Whittaker (1947-56)
Billy Wright (1962-66)
Bertie Mee (1966-76)

Chapter Three

"If"
RUDYARD KIPLING

So what had actually brought me to the marble hall of Highbury?

It all started a number of years before that visit to Highbury, in fact at the age of 19 in a RAF recruiting office in Plymouth. I had been a fairly successful athlete and footballer in my home county of Cornwall. Playing alongside me in my local football team of Gunnislake was Mike Trebilcock who later went to play for Plymouth Argyle and then fame at Everton with his goals at Wembly in the 1966 FA Cup final.

My sporting ability had gained me a place at the Royal Air Force School of Physical Training based at R.A.F. St. Athan in South Wales.

People today complain about the lack of sporting facilities, but the very first day that I walked into the huge gymnasiums at St. Athan was the very first time that I had ever been in a gymnasium of any description. I had only played 3 sports in my life, football, cricket and athletics, but in the next couple of years I was to be introduced to a full range of sports.

Two sports in particular were to bring me great pleasure and success, the great game of Rugby Union and Athletics eventually I was to play at county level and representing the Royal Air Force in both and so close to international level in athletics.

Sport in the RAF was to take me to a lot of places I normally would never have seen. It even saw me rising to fame in athletics, for during the

Arsenal to Armenia

season of 1963 I was to be one of the fastest sprinters in GB over 60yds indoors, I expect that only a few athletes competed that year, but it is still a good conversation point.

Britain at this time had a very healthy sprint team, with names like Peter Radford, Ron Jones, David Jones, Berwyn Jones, Menzies Cambell and Lynn Davies.

You only have to look at the dominance of these athletes in the AAA championships, during those years.

Year	First	Second	Third
100 Yards			
1960	Peter Radford - 9.62	Dave Jones - 9.70	Nick Whitehead - 9.80
1961	Harry Jerome CAN - 9.63	Seraphino Antao KEN - 9.84	**Dave Jones - 9.89**
1962	Serephino Antao KEN - 9.8	**Peter Radford - 9.9**	**Berwyn Jones - 9.9**
1963	**Berwyn Jones - 9.71**	Larry Questad USA - 9.74	**Ron Jones - 9.76**
1964	Enrique Figuerola CUB - 9.4	**Lynn Davies - 9.7**	Seraphino Antao KEN - 9.7
1965	Enrique Figuerola CUB - 9.64	Barry Kelly - 9.84	**Menzies Cambell - 9.96**
1966	Paul Nash RSA - 9.62	Wieslaw Maniak POL - 9.70	Barrie Kelly - 9.74
1967	Barrie Kelly - 9.91	**Ron Jones - 9.92**	Charis Aivaliotis GRE - 9.95
1968	Paul Nash RSA - 9.87	**Ron Jones - 9.92**	Barry Kelly - 9.94
100 Meters			
1969	**Ron Jones - 10.7**	Don Halliday - 10.7	Ian Green - 10.7
220 Yards			
1960	**Dave Jones - 21.31**	Dave Segal - 21.55	Mike Hildrey - 21.67
1961	**Dave Jones - 21.46**	Mike Hildrey - 21.53	Abdul Amu NGR - 21.69
1962	Serephino Antao KEN - 21.1	**Dave Jones - 21.40**	Len Carter - 21.8
1963	**Dave Jones - 21.26w**	Larry Quested USA - 21.29w	**Peter Radford - 21.56**
1964	**Menzies Campbell - 21.1w**	Seraphino Antao - 21.3w	Len Carter - 21.7w
1965	Pat Morrison - 21.84	**Menzies Campbell - 21.92**	Laszlo Mihalyifi HUN - 22.00
1966	Paul Nash RSA - 21.18	**Menzies Campbell - 21.60**	Dave Dear - 21.66
1967	**Menzies Campbell - 21.40**	Mike Hauck - 21.58	Dick Steane - 21.75
1968	PaulNash RSA - 21.20	Ralph Banthorpe - 21.36	Dick Stean - 21.42

Peter Radford
Date of birth, 20th September 1939 Walsall, West Midlands

Events:
100yds/100m, 220yds/200m, 4x110yds/4x100m

Championship Performances
Olympics: 1960 bronze 100m, bronze 4x100m.
European: 1958 bronze 100m, silver 4x100m.
Commonwealth: 1958 & 1962 Gold 4x110yds.

Career Highlight
World 200m record in 1960

Following his spectacular debut on the international athletics scene in 1958, Peter continued to improve over the next two years and on 28 May 1960 at Wolverhampton, he broke the world record for 220yds, setting a new time of 20.5sec. This time was also recognised as a new world record for the marginally shorter distance of 200 metres. This performance made him one of the favourites for the 200m at the Olympic Games in Rome later that year, together with Stone Johnson and Ray Norton who equaled Peter's newly-set world record at the USA Olympic trials. The only other serious contender was Italian Livio Berruti, who Peter defeated over 100m in an international meet between England and Italy three months before the Olympics. In Rome, Peter's first event was the 100m, in which he won his heat and semi-final. In the final, Peter was slowly away, but finished strongly to win the bronze medal. In the semi-finals of the 200m, he was a victim of some bad seeding which saw all three of the recent world record setters and Berruti placed in the same heat. As only three could qualify, someone had to miss out, and unfortunately it was Peter, who finished fourth in a time which would have placed him a comfortable second in the first semi-final. He was more fortunate in the 4 x 100m relay final, where Great Britain finished fourth, but was elevated to the bronze medal position after the USA team was disqualified. After 1960, his main successes came in relays rather than in individual events, which included membership of the England 4 x 110yd relay team which won gold at the 1962 Commonwealth Games and the Great Britain squad which set a new world record in that event on 3 August 1963.

Ron Jones

Born in Cwmaman, South Wales 1934 and was educated at Aberdare Intermediate School (the old Grammar school adjacent to Aberdare Park) before joining the R.A.F where his Athletic career took off.

In a 16-year career he was the Welsh 100yds champion 8 times, and 220/200 metres champion 6 times. He held the Welsh 100 metres record of 10.4 sec for a remarkable 24 years 1967-1991. He represented Wales in 4 Commonwealth Games. 1967 saw him become British 100-metre champion and he represented Great Britain in 35 full Internationals.

He took part in 2 Olympic Games and captained the Mexico team. The European Games Championships saw him represent Great Britain on 3 occasions. On retiring from athletics he became a football administrator, first with Queen's Park Rangers then Cardiff City and then Portsmouth between 1976 and 1989.

He was a member of the Sports Council of Wales, 1982-1985, also the chairman of the Sports Development Committee.

Menzies Cambell

A successful sprinter, who competed for the Great Britain and Northern Ireland team in the 1964 Tokyo Olympics. He was captained of the team in the 1966 British and Empire and Commonwealth Games in Jamaica. He also captained the UK athletics team in 1965 and 1966. He was also the former 100 metres British record holder.

Yes the former Liberal Democrate leader Sir Walter Menzies Campbell.

Lynn Davies

More commonly known as "Lynn the leap" for his long jumping ability, but Lynn was also a very successful sprinter.

He is obviously one of our most well known athletes, not only because of his Gold Medal in the 1964 Tokyo Olympics.

This is an article written by David Martin, PA Sport.

"Ask Lynn 'The Leap' Davies and he will candidly tell you that he won the 1964 Olympic Games long jump 4 years earlier than he had intended.

Although coming on leaps and bounds that year, never in his wildest dreams did the Welshman believe he would stop America's Ralph Boston from retaining his title.

Boston arrived in Tokyo having just set a world record jump of 8.24 metres to win the United States trials.

Rather than the sun shinning on the 22-year-old Bridgend born jumper, it was the harsh weather conditions, which assisted Lynn to his tremendous victory.

With the wind blowing in their faces and the temperature constantly below 15 degrees, the competitors were further hindered with puddles of water lying at several points on the cinder run up which were not conducive to world class long jumping.

Both Boston and the great Igor Ter-Ovanesyan, who preceded the American as world record holder, were suffering immensely from the freezing cold. Although after four rounds the American led his great Soviet rival by 8 centimeters with a clearance of 7.88m.

But in the next round Lynn totally transformed the top 3 positions.

Already knowing that fortune had smiled upon him when, in the morning's qualifying round, he only just made the final with his last attempt of 7.78m, he realised time was against him but he produced the leap of his lifetime.

Defying the horrendous conditions, and finding from somewhere the biggest jump of his career, he soared through the air to land into the gold medal position with a leap of 8.07 metres.

The pressure was now totally on his two great rivals.

Ter-Ovanesyan almost immediately replied with 7.99m, while in the 6th and final round Boston hammered down the runway as if his life and not just the gold medal depended on it.

He landed alarmingly close to the Welshman's mark.

Davies chewed on his lip, anxiously awaiting the judges to measure the world record holder's final attempt.

Then his face lit up as the figure 8.03 flashed upon the adjacent scoreboard. The gold medal was his!"

These were the athletes I was rubbing shoulders with!

But one of the important things that sport had taught me was that stars, internationals and sports personalities are only real people. Today so much emphasis is on the mega star sports image and personalities who seem to have taken over from the sporting aspect, players and athletes have become or trying to become bigger than the very sport they are involved with. They are not content in being stars, but now all want to be personalities!

I remember an athletics meeting in 1963, held at Motspur Park, I was involved in a guest 100 yards (yes, prior to the introduction of metres to athletics). The line up was very daunting as I gazed along the starting line, international and Olympic athletes filled each lane eccept mine, I was beaten before I had even started, as the thought of 'What am I doing here?' came into my mind. I finished a miserable 5th.

But it taught me a lesson, which was to help me in sport and also in my future career in professional football, they are only people.

That season also saw me at a meeting at British Nylon Spinners in Pontypool in South Wales, I had just finished the 100yards race, and I was approached by a gentleman from the Welsh AAA who asked various questions about me, including my birth place and did I have Welsh connections, to which I answered that my Mother was born in South Wales. Then he asked me my age to which I said 22 years, but disappointment was to descend on me as he was inquiring regarding the Wales under 19's (the Junior). So near and yet so far, wish those young features were still with me now.

Meanwhile the RAF gave me great opportunities to take up coaching awards in various sports and activities, but it also taught me how to empty a pint glass.

Forces life is a great life, but it also introduces you to a complete mans world and everything that goes with it, no wonder that the divorce rates are extremely high. I met and married Ann during my first 5 years in the RAF, she was a WRAF and had been brought up in the forces, her father and mother both serving in the Army. Her father Pat was in fact awarded the Military Medal, as one of the only soldiers to escape from being a Japanese POW and making his way back to England. But even this military background couldn't save this marriage. It is easy to blame the forces lifestyle, but it was me who went along with it and loved it; playing sport and loving it, training hard and loving it, supping ale and loving it' which eventually led to a separation after 8 years of marriage from Ann and my 6 year old son Gavin.

Dennis Loze

At the time of the Highbury visit I was stationed at Joint Services Medical Rehabilitation Unit Chessington in Surrey, which was the start of me moving into the field of medicine, and an interest in sports medicine. Chessington what a place, what an experience, a place of work hard and play hard, with tremendous results both medically and socially. The Medical unit first opened during the 2nd world war for the rehabilitation of wounded service personnel, this purpose was to continue until its final closure in the 1990's, when the unit combined with its sister unit at RAF Headley Court. The training at Chessington was second to none, but was hard as we had to squeeze a 3 year course into 18mths. This was compensated by an extremely good socially life centred around the Sgts mess, sport and great friendship. This started me looking towards the treatment of sports injuries, which combined well with my coaching and practical sporting abilities.

We certainly had a few characters there one in particular, a fellow RAF Sgt, Mick Skelton. Mick, well a one off, a person who could swear in the company of the Queen and get away with it, a person who liked his beer, betting on three legged race horses, but a person who you could trust your life with. Mick astounded us all when he started to go out with, and eventually marry Edie a very straight, no nonsense Geordie lass, a committed Christian. Would she tame him, only time would tell.

I well remember after a good full days drinking with Mick we ended up near Epsom, in a village with a great big duck pond in the centre. Well this was too much of a temptation, not to walk around, but yes to walk straight through, the water got deeper and muddier, the ducks flying off in disgust, water up to the chin, but the challenge was successfully completed Mick was OK as he was a lot taller than me - well nearly everyone is taller than me.

To think when Mick left the RAF he went to work in the House of Lords, as a member of staff under Black Rod.
Another was Ted Powell, an Army Warrant Officer. The number of hours that Ted, Mick and myself spent locked in the Sgts Mess bar, especially on Friday afternoons.

Chessington was also ideally placed regarding sport, and a number of the medical staff were attached to various semi professional football clubs. One such person was a fellow therapist, Mike Varney who was later to take up the position as club physiotherapist with Tottenham Hotspurs.

One of the semi professional football clubs in the area, made contact as they wanted someone to look after their injuries and were willing to pay for the expertise. A number of my colleagues were already involved with clubs such as Staines, Epsom, Corinthian Casuals, Leatherhead and a few others, so I was tempted and made enquires to Molesly FC, but one problem was that I was still playing weekend rugby, so it would mean a sacrifice.

My next move wasn't obvious but if I did want to get involved practically with sports injuries, it did mean that a sacrifice had to be made and I had to say good bye to playing civilian club rugby.

I first started playing civilian club rugby with Beaconsfield RFC whilst being stationed at RAF High Wycombe, then with Harrogate RFC whilst being in the north of England.

A potted history of Harrogate Rugby Union Football Club.

- **1871** Founded under the name of Harrogate Football Club.
- **1875** In 1875 the club acquired land at Dragon Fields opposite where Smiths the Rink is today.
- **1896** 19th December move to Claro Road
- **1903** Harrogate played Canada, result unknown.
- **1905** Winners Yorkshire Cup
- **1906** Harrogate Old Boys formed from 2nd XV.
- **1907** Winners Yorkshire Cup
- **1914** Harrogate becomes a soccer club. Rugby continues as Harrogate Old Boys.
- **1923** Harrogate R.U.F.C. formed. Played at the showground Knaresborough Road, now Shaw's caravan park.
- **1926** Harrogate Old Boys purchase Claro Road
- **1928** The current changing rooms were built – regarded as the best in the county if not country at that time

Dennis Loze

1936 Harrogate R.U.F.C. joins with Harrogate Old Boys.

1948 Saw the first Colts team form under the guidance of a Mr. G. Ashcroft.

1949 Winners Yorkshire Cup v Skipton

1957 Harrogate Georgians (Ex Civil Service, St Georges Road) join Harrogate R.U.F.C. name saved for posterity as our second team title.

1963 Present Club House opened

1965 Winners Yorkshire Cup v Wakefield

1968 Winners of Daily Telegraph Northern Merit Table

1971 Club Centenary

1972 The Bantams now known as the Mini/Junior section was formed as one of the first in the Country, and has thrived ever since, and has produced many a County and Schools player from the Under 15's upwards as the honours board in the Clubhouse can testify.

1981 Won Yorkshire Cup v Morley

1990 Promotion from Div. North 1 to Div. 4 North

1991 Winners Yorkshire Cup V Otley

1992 Winners Yorkshire Cup v Bradford & Bingley, Div North champions promoted to newly formed League 4. Finished 2nd and promoted.

1993/4 Division 4 finished 2nd

1994/5 Division 3 Club finished 7th

1995/6 Division 3 finished 6th

1996/7 Division 3 finished 5th

1997/8 Jewson National Division 1 finished 14th

1998/9 Jewson National 1 finished 12th

1999 - 2000 Jewson National 1 finished 6th

2000/1 National 1 finished 5th. Represented Yorkshire in National 7's Cup.

2001/2 National 2 finished 4th. Won Yorkshire Cup v Wharfedale. Represented Yorkshire in National 7's, winning the cup

2002/3 National 2 finished 4th (*again*) Won Yorkshire Cup (*again*) v Doncaster. Runners up in National 7's Cup representing Yorkshire

Arsenal to Armenia

I played for Harrogate 1st and the Georgians during the seasons of 1968 to 1970, and made many good friends.

As I wrote this, news has come through of the death of former team player of Harrogate, also Wales and British Lions hooker, Jeff Young, who was capped 23 times between 1968 and 1973. Our paths were to cross again in the RAF when he joined in 1971. We were to play in the same and also on opposite sides.

Also in the same team at Harrogate was Roger Shackleton who was capped 4 times for England at fly-half in 1969 and 70.

But when you finally say goodbye to playing Rugby the last club remains closest to you. That club was a local Surrey team of Effingham, who now are known as Effingham and Leatherhead RFC.

I spent the seasons of '73 to '76 playing at Effingham and had some great times and drunk a lot of beer, home games were handy, as for a short period of time I lived in Effingham which was just a short stagger from King Georges Hall club house.

I played my last game for Effingham in '77 and received this write up in the Leatherhead Advertiser:-

............*"Mention should be made of Dennis Loze who played his last game for the club. A gritty and determined winger, he will be remembered for his ability to make space for himself in awkward situations and a devastating burst of speed brought him many useful tries."*

A Brief History of Effingham RUFC.
The Clubs first game, was in March 1966, against a Guildford and Godalming XV. Although leading at half time it was not to be a successful debut. This first Effingham team consisted of players who had never played before on the one hand, to a player who had represented the Royal Navy on the other. From the records it appears that the Clubs first victory was a 19-10 win against a Battersea Ironsides XV on the 29 October 1966.

From here, the club gradually progressed. The mini rugby section was formed in 1975. In 1976 the new changing rooms were opened and a tenth anniversary game against Guildford and Godalming was played. Unfortunately victory yet again eluded the Club. In 1982 the junior section was formed.

By 1986 the Clubroom had been constructed and the occasion was marked by an official opening by the President of Surrey, and a game against a Surrey XV.

The introduction of Leagues into Rugby Union was well received by the Club. However, the decision by Surrey RFU to place Effingham in Surrey Division II was not. The Club, to coin a phrase, put its money where its mouth was and immediately won promotion to Surrey Division I.

1991 saw the 25th anniversary of the Club and a tour to British Columbia. Although the Club has enjoyed many tours both at home and in Europe, this was the first tour to North America and it certainly lived up to expectations with many firm friendships being formed.

Effingham in 1996 now boasts four senior sides and a vets side, at junior level we are represented at every age group from under 13 to under 18, at mini level we are represented at every level from under 6 to under 12. The mini section is currently the fifth largest group in the South East of England.

In the 1996/97 season the 1st XV won promotion from the Surrey 1 league to the London South West 3 league, a major milestone.

At the beginning of the 1997/98 season, the club changed its name to "Effingham & Leatherhead RFC" and we intend to promote the club under the nick-name "The Eagles"

The 1998/99 season was Effingham & Leatherhead's most successful ever, by winning "the double", of the London 3 South West league combined with the Surrey Cup. The league win gained the Eagles promotion to London 2. However, it was a struggle to remain in that division and for the 2003/4 season the "Eagles" reverted to London 3 South West.

At the time I played for Effingham, we had a good representation of service colleagues from Chessington – Pat Clash, Cas Clay, Nev Smith, Pat Fleming plus myself.

Although I made my farewell to civilian Rugby I did continue to play service Rugby for another 2 years, until finally leaving the RAF.

Arsenal to Armenia

So the move into the football world came through joining Molesey FC based in West Molesey in the Athenian league. For those who do not know the location it is a few miles west from Hampton Court.

I spent the seasons of '75/76 to '77/78 at Molesey and met some great characters, some of which I will explain after a bit of Molesey FC history.

Formed: - 1952. Although a junior side existed in the 1800's. In 1953 Molesey St Pauls joined forces with another Molesey team and the senior club was formed.
Nick Name:- The Moles
Capacity:-4,000
Record Gate:-1,255
Most appearances:-Frank Handley 453
Record signing;- £500 Chris Vidal 1988
Record Transfer:- £5,000 Chris Vidal 1989
Most notable player: Cyril Regis (West Bromwich Albion and England)

One person who must get a mention is John Sulley, who was manager during the period that I was there, he did more ducking and diving than Arthur Dalley. John would turn up at the club in so many different cars, also you could never ring him, his only contact number was to his local Chinese take away.

Pay day was an experience like getting blood out of a stone. Many an evening the players and myself have stood in the bar of the club house waiting for Sulley to appear, only to find out that he had already left, so another week without pay. I remember one Saturday after a home match, stood at the bar with a few of the players, a young lad came into the club selling the early evening paper, which had the football league results in, Jim one our players purchased a copy. Later Sulley appeared and asked about some of the results including Chelsea, so to ease the conversation Sulley was handed the paper, which after being consulted was handed back to Jim. Approx. an hour had passed and still no sign of money passing hands, the newspaper was opened to check on a result and a number of notes fluttered to the floor, Yes it was Jim's pay, pushed into the paper by Sulley, but again the rest of us had missed out.

On another occasion, after training, Sulley came to me at the bar asking about the injury situation. As he was talking I could feel something being pushed into my pocket, then a wink from him and he was gone. Have you ever tried to count notes in your pocket trying, to distinguish fivers from tenners? By the time I had done that and found I was short, but too late he had gone.

One of the young players at the club was a very promising centre forward, who was big and strong, and also a super genuine person, a lad I was to meet up with a few years later. A young man by the name of Cyril Regis.

Cyril was born in Maripasoula, French Guiana and moving to England in his youth, He started work as an electrician, playing for amateur team Molesey FC and later Hayes in his spare time. He was spotted by Ronnie Allen, he joined First Division club West Bromwich Albion in 1977 where, under manager Johnny Giles, he teamed up with another black player, Laurie Cunningham, and the following year (under Ron Atkinson) with Brendon Batson.

It was very unusual for an English club to simultaneously field three black players. The **Three Degrees**, as they became known, in reference to the contemporary vocal trio of the same name challenged the established racism of English football and marked a watershed that allowed a generation of footballers to enter the game who would previously have been excluded by their ethnic background. There was still enough residual racism, however, that Cyril, Laurie and Brendon (and Lutons Ricky Hill) were selected for far fewer internationals than many felt their talents warranted.)

Interestingly, after Big Ron Atkinson's famous on-air use of the word "…..", Cyril defended his mentor, suggesting that the word is less significantly offensive to people of that age.

A strong and fast traditional centre-forward, Cyril was voted PFA Young Player of the Year in 1978 and went on to win five England caps. He earned the Goal of the Season award in 1981-82, for his powerful long-range shot against Norwich City in the FA Cup. Cyril was also an FA Cup winner in 1987 with Coventry City, where he 'scored' a fine header before it was disallowed.

After leaving Coventry in 1991, he was transferred to their arch-rivals Aston Villa and partnered Dalian Atkinson in the 1991-92 season. He left at the end of the following season after being forced-out of the side by new signing Dean Saunders, and signed for Wolverhampton Wanderers. He had little success at Molineux, with first-team opportunities restricted by the strength of the Steve Bull - David Kelly strike partnership. His stay at Wolves lasted a single season before he joined Wycombe Wanderers.

After one season with The Chairboys, he was on the move again, this time to Chester City. Cyril played his last game in February 1996, aged 38, and retired from professional football nine months later, having never made a full recovery from an injury suffered in a match with Chester.

Since retiring from playing, he has worked in a variety of coaching roles before becoming an accredited football agent with The Stellar Group Ltd.

Cyrille is uncle of Blackburn Rovers star Jason Roberts and cousin of sprinter John Regis.

Meanwhile back at Highbury, after Fred had shown us around, and had a good discussion with Cliff, I asked Fred what it was like to work and be with the Arsenal, his reply was "Its just a job of work" which sums up Fred's laid back approach to life.

A huge surprise was to follow, in fact just as we were leaving, Fred asked me when and what I was doing on leaving the RAF in 4 weeks time. As I said previously, things are thrown at you, and are you prepared to deal with the situation that arises. What was initially a casual visit to Highbury was to end up with a fantastic surprise, one that would lead me into a world that millions of people can only dream of.

Well at that stage so much had been happening. After 8 years of marriage, and a trial separation, Ann and I now legally separated. A marriage which had had its great times, and through me its bad times. Ann had been a good wife and a great mother to Gavin, but it had been me in my selfish attitude to life that had destroyed something that was good.

I had started to meet up with Jane, who worked as a civilian Occupational Therapist at Chessington, and things seem to be working out well. I was convinced that being out of the forces would bring about a change in me, although I must admit that Jane didn't know the full problem side of me.

So the reply to Fred was positive, that Jane and I were moving to live just outside Honiton in Devon. Jane already had the promise of employment with the local authority, and I was looking at setting up a sports injury clinic. We had seen a house and were in the process of putting in an offer.

The next words were to drastically change those plans!

"Is it 100% certain that is what you are doing, because we are looking for an assistant physiotherapist here, and if you are interested it is yours."

From a social visit to an offer of a job with one of top clubs in Europe, and the top club in England, was I prepared for that? NO!

I was coming to the end of my career in the Royal Air Force, plus facing an ultimate divorce and the prospect of a fresh start with Jane my future wife, so was it an easy decision?

After a discussion with Jane that evening, a phone call to the estate agent to withdraw our interest in the Honiton property, it was time to confirm with Fred YES! What a time in the Sgts mess!!!

Chapter Four

∽

"We must use time as a tool not as a crutch"
J.F.KENNEDY

A new start, but a start for what, where, when and how? As I said in chapter one, we think we are prepared for what comes our way, or sometimes thrown at us. You think that something is for life and it is either taken away from you, or you throw it away, or sometimes you destroy it.

I still had a month or so of my RAF service to finish so I joined Arsenal at the end of their 1977-8 pre-season, and straight into the behind the scenes politics of football life.

I remember my first day, just like the new boy, but a new boy in an important role. Again walking up the marble steps, greeted by the door man in his full uniform and into the marble hall, I think, as I looked up to the bust of Herbert Chapman, that he had a look of expectation on his face, could I live up to this expectation?

I turned right into the long corridor that led into the action area, even this area had its marble floors! Past the door on the right, this led into the visitors changing room, then immediately off to the left, the tunnel leading down the steps out on to the field of play. Past the tunnel entrance off to the left was the staff changing room, which in turn led to the staff room.

The corridor then continued, with a further door off to the right which led into the treatment office, and a door from this into the treatment room, through into the home changing room.

Back into the corridor, which continued past the treatment room, through into the kit room off to the left, with the entrance to the changing room off to the right. The corridor continued to a set of marble stairs going upwards to a landing, off to the left was the laundry and drying rooms and to the right the gym and weight training room.

The main changing room with the normal benches etc. around the walls, a door leading into the treatment room, opposite this door leading to the showers, sauna, baths and off this was the boot room.

But Arsenal is not all about the buildings, although now they have moved to the Emerities Stadium, the memory of Highbury will always remain in peoples minds and hearts, including mine and the players!

The team had just returned from their tour of Singapore and Australia, or should I say that two had already returned, Alan Hudson and Malcolm MacDonald. I won't go into the main conflict that caused Huddy and Malcolm's early return; this is covered better by Malcolm in his book "Super Mac" and Huddys "The Working man's ballet". What it did show, and continued to show up in the next 10 or so years of my connection with pro-football, is of mangers and coaches inability or lack of man management skills. This is where the armed forces excel; it is not all about shouting and balling, man management is so high on the agenda.

I will only say that this was possibly one of Terry Neil's weak points, especially in the lack of ability in dealing with senior and experienced players and this was the situation in Australia. Don't get me wrong, I am not saying that Terry was a bad manger. The time I spent there, he performed with a very high degree of professionalism, something which is of the Arsenal blood line. His handling of the media was excellent - possibly the Irish blarney helped! I found him a very easy person to talk to and to get on with I respected him as a person, manager and ex player and I am certain he respected who I was and my role within the club.

An episode at Arsenal, prior to me joining them, showed the area of senior pro experience, that they need to be listened to as they are closer to the grindstone than any other member of the staff, both playing and non playing staff. It was an episode of Ballie (prior to his move to Southampton) with Terry and Wilf Dixon, who was then the first team coach. Bally was very forthright in his opinions, which are loud, and obvious and he was speaking not just for himself but for the other senior players, such as George Armstrong, Peter Storey and Peter Simpson, that Wilf was not up to the job. It got to the point that even in training the ridicule would continue. Terry would admit that he was not a coach but essentially the manager. But no matter how much the Irish blarney was used this was a major problem.

Wilf was pushed into the office and for the start of the new season (mine also) Don Howe was brought in. Man motivation and management was his strong point and his amazing coaching ability backed this up.

So this was the position at Highbury

My first taste of action was a mid week reserve team game at Cardiff. The team consisted of a blend of experienced and not so experienced players, but there was no evidence of any demarcation between the two. They were all Arsenal players, wearing the famous red shirts with the Cannon on the left breast.

Players like Peter Simpson who had one of the finest left pegs in the business, he could open a tin can with it! Peter was coming to the end of his illustrious career

David Price who was coming back after injury, a run out before going back into the first team squad. David was a very genuine person, who still traveled to the ground each day by local transport the bus. Something that you wouldn't see today

Geordie Armstrong, who like Simmo was coming to the end of a long and illustrious career.

John Devine who was to make his 1st team debut during my stay at Highbury.

Steve Walford, who made the journey from Spurs, and arrived the same week as myself; and

Steve Gatting, brother of England cricketer Mike.

I think I should take this opportunity to introduce the Arsenal Squad:-

Patrick Anthony Jennings OBE (born June 12, 1945 in Newry, Northern Ireland)

Pat played a total of 119 games for Northern Ireland a figure which at the time was a world record, in an international career which lasted for over 22 years. Pat is considered one of the greatest goalkeepers of all time. During his career he played in over 1000 top level games for club and country, he even managed to score a goal in the 1967 Charity Shield match.

Pat began his playing career with his hometown side Newry Town as a 16 year old. After making an impression within the team, he moved to English Third Division side Watford in May 1963. He again made a big impression in his first season in English football, during which he played every league game for his club, and was then bought by Tottenham Hotspur for £27,000 at the end of it. Pat spent a total 13 years at White Hart Lane, during which time he played in 472 league games for Spurs. During his time with Spurs he won the FA Cup in 1967, the League Cup in 1971 and 1973, and the UEFA Cup in 1972. In 1973 the Football Writers' Association named him as its footballer of the year, three years later he won PFA version of the award.

In August 1977, he was sold to Tottenhams arch-rivals, Arsenal. During his eight years with the Gunners he appeared in 237 league games. Whilst at Highbury he helped Arsenal to three successive FA Cup finals, in 1978, 1979, and 1980. However, Arsenal only managed to win the second of these finals, a 3-2 victory against Manchester United.

Pat made his Northern Ireland debut as an 18 year old, whilst playing for Watford. This game was on April 15, 1964, and was a British Home Championship match against Wales, Northern Ireland won the game 3-2; George Best made his international debut in the same game. The final international game fell on his 41st birthday, having returned to Tottenham Hotspur 6 months earlier and playing in their reserve side to maintain his match sharpness. This game was Northern Ireland's final group game in the 1986 World Cup, and was against Brazil, Brazil won the game 3-0. This was in fact was Pat's second World Cup. He had previously played in the 1982 World Cup.

Following his retirement Jennings has worked as a goalkeeping coach. He has worked at Tottenham in this capacity since 1993. In 2003 Jennings was inducted into the English Football Hall of Fame in recognition of the skills he demonstrated in the English league.

His son, also called Pat, is also a professional footballer, although he is far less successful. He has played for Eircom League clubs UCD and Derry

John Anthony Devine (born November 11, 1958)

Arsenal to Armenia

Born in Dublin, John joined Arsenal in November 1974 as an apprentice. He became part of a large young Irish contingent at Arsenal (which also included Liam Brady, David O'Leary and Frank Stapleton), he turned professional in 1976. A full back who preferred playing on the right, he made his debut for the Gunners on April 28, 1978, deputising for Pat Rice.

With Pat and Sammy Nelson occupying the Arsenal full back positions most of the time, John had a battle to break into the first team, although he did play in the 1980 FA Cup final (which Arsenal lost 1-0 to West Ham United) after Pat was injured. However, Pat returned to the Arsenal side for the Gunners' Cup Winners Cup final against Valencia. After Pat left for Watford in the summer of 1980, John stepped up to become Arsenal's regular right-back, playing 44 times in 1980-81. However, his tenure there didn't last; after he was out of the side due to an injury, John Hollins was moved back into defence as cover, and John could not reclaim his place once he had regained fitness. He went on to play only 23 games in his final two seasons at Highbury

John was capped for the Republic of Ireland at every level, winning thirty caps in all, with thirteen of those coming for the senior side. He made his senior debut on September 26, 1979 against Czechoslovakia, and his last cap came against Norway on October 17, 1984. He never played in a World Cup or European Championship finals, as Ireland did not qualify for any tournaments during that time. Most of his caps were won in European and World cup qualifying games.

John left Arsenal in the summer of 1983, having played 111 first-team matches for the club in nine years. He joined Norwich City, and played 69 games in two seasons for the Canaries and was an unused sub in the Canaries' League Cup final win in 1984-85. He then had a spell at Stoke City, but after breaking his leg his career was effectively over. He had brief spells at Norwegian club I.K. Start and Indian side East Bengal, before retiring from playing.

He returned to Ireland as a coach at Shelbourne. Shelburne's close ties with Manchester United led to him working with the English club and he has been Uniteds head of youth development in Ireland since 1997.

Patrick James Rice (born March 17, 1949 in Belfast)
Pat has spent most of his footballing career at Arsenal. Though born in Belfast, he grew up in London, and joined the Gunners as a youth in 1964. He made his debut in the League Cup against Burnley on December

5, 1967. Playing at right-back, he was a stalwart at the club through the 1970s, eventually becoming club captain. He won the Inter-Cities Fairs Cup in 1970 and was part of the League and FA Cup Double-winning side of 1971; in all he appeared in five FA Cup finals, but only won two (1971 and 1979).

Pat played 528 games in total for the Gunners, before moving to Watford in 1980. He played 137 times for the Hornets, helping the club gain promotion to the First Division becoming captain before retiring from playing in 1984. He also won 49 international caps for Northern Ireland between 1968 and 1979.

He rejoined Arsenal in 1984 as youth team coach, a post he held for the next 12 years, winning the FA Youth Cup twice in 1988 and 1994. In September 1996 Rice was briefly caretaker manager of the club after the resignation of Stewart Houston (who himself was caretaker after the sacking of Bruce Rioch). He managed the side for three FA Premier League matches (all of which Arsenal won) and a 3-2 defeat in the UEFA Cup away to Borussia Mönchengladbach. Upon the arrival of Arsène Wenger at the end of the month, he became his assistant, and has since played a key role in helping the club to their success in the 1990s and 2000s, including the Doubles of 1997-98 and 2001-02. He holds the distinction (along with Bob Wilson) of having taken part, as player or coach, in all three of Arsenal's Doubles.

George "Geordie" Armstrong (August 9, 1944 – November 1, 2000)
Born in Hebburn, County Durham, Geordie had trained as an electrician while playing in youth football, before joining Arsenal as a youth player in August 1961. Initially he had been a forward but was soon switched to the wing. He made his debut not long after joining the club; while still only 17, against Blackpool on February 24, 1962 in a match that Arsenal won 1-0. Although he started out as understudy to Johnny MacLeod and Alan Skirton, by the 1963-64 season, he had become a regular in the side, and in 1964-65 he missed only two matches.

Over his long career with the Gunners, he became one of Arsenal's most consistent players, who was noted for the quality and accuracy of his crossing and corner kicks, as well as for his tireless running up and down the wing; he primarily played on the left, but was also effective on the right. As he matured, he became one of the few players of the Billy

Wright era (along with Jon Sammels and Peter Storey) to become an integral part of Wright's successor Bertie Mee's Arsenal side, which ended the club's long trophy drought.

After losing two successive League Cup finals in 1967-68 and 1968-69, Geordie helped the Gunners win the 1969-70 Inter-Cities Fairs Cup and the 1970-71 League and FA Cup double. He was ever-present in the Double-winning team that season, and set up Ray Kennedy's winning header against Tottenham Hotspur, in the match that won Arsenal the League title. He was also voted Arsenal's Player of the Year in 1970.

He remained with the club through the 1970s, as Arsenal failed to win any further trophies after their Double win; he played at least thirty matches in each season he was at the club during that decade. However, after falling out with Mee's successor, Terry Neill, he moved to Leicester City in the summer of 1977 for £15,000. He played only 14 League matches in his single season with the Foxes, and finished his career with Stockport County before retiring in 1979.

Having spent fifteen full seasons at Arsenal, most of them as an ever-present, he at the time held the club's all-time record for appearances - 621 competitive first-team appearances, including exactly 500 in the league; his record has since been overtaken by David O'Leary and Tony Adams. He also scored 68 goals for Arsenal. Surprisingly for such a high-standing player, he was never capped for the full England side, despite plenty of youth and U21 caps; this was primarily because of England manager Sir Alf Ramsey's policy of not using wingers.

After retiring from playing, Geordie moved into coaching, and worked for a variety of clubs, including Fulham, Aston Villa, Middlesbrough and QPR as well as Narvik in Norway. In 1990 he returned to Arsenal as reserve team coach, a post he remained at for the remainder of his life, despite the many managerial upheavals the club underwent. On October 31, 2000, he collapsed after an unexpected brain haemorrhage whilst at a club training session; he died in hospital in the early hours of the following morning.

Samuel "Sammy" Nelson (born Belfast, Northern Ireland on April 1, 1949)

Sammy joined Arsenal on his 17th birthday in 1966. Originally a left-winger, he was later moved back into defence to become a left back. He was a regular in Arsenal's reserve side for several seasons, before making his first-team debut against Ipswich Town on October 25, 1969.

However, he was understudy to the Gunners' established left back, Bob McNab, and it wasn't until Bob was injured during the 1971-72 season that he become a regular in the side. When Bob returned from injury, Sammy was forced to step down to the reserves.

In the meantime, he had made his debut for Northern Ireland, as a sub against England on April 21, 1970 he went on to win 51 international caps, including two of Northern Ireland's matches in the 1982 World Cup.

When Bob left Arsenal in the summer of 1975, Sammy became Arsenal's first-choice left back. For the next five seasons he was ever present in the Arsenal side, and played in all three of the Gunners' successive FA Cup finals (1978, 1979 and 1980 – but only winning the middle of the three) as well as the Gunners' 1980 Cup Winners' Cup loss on penalties to Valencia.

An aggressive, hard-tackling full back, Sammy was a crowd favourite and known for his sense of humour. He was famously suspended by the club after an incident in a match against Coventry City at Highbury on April 3, 1979, having already scored an own goal, he then scored Arsenal's equaliser to make the score 1-1. Jubilantly celebrated by dropping his shorts and flashing his backside at his own supporters in the North Bank.

With the arrival of England international Kenny Sansom at the club in 1980, Sammy once again found himself in the reserves. He left Arsenal in 1981 to join Brighton & Hove Albion. In total he played 339 first team matches for the Gunners and scored 12 goals.

He spent two seasons at Brighton; although unable to save the side from relegation in 1982-83, he did reach another Cup final (his fourth) that season, losing to Manchester United 4-0 in a replay, after a 2-2 draw in the final. He retired from football that summer and after spending a season as a coach at Brighton, he left the game completely and went into the insurance industry.

David Anthony O'Leary (born in Stoke Newington, London on May 2, 1958)

He moved to live in Dublin at the age of three. As his father was born in Ireland, David decided to play for the Republic of Ireland.

Arsenal to Armenia

David signed for Arsenal as an apprentice in 1973. He soon progressed through the ranks at Highbury, playing in the reserves at the age of 16. He made his debut for Arsenal against Burnley on August 16, 1975, and despite being only 17, went on to make 30 appearances that season. For the next ten years he was a near ever-present in the Arsenal side, playing more than 40 matches each season (except for 1980-81, when he was injured and only played 27).

A calm and collected centre half, he was noted for his positional sense and elegant style of play. He won his first major honour with Arsenal when he played in their 3-2 win over Manchester United in the 1979 FA Cup final. He also played in the 1978 and 1980 Cup finals, and the 1980 Cup Winners' Cup final, all of which Arsenal lost. In 1982 he became club captain, but reliniquished it to Graham Rix eighteen months later.

David broke numerous appearance records at Arsenal; he was the youngest person to reach the 100 and 200 match milestones, and he made his 400th appearance while still only 26. He passed George Armstrong's all-time record of 621 first-team games in November 1989. By this time, he was no longer automatic first choice (with the partnership of Tony Adams and Steve Bould at the centre of George Graham's defence), but he still turned in over 20 appearances as Arsenal won the 1988-89 First Division title.

He won another League title in 1991 and an FA Cup and League Cup double in 1993, though by this time he was mainly used as a sub. He holds Arsenal's all-time record for appearances, with 722 first-team games, and over 1,000 games at all levels, in a twenty-year long association with the club.

He joined Leeds on a free transfer in 1993 after 19 years at Highbury. Throughout 1993-94, was a regular player in the Leeds side until he suffered an achilles injury, which ruled him out for the whole of the following season. He was still on the club's payroll at the beginning of the 1995-96 season but that September he gave in to his injury and announced his retirement from football at the age of 37.

His international debut with the Republic of Ireland came as a teenager in a 1-1 draw with England in 1976, but the highlight of his 68-cap international career came in the 1990 World Cup. With Ireland in a penalty shootout with Romania, Packie Bonner saved Daniel Timofte's last penalty. It was O'Leary who then stepped up to take the decisive final penalty to win the shootout 5-4.

When the former Arsenal manager George Graham was put in charge at Leeds United in September 1996, David was installed as his assistant. He remained in this position for two years until George moved to Tottenham.

The Leeds directors made an offer for Martin O'Neill to take charge at Elland Road but the deal fell through and David was promoted to the hot seat. At the end of 1998-99 Leeds finished fourth in the Premiership and qualified for the UEFA Cup. Their 1999-2000 campaign ended in the semifinals with defeat to the Turkish side Galatasaray, and it was after the game in Turkey that two Leeds fans were stabbed to death by Turkish hooligans. But on the domestic front, Leeds finished third in the Premiership and qualified for the Champions League - it would be their first campaign at this level since they were losing finalists in the European Cup in 1975.

Leeds reached the semifinals of the Champions League, where they lost to eventual runners-up Valencia. Their Premiership form also dipped slightly and David O'Leary's men had to settle for a UEFA Cup place.

2001-02 began well for Leeds. They constantly topped the table during the first half of the season and come the new year of 2002 they were Premiership leaders, a loss of form in the second half of the season saw them slump into sixth place - the last automatic UEFA Cup place. They had secured their place in Europe much earlier because seventh-placed West Ham had collected 12 less points.

The season was thrown into turmoil by the involvement of four players, including first-teamers, in an incident in Leeds city centre that ended in the assault and injury of an Asian student.

By June 2002 David had spent £100 million on new players in less than four years for relatively little reward. The club was in serious financial trouble and had relied on qualifying for the Champions League.

Although he had never finished outside the top five as a manager, he was sacked.

David remained out of work until June 2003 when he was appointed manager of Aston Villa.

Arsenal to Armenia

By the beginning of November 2003, Aston Villa were hovering just above the relegation zone and it looked as though he would be another of the club's unsuccessful managers. He remained at Villa and managed to get an already good squad to perform successfully so that by the final weeks of the season they were pushing hard for at least a UEFA Cup place and possibly even a Champions League place. But in the end their early season form had caught up with them and they had to settle for sixth place - this season one place too low for European qualification.

During the 2004-05 season, Aston Villa hovered just below the European qualification places, ending the season in 10th. Despite a bright start to the season, they lacked the consistency that was attributed to his first season in charge. He started to create a Villa side that bore his trademarks at Leeds United: a solid team that plays neat football, sparked to life by a sprinkling of younger players keen to make their mark.

The 2005-06 season brought a disappointing turn for the worse for him. Injuries and suspensions have decimated the squad. The frustration of the Aston Villa fans become more and more apparent, with chants for his dismissal following the 4-1 drubbing at Everton and banners began to appear amidst the Villa crowd. Many blamed his lack of motivation in the dressing room and it seemed with more and more excuses from him instilling little faith amongst the supporters, his three year reign as Villa manager would soon reach its end. With Aston Villa losing 5 - 0 at Highbury against Arsenal the calls for him to stand down may well intensify.

Peter Simpson (born January 13, 1945) Born in Gorleston, Norfolk.
Simmo' initially joined Arsenal as a member of the club's ground staff in 1960, before joining as an apprentice a year later, and turning professional the year after that. He made his first team debut in 1964 against Chelsea, but didn't break fully into the side until the 1966-67 season. A versatile player, he played in every position on the pitch (except as goalkeeper!), before settling into role of central defender usually alongside Frank McLintock.
He was a leading figure in Arsenal's success in the early 1970s, winning the Inter-Cities Fairs Cup in 1970 and the First Division and FA Cup Double in 1971. He continued to play for the club in the barren years following the Double, though by 1975 age was starting to get the better of him, and he was only a semi-regular in the last few years of his Arsenal career.

He left Arsenal in 1978, having played 468 times for the club. He had brief stints with the New England Teamen in the United States, and then Hendon, before retiring. Despite his long career at the top, he was never capped for England.

Steve Walford(Born Islington 1958)

Steve started his professional career at Tottenham where in 1975 he made 2 league appearances, but in the following season failed to make an appearance. But Terry Neil saw in him enough to pay £25,000 for him in the August of 1977. At Highbury Steve gradually eased himself in the first team squad so that by the end of his first season made 5 appearances. But 1978-9 made 33, 1979-80 made 19, and 1980-81 a total of 20 appearances. He was transferred in the March 1981 to Norwich for £175,000 and played a total 93 games until his transfer to West Ham in the August of 1983.

At West Ham he had an indifferent success, during the next 4 seasons making 115 appearances, but in the season of 1987-88 made no appearances, but included a loan period to Huddersfield making 12 appearances. The following season he again failed to break back into contention and serviced a further two loan periods to Gillingham 4 appearances and West Bromwich 4 appearances. Steve then played for a period of time in Hong Kong and also Turkey, before moving to Wycombe Wanderers. He commenced as a player but soon took up the post of assistant manager to Martin O'Neil, there the link was forged. Moving to Norwich with Martin in 1995, then to Leicester then the big move to Celtic in 2000, leaving together in 2005. Recently Steve accepted a similar post with Martin at Aston Villa.

William David "Willie" Young (Born November 25, 1951)

A large, physically intimidating centre back from Edinburgh, Willie first played for Aberdeen, and made 187 appearances for the Dons between 1970 and 1975. He was signed by Tottenham Hotspur in September 1975, and made 54 appearances for Spurs in two seasons. In March 1977, he signed for Arsenal for £80,000.

Willie immediately became a regular in the Arsenal first team, and played in all of the Gunners' trio of FA Cup finals; after losing to Ipswich Town in 1978, he was on the winning side the following year, with a 3-2 defeat of Manchester United. In his third Cup final in 1980, he infamously hacked down West Ham United's Paul Allen while Allen was clean through on goal. At the time, there was no specific rule against committing a professional foul, meaning Young got away with a booking, instead of being sent off; Arsenal however lost the final 1-0 after a goal by Trevor Brooking.

He continued to be Arsenal's first choice centre back until the 1981-82 season, when he was ousted by Chris Whyte. Having played 237 times for Arsenal, the 30-year-old Young joined Nottingham Forest in December 1981 for £50,000, and played 59 times in two seasons there. In 1983 he joined Norwich City, but with injuries dogging him, he failed to secure a place in the side; short spells at Brighton and Darlington followed, before retiring from the game in November 1984.

He left the game completely after his retirement, and now runs a pub near Nottingham.

Liam 'Chippy' Brady (Born February 13, 1956 in Dublin, Ireland)
Part of a footballing family (his uncle and two brothers having been players as well), he started his career as a midfielder at Arsenal, making his debut aged 17, on October 6, 1973 against Birmingham City F.C.

Renowned for his supremely elegant technical skills, most notably his famous left foot, his high-quality passing and close control, he gained the nickname "Chippy", although it appears this was on account of his dietary habits rather than his ability to chip the ball.

By 1974 he was a first-team regular; his passing providing the ammunition for Arsenal's front men such as Malcolm Macdonald and Frank Stapleton. With the Gunners, he won the 1979 FA Cup (helping set up Alan Sunderland's famous last-minute winner in the final against Manchester United), as well as being a runner-up in the 1978 and 1980 competitions. He was also a runner-up after Arsenal lost the 1980 Cup Winners' Cup final to Valencia on penalties. He, along with Graham Rix, missed in the shootout.

Chippy was the most talented player in what was then a distinctly average Arsenal side, which was unable to challenge for serious honours like the Division One title. He was voted the club's player of the year three times, and PFA Player of the Year in 1979. In the summer of 1980 he signed for Italian giants Juventus and spent two seasons there, picking up two Italian Championship medals, in 1981 and 1982; he scored the only goal (a penalty) in the 1-0 win against Catanzaro that won the 1982 title.

After the arrival of Michel Platini in summer 1982, he moved to Sampdoria, and went on to play for Internazionale (1984-1986) and Ascoli (1986-1987), before returning to London to play for West Ham

(1987-1990). He won 72 international caps for the Republic of Ireland, scoring 9 goals, although he never played in a major tournament, thanks to injury and a suspension accrued before Euro 88.

After retiring from playing in 1990, he managed Celtic between 1991 and 1993, and then Brighton & Hove Albion between 1993 and 1995. Neither spell was particularly successful, as at both clubs his tenure was overshadowed by financial problems.

He is remembered as one of Arsenal's all-time greats, playing 307 matches for the Gunners, scoring 59 goals and setting up many more. He rejoined Arsenal in 1996, as Head of Youth Development and Academy Director and has remained there since. He oversaw the club's FA Youth Cup wins in 2000 and 2001.

Jim Harvey (Born Lurgan, Northern Ireland)
Signed for Arsenal in 1974, sadly his 1st team opportunities were restricted with only making 3 league appearances. In 1980 Jim was given a free transfer to Hereford United, where he became a firm favourite with 278 league games under his belt.

In 1983 Bristol City purchased him for £25,000, but after making 2 appearances he went on loan to Wrexham, making 6 appearances. He was then transferred to Tranmere Rovers in late 1987. Jim was quickly made captain, making 121 league, 12 League Cup and 8 FA Cup appearances.

When he left Tranmere for Crewe Alexander, he had his first taste of player/coach under the great Dario Gradi. He then made moves to Southport in the Vauxhall Conference, then joined Chester City as reserve team coach and Director of the School of Excellence.

In 1994 he moved to Morecambe Town as assistant manager, and took over the management when Leighton James left.

Morecambe Town came alive over the next 10 years, winning everything they seemed to touch. Unfortunately in November 2005, Jim suffered a heart attack, and medical advice took time out from the game. In May 2006 the club released him from his contract.

Mark Heeley Signed from Peterborough in 1977, and played a total 20 games, before being transferred to Northampton for £33,000 in 1979.

Alan Anthony "Huddy" Hudson (Born 21 June 1951 in Chelsea, London)
Huddy was one of the most naturally gifted midfielders of his generation, a skillful and natural playmaker with tremendous vision and

comfortable using either foot, yet his career was marred by controversies and injury problems. World Cup-winning England captain Bobby Moore once said of him: *"Alan Hudson could have conquered the world, but there was no guarantee he was going to conquer his temperament."*

Born and brought up near the King's Road, he was rejected by Fulham as a schoolboy before signing for Chelsea Juniors. Injury denied him the chance to become Chelsea's youngest ever player aged 16 and he eventually made his senior debut 9 months later on February 1, 1969 in a 5-0 loss against Southampton.

He found himself in a Chelsea side noted for its flair and skill, complete with equally flamboyant footballers such as Peter Osgood and Charlie Cooke. It was during the 1969-70 season that he established himself as the team's playmaker, creating goals for Osgood and Ian Hutchinson, and enabling Chelsea to finish 3rd in the First Division.

He played in every match in Chelsea's run to the FA Cup final in 1970, but missed the final itself due to another injury when they beat Leeds United 2-1 in a replay at Old Trafford, having drawn 2-2 at Wembley. He did, however, play a major role in Chelsea's replayed European Cup Winners' Cup final win against Real Madrid in Athens a year later.

The debt burden caused by the building of the then new East Stand resulted in the sale of key players, and a spiral of decline began. Chelsea lost 2-1 to Stoke City in the 1972 League Cup final at Wembley, whilst a falling-out with manager Dave Sexton resulted in both Huddy and Osgood being placed on the transfer list in January 1974. Within a month, he had joined Stoke City for £240,000, and his career with Chelsea was over at the age of 22.

Stoke manager Tony Waddington saw him as the final piece of the jigsaw that would turn Stoke City into genuine championship challengers in 1975. He played some of the best football of his career under Waddington's shrewd leadership as Stoke finished just four points away from eventual champions Derby County in his first season with the Potteries club.

Owing to a ban from international football after refusing to tour with the England under-23 side, he didn't make his England debut until 1975, when sparkling performances earned him two call ups by then England manager Don Revie. He starred in the team that beat World Champions West Germany 2-0 at Wembley, and then in the 5-0 destruction of Cyprus. However, injuries and clashes with Revie meant that those two caps were the only ones he earned.

Financial troubles at Stoke forced his sale to Arsenal in December 1976 for £200,000. He helped Arsenal reach the 1978 FA Cup Final, which they lost 1-0 to Ipswich Town, but differences with Terry Neill meant that he moved to the Seattle Sounders of the NASL for £100,000 at the age of 27. He subsequently moved on to Hércules CF of Spain before returning to Chelsea, then in the Second Division, although illness and injury denied him the chance to play for them again. There was also a nostalgic return to Stoke, where he helped the club avoid relegation from the old First Division in the 1983-84 season.

Since his retirement, he has suffered a series of setbacks. He had problems with alcoholism, and in 1997 sustained serious injuries in a car crash (spending two months in a coma), after which he was not expected to walk again, but managed to make a recovery.

I was to meet up with Huddy again in the NASL.

John Matthews (Born 1955 in Camden)
Commenced as an apprentice at Arsenal, but signed as a pro in 1973 and making his debut in 1974. John struggled to secure a permanent midfield position with Chippy and David Price holding on to their places. John was transferred to Sheffield United in 1978 for £90,000 after playing 57 games in the 4 seasons at Highbury.

John played 103 games for the Blades before being transferred to Mansfield in 1982. He played a total of 82 games and was given a free transfer to Chesterfield in 1984. Plymouth Argyle was his next move in 1985, there he played a total of 135 games. It was then a move down the road to play 25 games for Torquay United. John finally finished his career playing non league for Dorchester Town.

Richie Powling (born 21st May 1956)
Richie joined Arsenal as an apprentice during the 1971/72 season. He had previously gained England Youth caps. Richie made his debut in Oct 1973 against QPR, although appearing only once more that season against Liverpool. The following season managing 8 appearances at centre half, but although his introduction was gradual by the 1975'76 season he was a regular and becoming a key figure, making 29 appearances. Although this season wasn't the most successful season for Arsenal, it was for Richie forming a good relationship with Macini, which proved to be valuable as Arsenal fought off relegation. When Terry Neil became manager in the summer of 1976, with the immediate arrival of Pat Howard from Newcastle, this pushed Richie out of contention, but

when Willie Young arrived from Spurs, Richies chances seemed to more limited. But during that season he still managed to make 12 appearances, three of them deputising for an injured Sammy Nelson. When the 1977'78 season started Willie and David O'Leary began to establish themselves at central defenders, but Richie was put into the midfield, starting the first 5 games, plus scoring two goals. Unfortunately he was to receive an injury that kept him out for the remainder of that season, although making a couple of appearances for the Stiffs. Unfortunately he never fully recovered, and retired from the game during the '79/80 season.

Richie was a very talented player, and one of nicest people I have met in football.

He has had some great successful management positions in non league football.

David James Price (born June 23, 1955)
Born in Caterham, Surrey, David was snapped up by Arsenal in 1970 having been already known as a prodigious young midfielder (he was captain of the England schoolboys team). He spent the next few years in the Gunners' youth and reserve sides, winning the FA Youth Cup in 1971. He had made his first-team debut aged 17 in a First Division match against Leeds United on May 9, 1973 (the final day of the season) but even after this, he still played mainly in the reserves for the next few years.

After a loan spell at Peterborough United, he fully broke into the Arsenal first team in 1977-78, playing 51 matches that season (he had only made 13 appearances in four years before then). His regular spell in the Arsenal side coincided with the Gunners' FA Cup runs of the late 1970s, reaching the Cup final three seasons running between 1978 and 1980, he played in all three. But as we now know Arsenal only won the one in 1979, 3-2 against Manchester United; David setting up Brian Talbot for the opening goal. He also played in Arsenal's Cup Winners' Cup defeat at the hands of Valencia in 1980, on penalties after a 0-0 draw.

He surprisingly lost his place to the veteran John Hollins at the start of the 1980-81 season, and was sold to Crystal Palace in March 1981, in a part-exchange deal which saw Peter Nicholas move the other way. In all he played 176 games for Arsenal, scoring 19 goals.

His spell at Crystal Palace was not happy one, being hampered by injury; he only made 27 League appearances in two seasons and after a brief spell at Leyton Orient, he quit the game because of injury, at the early age of 28. He is now a taxi driver in Croydon.

Graham Rix (Born October 23, 1957)

Originally from Doncaster, Yorkshire, Ricco joined Arsenal as an apprentice in 1974 and turned professional the year after. He made his debut for the club against Leicester City on April 2, 1977, and marked it by scoring the opening goal. He immediately became a regular on the left wing, replacing George Armstrong. Together with Liam Brady he formed part of an impressive attacking midfield, which helped Arsenal to three successive cup finals between 1978 and 1980. Ricco crossed for Alan Sunderland's last-minute winner, just seconds after United had equalised to level the score 2-2.

Arsenal reached the Cup Winners' Cup final the following season, against Valencia; the match finished 0-0 after extra time - a penalty shootout ensued, but he missed his kick and Arsenal lost. After the departure of Liam Brady to Juventus that summer, many believed he would also leave but he stayed at the club, and became captain in 1983. Arsenal's form slumped in the early 1980s, though, meaning he was unable to claim any silverware as skipper.

A series of injuries to his achilles tendon kept him out of the team in the mid-1980s, and he lost his starting place in the side to Martin Hayes. He spent a spell on loan at Brentford, before being released in 1988. In all he played 464 times for the Gunners, scoring 51 goals. After leaving the London club, he spent time at French clubs Caen and Le Havre, before finishing his playing career at Dundee in 1993.

He joined Chelsea as youth team coach in the summer of 1993; during an injury crisis, he briefly enlisted as a player for the club, playing a solitary Premiership match in May 1995 against his old side Arsenal. He became assistant manager in 1996 under new Blues boss Ruud Gullit, and continued in the same role under Gullit's successor Gianluca Vialli, winning the FA Cup in 1997, and the League Cup and Cup Winners' Cup in 1998.

In March 1999, he was sentenced to twelve months in prison; upon his release from prison six months later he immediately rejoined Chelsea in his old job. He won the FA Cup again in 2000 before leaving the club in

November that year, after Vialli was sacked by Ken Bates. He had unsuccessful spells managing Portsmouth and Oxford United; both times he was sacked after less than a year in the job.

On November 7, 2005, after speculation linking him with the Manager's job at Scottish Premier League club Hearts, it was confirmed that Ricco would take over at Tynecastle. He officially took the position of head coach on November 8, 2005. Hearts stated that a Director of Football with responsibility for signing new players would be appointed shortly. He was reported as saying he "will be happy to have someone else buying and selling his players." He states, "My forté is working with the players, motivating them and hopefully winning matches. Dealing with agents and the press does not really interest me."

Events reported in February 2006, by Scottish newspapers, suggested that he was unhappy with Vladimir Romanov's "hands on" approach and speculation increased that Romanov was involved in team selection.

On 22 March 2006 he was sacked as manager after just four months in charge with Hearts Chairman Roman Romanov stated that "Results were not what they should have been."

The future of Hearts still seems to be still guided by director or chairman's poor decisions making.

Trevor Ross (Born 1957 in Ashton under Lyne)

Joined Arsenal as an apprentice in 1972, and turned pro in 1974. He made his debut against Liverpool in 1975, but finally lost his place to David Price during the 1977-78 season. Trevor was transferred to Everton during that season.

He played a total of 68 games and scored 9 goals, before going on loan to Portsmouth. Sheffield United was his next move, followed by a series of moves to Greece, back to Sheffield, Bury and Altrincham.

Trevor won 1 Scottish under 21 cap.

Malcolm Ian "Supermac" Macdonald (Born January 7, 1950, Fulham).

Malcolm started out as a full back before switching to centre forward. He played for Fulham for one season (1968-69), before moving to Luton Town. At Luton he scored 49 times in 88 matches, which caught the eye of Newcastle United, who signed him for £180,000 in the summer of 1971. At Newcastle he quickly became a favourite of the fans, scoring a hat-trick on his home debut against Liverpool, and was the club's top scorer for five seasons in a row.

While at Newcastle, he made his debut for England (against Wales). On April 16, 1975, in a game for England against Cyprus he scored all five goals in a 5-0 victory, a record that still stands today. In all he played 14 times for his country, scoring 6 times (the only other game he scored in being a 2-0 win over then World Champions West Germany).

Malcolm left Newcastle for Arsenal in 1976, for the slightly bizarre fee of £333,333.33, and played two full seasons (being the club's top scorer in both). He suffered a knee injury in a League Cup match against Rotherham at the start of the 1978-79 season, from which he was unable to recover. After having spent a couple of months in Sweden with Djurgårdens IF he announced his retirement from playing at the premature age of 29 in July 1979. He never won a major honour but was on the losing side in two FA Cup finals, one each for Newcastle and Arsenal.

After retirement, he returned to Fulham to manage them for four seasons, and was later manager of Huddersfield Town between 1987 and 1988. In the years after his injury he struggled with, his health before becoming a radio commentator on the North East's Century FM.

Frank Stapleton (Born July 10, 1956 in Dublin)

Frank a subtle, intelligent player, held in esteem by many for his strategic thinking and accurate passing on the pitch. He started his career with Arsenal, joining them in 1972 as an apprentice. He made his first-team debut in 1975 against Stoke City, and would go on to form a potent striking partnership with Malcolm Macdonald; the two scored 46 goals between them in 1976-77. He was Arsenal's top scorer for the three following seasons, and helped the Gunners reach a trio of FA Cup finals; Stapleton scored one of the goals in Arsenal's 1979 3-2 win over Manchester United, and scored 108 goals in 300 appearances in total for the Gunners.

He went on to move to Man United in 1981 for £900,000 (a fee set by tribunal after the two clubs could not agree). He would help United win the 1983 and 1985 FA Cups. He left United in 1987, after scoring 78 goals for the club in 365 matches.

He then went on to play for Ajax Amsterdam, before returning to England with Derby County and Blackburn Rovers. He also won 71 caps for the Republic of Ireland, scoring a then record 20 goals. In 1991 he became player-manager of Bradford City, where he spent three seasons, and later went to the United States to coach Major League Soccer side New England Revolution.

Arsenal to Armenia

In the 2003-04 season he briefly returned to English football as a specialist coach of Bolton Wanderers. The Bolton manager Sam Allardyce wanted Stapleton to enhance the skills of the strikers at the club and saw the Irishman as an ideal candidate, given his successful playing career.

Kevin Stead
Played for Tottenham from 1976-78 making 14 appearances, before his move to Highbury. Kevin failed to make an impact, due to the strength of the squad there and only managed 2 first team appearances during his stay there.

Steve Gatting (Born Willesdon, North London)
Steve carved out a great career in football, after having to make a decision of County Cricket or football, he choose not to follow his brother Mike.

Steve joined Arsenal in 1977, but didn't make his debut until 1978. He played a total of 58 league appearances until moving to Brighton in September 1981. Steve went on to play a total of 316 appearances, until joining Charlton Athletic in August 1991. He played a further 64 games during the next two seasons before calling it a day.

It seems that the dual sports talent runs through the family, with his son Joe turning down County Cricket to join Brighton, where he is certainly setting the club alight.

Brian McDermott (8th April 1961 in Slough, Berkshire)
Brian joined Arsenal as an apprentice in January 1977 and signed professional forms with the club in February 1979. He was a regular in Arsenal's reserve team, finishing top scorer in the London Combination in 1978-79, before making his debut as a substitute against Bristol City on March 10, 1979. He did not properly break into the Arsenal first team until the 1980-81 season, notching 45 appearances (14 as sub) in all competitions in that season and 1981-82.

Unable to match his goal scoring rate at the top level, he featured much less in the 1982-83 and 1983-84 seasons and was loaned out twice, once to Fulham in 1983 and once to IFK Norrköping between April and October 1984, where he was named Sweden's Player of the Year.

He moved to Oxford United in December 1984, having played 70 games for Arsenal, scoring 13 goals.

His later career included a spell at Huddersfield Town on loan, before stints at Cardiff City and Exeter City.

He joined Reading as Chief Scout in September 2000, taking over from the late Maurice Evans.

Alan Sunderland (Born July 1, 1953)

Born in Mexborough, Yorkshire, and began his career at Wolves in 1970; initially a midfielder, he eventually switched positions to centre forward. He made over 200 appearances for the Midlands side, and won the League Cup in 1974 and the Second Division in 1977. In November 1977 he joined Arsenal for £220,000 and immediately became a regular, playing in the 1978 FA Cup final (which Arsenal lost to Ipswich Town).

Alan's most famous moment came in the FA Cup final of 1979; Arsenal had gone 2-0 up against Manchester United, with goals from Brian Talbot and Frank Stapleton, and looked set for victory with only five minutes remaining. However, United scored twice in three minutes, with goals from Gordon McQueen and Sammy McIlroy and extra time loomed. In the very last minute of the match however, Arsenal pushed forward in a desperate counter-attack; Liam Brady fed Graham Rix on the left wing and his cross was converted by Alan at the far post to make the score 3-2.

He stayed at Arsenal for another five years, forming an impressive partnership with Frank Stapleton; he was the club's top scorer in 1979-80 and 1981-82, and featured in the Arsenal sides that lost the 1980 FA Cup and Cup Winners' Cup finals. He also won a solitary England cap, against Australia. However, after a spate of injuries and the arrival of Charlie Nicholas, found himself pushed out of the first team.

He joined Ipswich Town on loan in February 1984 and made the move permanent later in the summer. He played for Ipswich until 1986 and then had a brief stint at Irish club Derry City, before calling it a day.

Following retirement, he opened a pub in Ipswich, before emigrating to Malta.

Chapter Five

∞

"Honest differences are often a healthy sign"
MAHATMA GANDHI

I remember Don with his man management and motivation, being used in a positive sense. We had had Huddy who had been out with a bad shin injury, so that week I had done a lot of physical work with him, on the track and the training ground, especially on the Wednesday and Thursday, with no reaction from the injury. This was now early Friday morning, and we, Fred, Don, Terry and myself were discussing the players for the Saturdays game at home versus QPR. I was able to say that Huddy had come through two extremely hard days with no reaction and although he hadn't played in a competitive game for a number of weeks, he was needed for that match. Just as I had given my report on him, a limping person passed our room, heading towards the 1st team changing room; it could be only one person Huddy. He was always one of the first to appear at the ground, suddenly a sinking feeling crept into my stomach, but I hoped that it didn't show on my face. Don said leave it to me and went into the changing room. After a couple of minutes, he reappeared saying that Huddy is OK just that his shoe was slipping off, which caused the limp. So he played on the Saturday, at home versus QPR. In real fact what really happened was that Huddy knew he would be playing on that Saturday but away to Bristol, but who wants to play a reserve team game on a Saturday traveling all the way to Bristol, hence the limp. So Don knew how to handle players!

People ask and still ask what it is like to work in professional football, especially working alongside international players and well known coaches etc. Although being Club Physiotherapist and being part of the management, your work is with players on a more intimate nature than any other member of staff, players are with you on a one to one basis and you get to know them as a person their like's dislikes, their family etc. You become one of them so you are sandwiched between the players and the management staff.

This is something I learnt whilst in the forces at Chessington early on in my medical training. We used to have lads and lasses from all the 3 services who were injured. We had a lot of lads who had received injuries whilst serving in Northern Ireland and also from the IRA pub bombings. Lads with serious head and subsequent brain damage, limbless young soldiers. One lad in particular had been caught by the IRA as a suspect informant (the lad was a member of the Irish Rangers). He was taken to the outskirts of Belfast and his body riddled with bullets and left in the snow to die. The same people drove by a number of hours later, and were amazed to see him still alive. A pistol then was applied to his nostril and the bullet went through the brain and out of the head, he was left again. A military patrol passed by and saw a body lying in the snow and yes, he was still alive. After months in hospital, he came to us for rehabilitation. So working with International players is nothing after dealing with people like that lad.

Also lads just couldn't wait to get back to the streets of Ireland, if they heard that their regiment was returning to Ireland, you became bombarded by questions like when will I be discharged from here and back with my regiment? When talking to them, they would say, that they want to be with their mates and to do the job that they joined up to do, a job that they were trained to do.
These lads had feelings; they had friends, family, a background and a future. They weren't just an injury, a diagnosis, but a human being.

So I would use this in my football career, getting to know the players, what motivated them, their interests, even the name of their dog or their wife, girl friend etc. A closeness to them, a person who would genuinely listen to their problems, not blabbing back to the management. I use to find it hard on away matches, where management would eat separately from the players etc. I knew where I wanted to be.

This also meant a lot of drinking especially Saturday after the game, or a mid week game. The pain from a bruised shin is sometimes better dealt with a few of pints rather than a pain killer!

Arsenal to Armenia

It didn't take the players long to realise that I was one of them. Not long after I had been at Highbury, Pat Rice had his Testimonial versus Spurs in a mid week evening game. Just as the players were leaving to hit the bars, Malcolm Mac, stuck his head around the treatment door and said, come on you're with us. So off I went to pass a few beers down my throat - the only member of the management staff to be asked and also I was told in strong terms that my money was to stay in my pocket. I was accepted.

A character used to be seen hanging around the main entrance especially on a match day. I remember meeting him on my first home game, I walked up the marble steps to the main entrance and there seemingly blocking the main entrance, was this rather large person, or should I say fat person. As I eased my way around him, he whispered in my ear, "Want a ticket?"

My reply was that I was a member of staff, to which his reply was "Got any tickets you don't want?" It was the famous or should I say infamous ticket tout Stan Flashman. If he couldn't get you a ticket for any event then nobody could. No, I didn't have any spare tickets.

People ask me even now who were the best players at Arsenal, a very difficult question to answer, as the names I mentioned in the previous chapter were all world class players. The most talented player in my opinion was Huddy. What a shame that he and Ballie didn't feature together at Highbury, now that would have been something tremendous. Both dedicated professional players, both flamboyant on and off the pitch, both had passion for the game, both hard trainers, both extremely fit, and boy couldn't they make that ball sing.

A number of years later, when I was with Vancouver Whitecaps (Canada) in the North American Soccer League, we played a pre-season friendly against Seatle Sounders. When the players lined up for the traditional National anthems, two pairs of eyes met, Huddys and mine and we met like two old mates, Huddy leaving his line up and me away from mine, to the tune of the American national anthem.

One of the nicest lads at Highbury, would have to be big David O'Leary, a really genuine player and person, also fitting into this category was Frank Stapleton. Both of them would spend hours with a young disabled lad who lived near to the ground, bringing him into the ground, taking him out for meals, and not for the cameras or publicity, which seems to go on in our present game.

Richie Powling must get a mention, although injury was to bring a close to his career at Arsenal whilst still in his early 20's. He was injured during a first team game, and then sustained a further injury whilst playing for the stiffs at Ipswich. During his long term injury, you never heard Richie complain. The calmness about him when his career was falling apart, remained with me and still does. It all became apparent when a number of years later I found out that he was a committed born again Christian - it certainly showed.

Sammy Nelson must receive the award of the comic. When he was away from the ground on International duties, it was so quiet, but then again, his straight man Pat Rice was away at the same time. It used to be so quiet at the ground when Ireland was involved at International level.

Chippy Brady, a character who I would say had the most talent; in fact probably had more talent in his left toe than some players in football had in their whole body. He was a person who knew what to do and if he made his mind up no-one could change it. He was single minded on and off the pitch, but what skill.

I remember Terry giving me a shout one afternoon that Chippy had received an injury whilst on International duties and was coming to the ground straight from Heathrow, but it would be early evening, so it meant hanging around at the ground because I didn't really know what time he would be arriving. When he arrived, he said, well if I wrote what he did say it would contain a lot of expletives, and also some people's names would be mentioned, in other words he was fine and some people should keep their nose out of things, and he wanted to get home and that he was sure that I wanted to as well!

Malcolm Mac. he would have to have a mention, not just because he was known as the Mouth, but for the person he was. Malcolm like Huddy, was flamboyant on and off the pitch, in dress and in attitude, confidence oozed out of him, hence his scoring ability and record. He was confident that he could beat any defender and score. How we could do with players like him back into football today.

Arsenal to Armenia

It was a great shame that the 'MacDonald knee' would force him to retire from the game so early, in his career. We would spend a lot of time together , when he would have to sit out of some of the training sessions to either rest or to protect the knee, a legacy of playing too soon after knee problems (not at Highbury but earlier on in his career). We are talking about a time when medical professionals were not in charge of injuries. Even in the 1st Division, only a handful of clubs had qualified staff, but used to rely on retired players, (jobs for the boys).

Jane and I had now moved from Surrey to live in Highbury, in a club flat with the biggest back garden in the whole of London, the Arsenal Stadium, so not far to walk to work. On a Saturday evening, Jane used to ask what the score was, as there must have been a lot of goals scored because of the noise!

The only problem was that Jane suffered consistently from colds and 'flu, from the time we moved into the flat. But no other accommodation was available. The flat was the ground floor of a Victorian Terraced house, which had damp problems and with winter coming I was a bit worried about her.

Tony Donnelly the kit man, lived with his wife and family a few doors down from us and were a great help to us during this period. They introduced me to Panatone cake, so when ever I see some my mind clicks right to them. It is strange how things happen, but a number of years after leaving Arsenal, I had a Sports Injury Clinic in Leyland, Lancashire. It was in a private health club of which I was manager and one of the members was in fact Tony's brother. We used to have long chats about Arsenal.

Things were working out great at the club, although my main responsibility was towards the reserves or "Stiffs" and the youth, Fred and I worked well together and shared the treatments and rehabilitation. Either one of use would be in the treatment room or I with the rehab side of the treatments, in the gym or out on the track or indoor pitch, or out at London Colney.

I was extremely happy at Highbury, and found the work enjoyable, I had always wanted challenges in my life, and I realised that I had got a job at the top of the ladder, working with the best club in England I could see myself working there for the next 20-30 years.

During this time I had a phone call from my brother who lived in North Devon, who asked if both I and Arsenal could help him out. He was chairman of Bideford Football Club (South Western League). They were drawn in the FA Cup against Portsmouth away and one of their important players was injured, could I help out?

So two days later Mickey Hilson appeared. You would have to know Mickey to understand this fully, but I shall try to explain. Mickey was a local builder, with a wife and young family, who lived at Instow. You could tell his house, because an old cement mixer was always in his front garden. Also I don't believe that he had ever been anywhere outside of Devon and Cornwall, so coming to the big city was a massive undertaking for him. The Arsenal players were tremendous towards him and treated him as one of them, Mickey stayed for treatment for the week, but he never ventured out of his hotel, only to come to the ground and back again. No matter what he was tempted with, "No" was the answer. He did play for Bideford at Portsmouth but unfortunately lost. However Mickey had been to Highbury, met and mingled with the top players in the UK and played at Portsmouth a real Roy of the Rovers touch.

Chapter Six

∞

"Time to finish this game, and then the Spaniards"
SIR FRANCES DRAKE

One day out of the blue, Terry came to see me, to say that Plymouth Argyle had contacted him and they wanted to speak to me about their position of Club physiotherapist.

Terry said that he wouldn't stop me from talking to them, but he didn't want me to leave as he was very happy with my work and the way that I had settled in, and that was the general opinion of everyone at the club, players included.

What now, would it work out, is it giving up the best for something less? Plymouth Argyle was a team I had watched from a young lad, going with my Dad. It was only 20 miles from my family home in Cornwall. Would it end up as a big **IF** only I had or hadn't?

So the following Sunday, I traveled by train to Plymouth to meet up with Mike Kelly the manager of Plymouth. As I said before, Plymouth was only 20 miles away from my family home and where I was born. It was the club I first supported with my Dad, since I was able to walk. The days of Bill Short, the Welsh international in goal, my hero Jimmy Gould up front, George Dews of the long shorts, who also played county cricket. So many memories of standing on the terraces with 40,000 others, being passed over the heads of people so that I could stand at the railings and at the final whistle, wait until my Dad came down to the front to collect me. Walking, or it should be carried along with the crowd, my feet not touching the ground as the crowd surged towards the exits. Being part of it felt as if the whole of Cornwall used to cross the border onto the foreign soil of Devon on match days.

Dennis Loze

Yes, as I got nearer to what used to be Plymouth North Road Station, I was excited, but should I even be thinking of leaving the top club to be with a club who were struggling in the 3rd division?

I was met by Mike at the station, who then drove to Home Park. I was already impressed my Mike and his attitude. Yes, I could work with him. A look around the ground, a look at the antiquated treatment facilities; at least they did have a weight room, even if it was in a wooden hut with no heating. A quick chat to the chief scout Ellis Stoddard, who had been with Argyle for so many years and who in fact had managed the club on two occasions. Ellis was a super person he had a little red book which never left him. If your name and contact number didn't appear in that book then you shouldn't be in football. A real down to earth Northerner. Then meeting Billy Harper (see chapter one) Billy was transferred to Plymouth from Arsenal way back in the early 30's. A Scottish International goalkeeper, he now looked after the boardroom, what a character.

Then off to lunch at the Magnet restaurant in Cornwall Street, which is now a Burger King. The Magnet was run by the Williams family Father and son, who were both Club Directors. I used to go to the original Magnet premises, which was on the way to the Barbican, with my parents. When I was about 5 years of age, sweets etc and so many things were still on ration from after the war, and I remember that the waitress used to secretly give me a couple of sugar lumps.

After being introduced to the Williams, Mike and I discussed contracts etc, all which seemed very favourable. After we had finished the meal, I was surprised that Mike actually paid for the meal himself and no receipt for claiming expenses, was this a sign of the financial aspect of Argyle?

We then drove towards Plymstock to Mikes house to meet his wife and family, and to discuss terms. They would match what Arsenal were paying me, pay for the removals, and the club would look for a flat to rent whilst Jane and I could look for a house.

This decision was to take a little longer than the Arsenal one, Jane and I had already discussed the possibility of a move and she was happy if I was happy with things.

But it would only be right that I discussed it with Arsenal before even considering taking up Argyles offer. Oh, just little point, as well as Argyle, struggling in the league, they had the most horrendous injury list imaginable!

So it was on to North Road Station and then back to Highbury to Jane and to talk things over.

The decision was made easier for me as I went into our flat Jane was still in bed where I had left her earlier that morning. Yes, the 'flu had re-appeared. In fact, I think it had never gone away, as the flat was so damp, no matter how much heating we had on the dampness remained.

So the next morning, after a chat with Fred, Terry and Don I informed them of my decision. We were to be Plymouth bound, in 4 weeks time. What would Plymouths position in the league be then, what would the injury list be like? I was soon to find out.

Arsenal were very good about my decision. They didn't want me to go and deep down I didn't want to go, but my heart ruled my head. Would it be a decision I would regret?

The furniture van - a local Cornish firm, Callington Carriers, was packed and Plymouth bound. Breakfast with Terry Donnelly and Fred the grounds - man in one of Highbury's restaurant and into Jane's old mini "Macintyre" and West Country here we come. We were going to stay with my Father and put our furniture etc. in store.

Plymouth Argyle

Argyle was born in 1886, when two friends decided the town (as Plymouth was then) needed a football team which local people would be proud to play for and support. The friends, F. Howard Grose and W. Pethybridge, arranged a meeting at The Borough Arms. After a discussion, the name "Plymouth Argyle" was agreed on.

The name "Argyle" is unusual, but controversy surrounds how the name was adopted. Many fans still believe that it stems from the name of a street in Plymouth where the original committee for the club use to meet. (*The Argyle Hotel-now owned by the Plymouth Argyle Development Trust*) is situated where the road used to be-and it pointed straight towards Home Park. In a letter from Howard Rose, a founder member of the team written in 1934, he recalled the setting up of the club. He was at Dunheved College in Launceston when he and W. Pethybridge met in 1886. They also met with other interested parties (*mainly old boys of the college*), and one name that was favoured was "Pickwick", but fortunately it was not adopted. To quote Howard:

"I recollect holding forth on what our club should aim at achieving in the football world viz.: to emulate the style of play adopted by the Argyll and Sutherland Highlanders who I believe in the previous year won the Army Cup. I then explained that anyone who had watched them play would be struck with the excellent team work shown, the fast low passing from backs to forwards, wings to centre followed by short swift shooting at the opponents' goal and we should endeavour to play on the same lines. Then someone said "Why not Plymouth Argyle?" "That's the name that could be applied locally." When put to a vote it was adopted unanimously."

The club has always been associated with the colour green and normally plays in some combination of green, black and white.

The club took its nickname, the Pilgrims from the vast number of people who left Plymouth for the new world, on the Mayflower, which appears on the clubs crest.

Turned Professional   1903
Ground
- 1886-7   No ground (played all games at opponents grounds)
- 1887   Mount Gould area
- 1889   Marsh Mills area
- 1890   Home Park (Formerly Devonport Albion Rugby ground.

Ground Capacity   22,500 (after year 2000)
Record Attendance 44,526 - Huddersfield 1934
Highest Scorer   32 goals -Jack Crock 1951-2
Record Appearances 530 - Kevin Hodges 1978-92
Managers
- 1903-05   Frank Brettell
- 1905   Bob Jack
- 1906-10   Bill Fullerton
- 1910-38   Bob Jack
- 1938 48   Jack Tresarden
- 1948-55   Jimmy Rae
- 1955-61   Jack Rowley
- 1961   Neil Dougall
- 1961-63   Ellis Studdard

1963-64	Andy Beatie
1964-65	Malcolm Allison
1965-68	Derek Ufton
1968-70	Billy Bingham
1970-72	Ellis Studdard
1972-77	Tony Waiters
1977-78	Mike Kelly
1978	Lennie Lawrence
1978-79	Malcolm Allison
1979-81	Bobby Saxton
1981-83	Bobby Moncur
1983-84	Johnny Hore
1984-88	Dave Smith
1988-90	Ken Brown
1990	John Gregory
1990-92	David Kemp
1992-95	Peter Shilton
1995	Steve McCall
1995-97	Neil Warnock
1997-98	Mick Jones
1998-00	Kevin Hodges
2000	Kevin Summerfield
2000-04	Paul Sturrock
2004	Kevin Summerfield
2004-05	Bobby Wilson
2005	Tony Pulis
2006	Ian Hollaway
2007	Paul Sturrock

Chapter Seven

"A fanatic is one who can't change his mind and won't change the subject"
WINSTON CHURCHILL

My first day at Argyle was strange, moving from a club were the medical side of things were top drawer, to one of chaos, from treating players with household names, to players whose names didn't really ring a bell, from players who knew what true professionalism was, to some players who didn't seem to know what it was all about.

Also an injury list that had grown to immense proportions. So much so that I didn't actual carry out any treatments that day, just assessments and to diagnose what the actual player's problems were.

Also in fact who was actually injure, and those who were swinging the lead! Yes, this was 3rd Division and a club struggling in the league. A difference from what I was used to, where injured lads couldn't wait to get back to the "muck and bullets."

The best part of the first day was the drive from Calstock to Plymouth, passing areas that I remember as a younger person, Kit Hill and my old Grammar School in Callington, over the Saltash Bridge, which runs alongside Brunels famous railway bridge, looking down into the water seeing where the old Saltash ferry used to run, prior to the building of the road bridge and finally into the Argyle car park.

The next day I split the lads into three groups, based on my assessments of the day before, oh and yes, I had more players than were on the actual training pitch. Group one with genuine recent injuries, group two, those who had been injured but needed rehabilitation and an encouraging push, group three with those who needed a kick up the backside!

Arsenal to Armenia

The joy about the position of Home Park if you have never been there is that it is right in the middle of Central Park, on a slight hill, so plenty of space and areas to do physical work. The pitch, like that of Highbury, had a track around the outside, ideal for running also, a decent high stand, not as steep as the ones at Highbury but ideal for cardio vascular and leg work.

The first group I worked with in the morning and then the second and third groups, in the afternoon. They were immediately unhappy about this as afternoons were normally their snooker time.

Well, after a good session in the park, the running track and then the terraces, you could see in their eyes that they wanted to go back to the training pitch, so in two days, the injury list was halved. Treatment of injuries is not all sitting having treatment done by waving around an ultrasound etc. but combined with hard physical individual rehabilitation.

For years the treatment of injuries in football was very unscientific to say the least, also in some clubs the injured players were treated as if they had the plague. Treatment times were hit and miss and they were humiliated by the coaching staff. In fact the treatment rooms were looked upon as a no go area, so an injured player would have no contact with the rest of the squad and be an outsider, being forced to rejoin the squad even when the injury was still acute.

I have just been looking at some of my books on football and came across a Football League booklet called "Review" dated 1971/72 season. In one of the articles is about Bob Paisley who was at that stage Assistant manger to Bill Shankley at Liverpool.
Quote from the "Review".
" ……..has worked his way up the ladder from player to second team trainer, to youth chief, to first team trainer – a job he held for 10 of the most successful seasons in the club's history"……….. "Paisley believes that a large part of a trainers job when he attends an injured player on the field is good, old fashion kidology. "They call it the magic sponge," he points out, "but often what you say to a player tends to work the biggest cure".
But then Bob states the obvious *"Every routine we do in training has a specific reason behind it. In the old days it was mainly a case of going through the motions of keeping fit. Football technique has advanced dramatically, so has the medical side and the treatment of injuries."*

Dennis Loze

It took a lot of years for football to heed these words of Bob Paisley.

One of Richie Hessions poems seems to sum it all up:-

Bucket and Sponge by Richie Hession

I stand on the sidelines
Watching the game,
And wait a torn hamstring,
Or a groin to inflame.
A scything tackle,
A cynical lunge,
And on I shall come
With my bucket and sponge.
To tend to the wounded,
Those hurt and in pain.
With my magical might,
I rival David Blaine.
I've no first aid experience,
Read no books or manuals,
But it's as though I am blessed
With the powers of Paul Daniels.
If it's a dislocated shoulder,
Or a twisted knee,
My magic sponge can heal
Any injury.
So, if your favourite player
Should trip, fall or plunge
To the ground, pray I'll be there
With my bucket and sponge.

The injury list shortened over the week, but the results on the pitch didn't change on my first game away to Preston North End who were flying high in the league. We ended up on the end of a real thumping and yes you've guessed right, more injuries!

In the book "Plymouth Argyle The Modern Era" by Andy Riddle this match is summed:

Arsenal to Armenia

"Bason returns on a £35k transfer. Foster celebrates his 50th league appearance with a goal but Preston strike three times in 15 minutes. New Argyle physio Dennis Loze is kept busy. Johnson scores from the spot after he was fouled by Doyle. Nobby Stiles' men continue their promotion push.

Time to introduce you to the players at Argyle:

Terry Austin (FD)
Born Isleworth 1954
Signed for Crystal Palace (Juniors) 1972.
Transferred to Ipswich Town 1973, played 10 games.
Transferred to Plymouth (part of the Paul Mariner fee) 1976, played 58 games.
Transferred to Walsall 1978, played 44 games.
Transferred to Mansfield 1979, played 84 games.
Transferred to Huddersfield 1980, played 39 games.
Transferred to Doncaster 1982, played 30 games.
Transferred to Northampton 1983, played 42 games.

Paul Barron (GK)
Born in Woolwich 1953
Signed for Slough Town in 1976.
Transferred to Plymouth 1976, played 44 games
Transferred to Arsenal 1978, played 8 games.
Transferred to Crystal Palace 1980 played 80 games.
Transferred to West Brom 1982 played 63 games.
Transferred to QPR 1985 (1 game loan to Stoke City), played 32 games.

Brian Bason (MF)
Born in Epsom 1955
Apprentice at Chelsea 1972 played 18 games.
Transferred after loan period to Plymouth 1977 played 127 games.
Transferred to Crystal Palace 1981 played 25 games.
Loan to Portsmouth 1982, played 8 games.
Transferred to Reading 1982, played 41 games.

Geof Banton
Born in Ashton under Lyne 1957
Apprentice at Bolton Wanderers 1973, 0 games
Transferred to Plymouth 1975, played 6 games.

Transferred to Fulham 1978, played 37 games.

Fred Binney (FD)
Born in Plymouth 1946
Signed for Torquay 1966, played 24 games
Loan to Exeter 1969, played 17 games
Transferred to Exeter 1970, played 160 games
Transferred to Brighton 1974, played 68 games
Period in NASL St. Louis 1977
Transferred to Plymouth 1977, played 67 games
Transferred to Hereford 1980, played 21 games

John Craven (DF)
Born in St. Annes 1947.
Apprentice at Blackpool 1965, played 154 games.
Transferred to Crystal Palace 1971, played 56 games.
Transferred to Coventry 1973, played 86 games
Transferred to Plymouth 1977, played 45 games
Transferred to Vancouver Whitecaps NASL 1978

Jon Delve (MF)
Born in Ealing 1953.
Apprentice at Queens Park Rangers 1971, played 9 games.
Transferred to Plymouth 1974, played 127 games.
Transferred to Exeter 1978, played 215 games.
Transferred to Hereford 1983, played 116 games.
Transferred Exeter 1987, played 12 games
Transferred Gloucester 1987.

George Foster (DF)
Born in Plymouth 1956.
Apprentice at Plymouth 1974, played 201 games.
Loan period to Torquay 1976, played 6 games.
Loan period to Exeter 1981, played 28 games.
Transferred to Derby 1982, played 30 games.
Transferred to Mansfield 1983, played 373 games.
Player Manager at Mansfield.
Manager at Telford.
Coach at Lincoln City
Youth Coach at Birmingham

Chris Harrison (DF)
Born in Launceston 1956.
Apprentice at Plymouth 1974, played 315 games.
Transferred to Swansea 1985, played 114 games.

Martin Hodge (GK)
Born in Southport 1959
Apprentice at Plymouth 1977 played 43 games
Transferred to Everton in 1979 played 25 games
followed by a series of loans to Preston 1981, played 28 games.
Oldham Athletic 1982, played 4 games.
Gillingham 1983, played 4 games.
Preston 1983, played 16 games.
Transferred to Sheffield Wednesday 1983, played 197 games.
Transferred to Leicester 1988, played 75 games.
Transferred to Hartlepool 1991, played 69 games.
Transferred to Rochdale 1993, played 42 games.
Transferred to Plymouth 1994 played 17 games.

Mick Horswill (MF)
Born in Annfield Plain 1953.
Apprentice at Sunderland 1970, played 68 games.
Transferred to Manchester City 1974, played 11 games.
Transferred to Plymouth 1975, played 98 games.
Transferred to Hull City 1978, played 82 games.
Transferred Carlise in 1983 played 1 game, then to Hong Kong.

Brian Johnson (FD)
Born in Isleworth 1955
Apprentice at Plymouth 1973, played 186 games.
Loan to Torquay 1979, played 5 games.
Loan to Torquay 1981, played 2 games.

Gary Megson (MF)
Born in Manchester 1959
Apprentice at Plymouth 1977, played 78 games.
Transferred to Everton 1979, played 20 games.
Transferred to Sheffield Wednesday 1981, played 123 games.
Transferred to Nottingham Forest 1984, played 0 games.
Transferred to Newcastle Untd 1984, played 21 games.

Transferred to Sheffield Wednesday 1985, played 107 games
Transferred to Manchester City 1989, played 78 games.
Transferred to Norwich City, 1992, played 42 games.
Transferred to Lincoln City 1995, played 2 games.
Transferred to Shrewsbury 1995, played 2 games.

John Peddelty (DF)
Born Bishop Auckland 1955
Apprentice at Ipswich 1973, played 44 games.
Transferred to Plymouth (part of Paul Mariner Deal) 1976 played 30 games.
Forced to retire from football 1978 due to injury.

Alan Rogers (FD)
Born in Plymouth 1974
Apprentice at Plymouth 1972, played 107 games.
Transferred to Portsmouth 1979, played 154 games.
Transferred to Southend Untd. 1984, played 84 games.
Transferred to Cardiff City 1986, played 25 games.

Kevin Smart (MF)
Born in Newcastle 1958.
Apprentice at Plymouth 1976, played 32 games.
Transferred to Wigan Ath. 1978, played 48 games.

Dave Sutton (MF)
Born in Tarleton 1957
Apprentice at Plymouth 1974, played 60 games.
Loan to Reading 1977, played 9 games.
Transferred to Huddersfield 1978, played 242 games.
Transferred to Bolton Wanderers 1985, played 96 games.
Transferred to Rochdale 1988, played 28 games.

Brian Taylor (MF)
Born in Gateshead 1949
Died Motor Neuron Disease 1996
Signed Coventry City 1968 played 0 games
Transferred to Walsall 1971, played 204 games
Transferred to Plymouth 1977, played 34 games
Transferred to Preston 1978, played 93 games

Loan to Wigan 1982, played 7 games.

Mike Trusson(FD)
Born in Northolt 1959
Apprentice at Plymouth 1977, played 65 games
Loan period to Stoke 1978
Transferred to Sheffield Untd 1980, played 125 games.
Transferred to Rotherham 1983, played 124 games.
Transferred to Brighton 1987, played 34 games
Transferred to Gillingham 1989 played 69 games.

John Uzzell (DF)
Born in Plymouth 1959
Apprentice at Plymouth 1977, played 292 games.
Transferred to Torquay Untd 1989, played 91 games

Apprentices

Kevin Hodges
Born in Broadwindsor 1960
Apprentice at Plymouth 1978, played 502 games
Loan to Torquay 1992, played 3 games.
Transferred to Torquay 1992, played 49 games
Manager at Torquay 1997
Manager at Plymouth 1998-2000
Now coach at Yeovil 2005 to date

Mark Graves
Born in Isleworth 1960
Apprentice at Plymouth 1978, played 24 games

Colin Upton
Born in Reading 1960
Apprentice at Plymouth 1978 played 2 games

Tony Levy (FD)
Born Edmonton 1959
Apprentice at Argyle 1977, played 0 games
Transferred to Torquay 1979, played 8 games.

Dennis Loze

I remember one morning, during the first few weeks, I took some of the players to the weight room (couldn't call it a gym) a wooden hut beside the Far Post Club. It was freezing cold and we had had some snow that morning. As we started to walk down to the room, a snow fight was started, by Brian Taylor. If you knew Brian, he was always in the centre of things. Brian had recently had the plaster cast removed from a blood poisoned foot. The bombardment was aimed at one of the players, whose name I will not mention so we will call him Pete. Pete had not played for a number of weeks complaining of a knee problem. He might have had one to start with, but now there was little or no sign of a problem, but he still walked with a limp. The snow balls were then aimed at Pete, he was under a real bombardment and to get away from it, suddenly broke into a sprint down a slope (which was clear of snow) and out onto the pitch. No sign of a limp or any discomfort.

The next morning I was taking the same group of players, who were nearing the end of rehab prior to moving back to squad training. I arranged that these lads could come in at mid morning giving me time to sort out some of the more acute injuries. All the players had arrived and were ready for the run etc., all but Pete. So off we went, but I left instructions with the gateman where we were going so he could tell Pete when he arrived. We had a really good session, but no sign of Pete. When we got back to the ground, the gateman said that he had arrived and the message had been passed on. Also that Pete had changed and run out of the gate about 10mins ago. Well in about 5mins Pete arrived back into the ground as we were all ready for the showers, so I said to him to get his water-proofs and tracksuit off and I would do some work with him on the track, but as he got undressed, his training gear was dry. Yes, the old trick of getting into the shower with your tracksuit on and it would look like sweat. Soon the training gear was wet but from real sweat this time.

However, worse than our previous results was to follow, with the management hearing a rumour that the chairman was going to bring in Malcolm Allison as a consultant, even though Malcolm was having a very unsuccessful time coaching in Turkey.

Mike went to see the Chairman, and the outcome was not good with Mike resigning as manager. In fact it was a very stormy departure. So with in a matter of days, I had moved from the best club in the UK to a club struggling in the 3rd Division and now without a manager. Mike was a person who I was starting to have a good working relationship with, and in fact it was his positive attitude that had persuaded me to move.

Lenny Lawrence was to take over as caretaker manager, but in the back of everybody's mind Malcolm was appearing. Lenny had a reasonable start and players began to back him Brian Taylor who was Club skipper and George Foster who was team captain, went to see the chairman about Lenny being given a decent run. The days of players being listened to hadn't yet arrived to these shores.

Then a double blow of also losing John Craven our central defender, who had been wooed by one of Argyles previous mangers Tony Waiters, who was now head coach of Vancouver Whitecaps in the North American Soccer League.
Now, looking back, it seemed strange to meet with Tony that day and hand over Cravo's medical notes, as in time I too would be meeting up again with him and Cravo.

Money at the club started to become tight, with overnight stops and hotel meals, being down graded. If you know your geography, then you will know that every away game was a mammoth undertaking. For example, fancy Carlisle away, by bus, with limited overnight accommodation!

One of the weekly highlights, was to meet up with the commercial manger Bill Pearce, a good fellow Cornish man and his team. Bill had the great position of being the first person to introduce a lottery into the football league, so Plymouth were 1st in something. This meant on a Wednesday evening traveling to various venues in Devon and Cornwall, pubs, clubs etc. to carry out the actual draw.

Our group consisted of Brian Taylor and his wife Wendy, George Foster and his wife Sue plus Jane and myself. We would actual assist with carrying out the draw, and shift pints. It was good to meet up with the supporters who were still willing to pay money to stand on the terraces, even through we were going through a sticky patch. The Cornish supporters were and still are strong Argyle supporters, even though Cornwall is a rugby county. Argyle were and still are known as 'The best team in Cornwall'. But when we were in Plymouth, it was a different story. Support was poor, even to the extent of receiving a certain amount of verbal abuse, but if the beer was good all the comments went over our heads.

Our friendship with Brian and Wendy, would continue for a number of years, I am Godfather to Peter their eldest and Jane is Godmother to Caroline. Brian would later be transferred to Preston North End and we would link up again when we too moved to Lancashire. More of that later. George and Sue we are still in contact with. George works with Birmingham City. The story of Brian and Wendy would end in tragic circumstances, with Brian later dying of Motor Neurone disease and shortly afterwards Wendy dying of cancer.

Chapter Eight

"You must be the change you want to see in the world"
MAHATMA GANDHI

Work at the club continued, with the eventual arrival of Malcolm Allison as manger. This would be Malcolm's 2nd term as manger at Plymouth. "What would this bring?" That was the main questions on peoples lips. What changes would happen within the playing staff? This period of uncertainty was going to affect a lot of peoples lives.

I remember having Mickey Horswell in the treatment room having sustained an ankle injury, when the news came through of Malcolm's appointment. Mickey's reply was, "Well I might as well go home and pack, because Malcolm never fancied me when he and I were at Manchester City". Micky was at the time the youngest person to receive a Cup winners medal, with Sunderland and their unbelievable win over Leeds. Mickey's words turned to be true as he was the first to appear on the transfer list.

To other players, the response was amazing. Players who had been hiding in the woodwork and just picking up their wage packet, started to play. This was much to the disgust of players who had been playing their hearts out. People like George Foster, who if at that time you took blood off him it would be green and black, Argyles colours.

Also money was found from somewhere. Overnight stops and hotel meals were to appear back on the agenda. I no longer carried an emergency cash kitty as Malcolm was in charge of that. Cigars, wine and champers appeared on away trips. However the standard of football was no different, and we were struggling.

Humour was great at the club, although a great cloud was hanging over its future. An example of this humour was from good old George

"Robbo" Robertson. We were playing away versus Sheffield Wednesday. We had traveled up by coach on the Friday, and on the Saturday morning whilst I was having breakfast, the receptionist called me and said that I had a phonecall from Manchester. A Scottish accented voice announced that it was Alex Ferguson (now Sir), from United and that he had heard good reports about me and would I consider taking over as Physiotherapist at United. A little voice in the back of my head was saying to me that this was George Robbo, so the conversation kept going, until both of us fell about in laughter.

George was a fantastic person. As a player he had joined Argyle from his native Scotland at the age of 19 in 1950. He played at full back until 1963/64 season, making 358 appearances and even scoring 2 goals. George was one of the players I used to watch as a youngster with my Dad. He then came back to Argyle as groundsman and then he and his wife ran Elm Cottage, which was a smashing house about 100 yrds from the ground where the apprentices and some of the junior pros lived. George also acted as trainer for the Stiffs, and also looked after the laundry. This was until real financial problems hit the club and Elm Cottage was sold to a firm of solicitors as offices.

Ellis Studdard was another person with great wit and a real Northern dryness about him. Nothing seemed to get him down. He used to say that he had seen everything in football and nothing ever surprised him. Every lunchtime Ellis used to come to the treatment room and give me a shout that food was calling. The two of us used to walk the short distance to the Far Post, which was a sponsored watering hole, in a prefabricated building I think was obtained by Bill Pearce. It had been refurbished and provided a bar and café style eating house. The club at this time was run by Gordon Ward and as soon as Ellis and I walked in, Gordon would shout out "Two ham, eggs and dips." Ellis always called them dips as that is what you did with your chips, into the eggs. On the walls of the Far Post were cartoon drawings of the current playing staff, which were done by Chris Robinson, a life long supporter and match day announcer.

Ellis knew everyone in the game. During one of his two spells of manger at Argyle, he attended the annual Mangers do in London, and with him was Graham Little the club secretary. Graham told me of this great occasion, being surrounded by people with names that he just used to admire from afar and was completely over whelmed by the affair. He was sitting with Ellis, when suddenly Ellis shouted across the room to Alex Ferguson, "Come over here me ole mucker and sign this for me mate ere." Graham said he could have died with embarrassment, but over came Alex, and said anything for you, you old*****, and signed the menu for Graham. Good old Ellis, who unfortunately has since died, but in our cabinet in the lounge is a beautiful dish, given to Jane and I as a wedding present by Ellis and his wife.

Billy Harper must now get a mention. As I said earlier Billy had been at Arsenal (see beginning for details). He was now acting as steward in the Directors room. Also, it was nothing to see Bill helping out with ironing the team strip. Sunday mornings were to be remembered as about mid day when I was about finishing with the knocks and bumps from Saturday, Bill used to give a shout from the kitchen which led from the Directors room, "Dennis!" I would then have to go through the ritual of opening the treatment room door where I could see Bill and he would then point under the counter and grin. Under the counter use to be the biggest tot of whiskey you had ever seen I always used to have a drop of ginger with my whiskey but Bill would have none of this. It spoils a good blend he used to say, both of us use to enjoy a tot each before going home.

Billy used to drive an old Triumph Herald, but due to hip problems, he had difficulty getting his right leg into the car, so he had a bent metal coat hanger and used the crooked end, get it into his laces of his shoe and lift his leg in, and off he used to go. He also used to say that late on a Saturday night he used to go home "by rail." After a home game and numerous whiskeys he used to go to his local working mans club with his mate. He was not able to drive home, so the railings in front of peoples houses were his guide and helper in getting home. Hence "going home by rail"! A super humble person.

Players were soon being transferred or put on loan, with new faces appearing but still things were not going right and we were nearing the bottom of the league.

Soon Paul Barron was to be snapped up by my old club Arsenal. We were playing at Chesterfield and Don Howe had come to run his eye over him. Don and I were to meet after the game, and he asked how things were going and said that Arsenal were still there for me, but I had made a decision and was going to stick by it. Don said that I was dealing with far different types of players, not just the skill factor but a different mind set. You can say that again!

Dennis Loze

In fact, our season was saved by a freak snow storm in February. This was just after Mike Kelly had left and was Lennie's first game in charge, which turned out to be one of the most bizarre games at Home Park. We were playing at home against Bradford City on a bitterly cold day. Only 2,843 people had braved the sub zero temperatures. City took a 25th minute lead by McNiven, who was soon was to be assaulted by Mick Horswill, (they had clashed earlier). This time the red hair of Mick took over and he seemed to run half the length of the pitch to get at McNiven. Mick took no more action in that game. The weather worsened and we were losing when a snow blizzard blew in from Dartmoor and the temperature dropped. I remember poor Gary Megson our then young mid fielder, looking like a block of ice as his movements became slower and slower we were saved by the referee who abandoned the game. In fact the referee had to receive medical attention in the referee's room. The only happy person was Mick who had had a nice hot bath and was set for the evening. The game was to be replayed but not until the very last game of the season. This result was to prove so important in the future of Argyle. (see later on in the chapter).

After the abandonment we all piled into the Vice Presidents club for warmth and some cold beer. The weather started to close in, so it was time to go, as Jane and I were still living with my Dad and we had to cross Dartmoor in her old mini. We got to the outskirts of Plymouth and the snow was getting deeper, so we returned to Home Park, left the car there and walked, or rather blown across Central Park, in bitter winds to Plymouth Station and we were fortunate that a local train to Calstock was due to set off in 30 mins time, so we did manage to get home.

We were saved from losing 3 valuable points as the game was in fact replayed as the very last game of the season. This turned out to be the saving of Argyle in Division 3.

The departure of Paul Barron to Arsenal opened the door to a young goalkeeper who was to continue to have a very lengthy and successful career, Martin Hodge.

Martin made his debut at home to Peterborough. On the Friday, the day before the game, when the reality of it all had hit Martin, he was a bag of nerves, even though we could rely on Robbo and his wife to help calm him down as Martin was still living at Elm Cottage. I gave him a very mild sleeping tablet to help him sleep. The Saturday lunchtime saw Martin walking into the ground with the big smile on his face. Those who know Martin would know that he is not often seen without a smile, only when he is giving his back four a bit of stick, but this one was huge. As he saw me it got even bigger, as he explained his nights sleep. Robbo had been good to his word and settled Martins evening routine, plus an early night, then Martin remembered the tablet, do I need it or don't I. He remembered that I said that it should be taken early and only if he thought he really needed it. Taking it out of his bag to place on his bedside locker, he dropped it, but then tried to flick it up with his foot as it was dropping, resulting in the tablet being sent across the room and disappearing. He set off looking for it, and after an hour or so, it still hadn't appeared he felt so tired that he lay on the bed and crashed right out, not waking until Robbo gave him a shout for breakfast. Did he have safe hands, or was his footwork not what it should have been?

During the season, Jane caused a laugh amongst the players and also the wives and girlfriends. Jane is not really interested in football, so much so that she only saw one game at Highbury and non at Plymouth. At home games she used to drop me off at the ground and then spend the afternoon in Plymouth City centre, then come back to the ground when the game had finished. Her timing used to be excellent as she always appeared in the Vice Presidents Room just as the rest of the girls came in from seeing the match. They would start talking about the game and when Jane was asked her opinion she would say that she hadn't seen the game but had gone shopping! The look on the girls faces use to be a mix of uncertainty and jealousy.

My Dad was still a regular spectator and just loved the fact that I supplied him with a free ticket, and that he used to attend the Vice Presidents and meet up with people. One of these used to be Billy Harper. My Dad was not a drinker and 1 bottle of stout used to be his lot, but Billy used to persuade Dad to have another. You could see Dads face getting redder and redder as the 3rd bottle was taking effect.

As the end of the season neared we had 2 games left - Port Vale and the rearranged game against Bradford. Port Vale had lost three games on the trot and for them their last game of the season, they were 1 point ahead of us and we were occupying a relegation spot.

The Port Vale game ended right for us as we managed a 3-2 win. You would have thought that we had won the league instead of just avoiding relegation. Players were carried off the pitch on the shoulders of jubilant spectators. In fact, we had 9,474 people watching the game, the highest home gate of the season.

We were saved. But in fact it was that abandoned game against Bradford that had saved us.

The following Saturday we played that game against Bradford, but for them it was not worthwhile as they were relegated because of our win over Port Vale the previous week.

I felt sorry for them because if our earlier game hadn't been abandoned and the score had stayed the same, it would have been us who would have been relegated. I think most of the Bradford team had been drowning their sorrows on the journey down as we thrashed them 6-0.

What was next season going to bring?

Chapter Eight

"Success is the ability to go from one failure to another with no loss of enthusiasm."
WINSTON CHURCHILL

Well it would see a succession of players coming and going, combined some eccentric or erratic decisions by Malcolm. We had had a terrible preseason run, as we lost to the local South Western side of Truro and only managed a draw against another local South Western side, St Austell.

We did manage to pick up a few points earlier in the season. One of Malcolms eccentric actions was during the week before our second game of the season at home to Lincoln. We had a young player called Tony Levy, who had just signed a pro contract after his apprenticeship at Argyle. Malcolm paraded this young lad in the senior pros changing room as the future and saviour of Plymouth Argyle. Tony's name was added to the team sheet as sub. So Saturday arrived, Tony was to come on as sub after 25 minutes when Brian Taylor had received a nasty gash to his ankle. Poor Tony was out of his depth, but he battled to come to terms with the occasion although nothing went right for him. We did end up winning 2-1 though.

On Monday morning as the players were coming in for training, I happened to be in the corridor outside the treatment room as Tony came in through the main entrance Malcolm was walking out of it, Malcolm totally ignored Tony who was looking up at Malcolm, like a lost puppy looking to his master. Tony never appeared on the team sheet again and was back in the Stiffs and youth set up.

That experience left a bad taste in my mouth. Was this what football was all about?

Dennis Loze

Soon more players were on the move but still results were hard to come by.

Loan Players

Lee Chapman (FD)
Born in Lincoln 1959
Signed Stoke City 1979, played 95 games.
Loan to Plymouth 1978, played 3 games
Transferred to Arsenal 1982, played 15 games
Transferred to Sunderland 1983, played 14 games.
Transferred to Sheffield Wednesday 1984, played 147 games
Transferred Nottingham Forest 1988, played 48 games
Transferred to Leeds Untd, 1990, played 133 games.
Transferred to Portsmouth 1993, played 5 games.
Transferred to West Ham Untd 1993, played 33 games.
Transferred to Ipswich 1995, played 11 games.
Loan to Southend 1995, played 1 game.
Loan to Leeds Untd 1996, played 2 games
Transferred to Swansea 1996, played 7 games
Later signings

Steve Brennan (MF)
Born in Mile End 1958
Apprentice at Crystal Palace, played 2 games
Transferred to Plymouth 1978, played 6 games

Tony Burns (GK)
Born in Edenbridge 1944
Signed for Arsenal 1963, played 31 games
Transferred to Brighton 1966, played 54 games
Transferred to Charlton 1969, played 10 games
Signed for Durban SA 1971
Signed for Crystal Palace 1973, played 90 games
Loan to Brentford 1977, played 6 games
Signed for Memphis NASL 1977
Signed for Plymouth 1978, played 8 games.

Colin Clarke (DF)
Born in Glasgow 1946
Signed for Arsenal 1963, played 0 games

Transferred to Oxford 1965, played 443 games
Signed for Los Angeles NASL 1977
Signed for Plymouth 1978, played 35 games.

Keith Fear (FD)
Born in Bristol 1952
Signed Bristol City 1969, played 126 games
Loan to Hereford 1977, played 6 games
Loan to Blackburn 1977, played 5 games.
Transferred to Plymouth 1978, played 40 games
Loan to Brentford 1979, played 7 games
Transferred to Chester City 1980, played 41 games.

Clevere Ford (FD)
Born in London 1958
Signed for Plymouth 1978, played 4 games

Tyrone James (DF)
Born in Paddington 1956
Signed Fulham 1974, played 18 games
Transferred to Plymouth 1978, played 77 games
Loan to Torquay 1983, played 13 games.

Brian McNeil (MF)
Born Newcastle 1956
Apprentice at Bristol City 1974 played 0 games
Transferred to Plymouth 1978, played 47 games.

Steve Perrin (FD)
Born in Paddington 1952
Signed Crystal Palace 1976, played 45 games.
Transferred to Plymouth 1978, played 34 games.
Transferred to Portsmouth 1979, played 18 games
Transferred to Northampton 1981, played 22 games.

Barry Silkman (FD)
Born in Stepney 1952
Signed for Hereford 1974, played 18 games
Transferred to Crystal Palace 1976, played 40 games
Transferred to Plymouth 1978, played 14 games
Loan to Luton 1979, played 3 games

Transferred to Manchester City 1979, played 19 games
Transferred to Brentford 1980, played 14 games
Transferred to Queens Park Rangers 1980, played 22 games
Transferred to Leyton Orient 1981 played 133 games
Transferred to Southend 1985, played 38 games
Transferred to Crewe Alexandra 1986, played 1 game.

Then came the disastrous game against non league Worcester in the FA Cup, losing out 2-0. You could see in Malcolms eyes it was time he moved on.

Unbeknown to me at that time, it would be me to moving from Argyle, before Malcolms return to Manchester City. It was over one of our ham, egg and dips lunch with Ellis, that he took out from his famous red book a scrap of paper torn from one of the national papers. It was an advert for the post of Club Physiotherapist with Vancouver Whitecaps. Ellis and I had a lengthy talk about it, and his advice was to go for it.

That night Jane and I had a lengthy talk about it, as we had only just recently bought and moved into a house at Tamerton Foliot and the thought of moving from Argyle had never entered our heads. Jane had obtained a good post at a Young Disabled Unit at Derriford. However an application was sent off during the next couple of days. I was soon to hear from Tony Waiters, manager of Whitecaps asking me to meet up with him, as he was back in England and staying in Modbury, just outside of Plymouth.

A couple of days later Tony and I met and agreed terms, but he wanted Jane and I to have a meal with him and Ann his wife, to talk about Vancouver. To cut a long story short I got the job and handed in my resignation with Argyle but agreed to stay on longer than the months notice, giving them time to get a replacement.

The local papers and TV had got hold of the news by now and it was news for a few days.

We had at this time taken a young player on loan from Stoke by the name of Lee Chapman, who would go on and make a real name for himself in football. Lee spent a month with us, and as it was his 3rd week of

Arsenal to Armenia

the loan period, I asked Malcolm if I should arrange the necessary medical etc.(you could see the potential in Lee) Malcolms reply was "No, I don't fancy him!"

The Christmas fixtures saw us playing away to Brentford on Boxing Day. This was to turn out to be my last game for Argyle, although I didn't know it at the start of the trip.

We traveled up by coach early on Boxing Day morning, and as we were nearing the ground the bus started to act strangely and finally conked out in the car park itself. The driver, who had been our team driver for the past number of seasons, said that he would get on to Trathens the company and get a replacement.

About 30mins before kick off, a message was passed to me that the driver had failed to get a replacement bus, but that the directors etc. were coming by coach and they could possibly take us on board for the return trip. I then passed a message on to the club chairman about the problem and asked if we, the team, could travel back in their bus.

After the game which we lost 2-1, a message was passed on to me via our driver that the chairman had agreed and that our normal driver would be driving the coach, whilst the other driver would remain with the broken down one.

When we had all changed, we piled into the bar, to replace some fluids - well sounds good doesn't it? We had been there about 30 mins or so when one of our directors came up to us at the bar and said to one of the Brentford players, "Come on hurry up we want to leave", then he walked out. So we decided to stay as he hadn't said anything to us. About another 15 mins had passed and in came the frustrated director. He caught hold of the same Brentford players arm and said if he wasn't on the bus with the rest of the team, it would go without him. See what I mean about behind the scenes in football, a director who didn't know his players? We got onto the bus carrying enough bottles of beer to keep us going for a while. The looks we got from the chairman and the directors was enough to turn milk sour, but they should remember that they had eaten and drunk well over Christmas, whereas this was the teams first chance to have a drink. It did seem funny that all the directors and guests were all sitting at the front of the bus, with their cases of wine and we were shoved to the back of the bus with our bottles of beer.

Dennis Loze

After a number of hours we were nearing the outskirts of Plymouth, when the same director who was involved in the Brentford fiasco came back to tell me that the Chairman wanted to see me, so off I went to see him. I was greeted by a very stern face and the words telling me that part of my job was to tell the driver where the players needed to be dropped off. That was like a red rag to a bull, so I told him that it wasn't in my job description as I didn't have one and also next time he wanted to see me, he could do it himself and not send one of his minions to do his bidding. The stern face had now turned a violent red and I thought don't have a heart attack as I would have to give you the kiss of life. He then leapt to his feet and started to splutter, so I helped him by saying that the driver had driven us for the past couple of seasons and knew exactly where the players lived and needed dropping off and in fact he knew the players better than some of the directors, and he had attended more matches than you Mr. Chairman!

His face was full of anger, so I advised him to sit down as if he continued I would have to punch him straight through the windscreen. Then up jumped his son and he received the same instructions, to which the chairman said that my time at Argyle was at an end, my contract terminated and that I was to see him at the ground the following morning. My final reply was that I had already worked my notice at Argyle. This again showed his lack of knowledge and interest in the club. Turning my back on him I walked back to my seat, through the maze of stunned directors and then the grinning players. We then shared the couple of bottles of wine that I had picked up on my way back.

When we finally got back to the ground, George Foster, Fred Binney and myself found ourselves in one of the local hotels and cracked open a couple of bottles of champers in celebration.

Arsenal to Armenia

Good forces training. My drinking mate Pete Stubbs and myself (on right) at RAF High Wycombe.

Winning the 100 yds Bomber Command Championship

Dennis Loze

RAF Training Command Champions RAF Cosford (Me front row left)

England vs. East Germany indoor International Athletics. (Me carrying East German flag.)

Arsenal to Armenia

Joint Services Rehabilitation Unit Chessington
Christmas show, for the patients. Me in the dance of the Seven Army Blankets.

My Arsenal pass.

[101]

Dennis Loze

FA Coaching Course Loughborough. Me back row 4th from left.

Plymouth Argyle Lottery night. Right to left - George Foster (Team Captain), me, Jane, Sue Foster, Wendy and Brian Taylor (Club Captain), Vernon Penprase (British Featherweight Champion) and his wife.

Arsenal to Armenia

Lottery Night at the Tamar Inn Calstock.

Chapter Nine

∞

"Faith is taking the first step, even when you don't see the whole staircase."
MARTIN LUTHER KING JR.

Tony Waiters took the news well about my blazing exit from Argyle, when I phoned him the next morning, by him saying not to forget that he had worked under that board for a couple of years! He had taken them from the 3rd, to the heights of the 2nd and they failed to back him, so forget it.

Harley Lawler who was Sports Editor of the Sunday Independent contacted me to say congratulation. Not so much for my position with the Whitecaps, but for the way I had left. He said that he would have given anything to have been there and seen it all with his own eyes, not to print it but to see it.

Just one scare came in the form of getting a work permit for Canada, as they are rightly protective of allowing a non Canadian to do the job of a Canadian. So the wording was changed from that of Physiotherapist to one of Physiotherapist/coach - another advantage of my coaching qualifications, as not many Canadians would have an FA coaching award as well as a medical qualification.

At least it now gave Jane and I a couple of clear weeks to get everything sorted, even the wedding arrangements.

At this present moment in time we are helping to prepare for our daughter Morgana's wedding she is normally a very down to earth girl, but she has got the wedding fever and things must be right. She is a great arranger and doer, but what a contrast to our wedding!

We were married at Plymouth Registry office, with members of our families, and work colleagues of Jane's, plus some of the players and wives. We decided on a registry wedding as I was divorced, but also we didn't attend any church, so it would be wrong to be married in one. The wedding cars were easy, my brother had a Saab Turbo, so I traveled in that and Jane's brother also had a Saab Turbo so she traveled in that. Our photographer was from the local paper who used to take match photos, Bernard Prince.

After the wedding we drove to the Young Disabled Unit where Jane had worked so that the residents or now they would be named "clients", could see us. We were traveling along and suddenly realised that I was still in my brothers car, and Jane in her brothers, so a quick stop and move around and we arrived at the Unit.

From there to the reception, which was at our house and Jane had done all the preparation except the wedding cake, which Wendy Taylor had made. They were now in Preston as Brian had already joined North End, so couldn't attend.

The rest of the players and wives turned up and we had a great time, so much so that I rang through twice to the Hotel we where staying at, to say we would be late.

The Hotel was the Bedford Hotel in Tavistock a grand total of 12 miles away, and we were finally let in by the Night Porter. We only had a couple of days there as Jane had to go back to work, in fact her uniform went with us so she could travel straight to work. Talk about a shoe string wedding, but it was a great occasion.

We were also due to fly out to Canada in a couple of days so things were getting a bit hectic.

The day before we were due to fly out, the weather forecast was a bad one with heavy snow for the next couple of days, so we decided to travel up a day earlier, I had rented an Hertz car which we could leave at the Airport. But what a drive up, it took us over 8 hrs to travel a journey which would normally take 3-4 hrs, so bad in fact looking back how we made it I shall never know how. Well we did make it, only to be greeted by the news that all flights were cancelled, and there would be at least a 24hrs delay. We were both absolutely tired out, all I could still see was snow beating against the windscreen, frozen wipers trying to clear the snow away, and the head lights peering through the white blizzard; so we had to stay at the airport for a grand total of 36hrs before finally flying out. By this time we were both so tired, that they could have flown us anywhere, what a start to our new life!

The flight over was great although I had spent 14yrs in the RAF, this was in fact the first time that I had flown, well it would be the first time, that I had taken off and landed, as previously after taking off I would be jumping out with a parachute. Even during my Land and Sea Survival training, the rescue was by helicopter, which had already taken off, so this was to be my first complete flight.

The crew on Air Canada were great and we had a good restful, uneventful journey.

We finally landed at Vancouver a bit jet lagged, but not too bad, Jane was to experience the first aspect of being married. She had always been a very independent person, own car, own life, etc. but as were going through immigration, it was only me that they were interested in, as I was the one with the work permit, and Jane seen as an appendage. It still riles her to this very day, sitting waiting and being ignored. We were met by Les Wilson plus the P.R. from the Whitecaps. They presented Jane with a lovely bunch of flowers, which did go a long way to ease her frustration. Les drove us to our hotel, the Rembrant. As it was night time, we didn't see much around us, but soon we would enjoy the beautiful scenery of Vancouver and its surrounding areas.

All I could think of was a good nights sleep and a couple of days rest, before work, but no. I was to be collected from the hotel at 8-0 o'clock the next morning for a press meeting, then the office to meet all background team and then to be seen fulfilling part of the new job description to be involved in a training session that late afternoon and evening with some young players, plus some of the Whitecaps Squad at the Empire Stadium, our home venue.

I was now in a complete daze, when I met up with Jane later on. We managed to find a small restaurant and experience the amount of food that North Americans and Canadians ate.

During these first couple of days I renewed my friendship with Barry Crocker. He was the ex-pat who had applied for the post I was now filling. Barry and I had met previously whilst in the RAF. I was on short term attachment at RAF Conningsby, a Bomber station in Lincolnshire, where Barry was stationed. We went to his house one evening to meet

Arsenal to Armenia

his wife and some of his Canandian friends. On meeting them Barry asked me to tell them the story of the chicken. he had told them previously but no-one would ever believe him. This is a true story which involved Barry, his first wife and myself.

One weekend at Conningsby, Barry invited me to stay with them and we would go to watch Leicester play on the Saturday afternoon. Barry was renting a cottage on a farm, in fact the cottage was just off the farm yard, which was the feeding ground for the farmers chickens, who just wandered all around the farm. On the Saturday morning, during breakfast, I asked to Barry if he had ever been tempted to catch and eat one of the chickens. His reply was "No", as the farmer would know how many there were and secondly, how would he do it without the chickens creating enough noise to draw the attention of the farmer to what was happening. My answer was "no problem just watch me." So I set out a trail of corn (taken from the farm yard) leading into the entrance of the scullery of cottage, then I placed a string noose on the floor, with more corn inside it, the end of the string leading to behind the door where I would stand. The idea was to entice a chicken to follow the trail into the scullery, for it to stand inside the noose, when I would pull the string, and result in the chicken being caught. Well after about an hour, one followed the trail into the scullery, yes and stood inside the noose it was a nice plump chicken. A quick pull of the string and yes, success - a captured chicken. The idea then was to push the chicken into a bag, take it into the kitchen, where I would kill and bleed it, ready for plucking. Roast chicken for Sunday lunch. However the chicken had a different plan. With the noose firmly around its legs, it started to flap its wings so hard that it took off, with me holding onto the string. Have you ever seen a model aeroplane on control lines, which circles around the controller, well this is what happened, the chicken flew around the scullery with me on the end of the string. It must have done about 4 circuits of the room before I managed to get it down, tie its legs and pop into the bag. Barry's wife was now a bit squeamish about me killing the chicken and also it was time for us to get to Leicester for the game, so her father who lived nearby would come and do the deed.

Sunday morning, one dead chicken ready for plucking, so I started. If you have never plucked a chicken, let me tell you that the feathers do tend to float around a bit, especially if you are suffering from a hangover! I was about half way through and a knock came to the door, yes you've guessed it the farmer, he had come for the rent. Normally he comes into the kitchen and has a cuppa, whilst the rent is sorted. Panic stations, feathers everywhere so Barry grabbed the rent, rushed to the door and told the farmer that he was just going out, as he had been called back to camp. Well the farmer bought it and 10 mins later, the plucked chicken handed was over to Barry's wife and we beat a hasty retreat to the local pub, whilst the chicken was cooking. But the chicken did have the last laugh. It was the oldest, toughest chicken you have ever tasted, I think the chicken believed in euthanasia, and decided to end it all, using me.

Back in Canada at Barry's apartment, we just sat back and drank to the health of the chicken, with Barry's friends now believing the chicken story.

In a couple of days we found an apartment in Burnaby, the eastern side of Vancouver, and it was great to be settled after the past hectic few weeks.

This only lasted a few hours, as that night were could hear a constant knocking which seemed to come from the wall dividing the bedroom from the lounge. It would come and go, and when it stopped, you would lie awake expecting it to start again. In fact, it was the central heating. As the heating came back on and the water rushed through the pipes they would vibrate against each other. We called it Harvey Wall banger, and arranged to get it fixed.

I was soon on the road to our training camp in California, near to Santa Barbara. Jane in the meantime was going to see some old family friends of hers in Kamloops and I would meet up with her there on my return.

So what was all this NASL about how and when did football start in North America?

N.A.S.L.
North American Soccer League
Founded 1967

Although the North American Soccer League was only founded in 1967, people actually think that football as we know it was not played in North America until the formation of the NASL. This is not the case even though one of the strangest aspects of football around the world is that the game had never become popular in such former British territo-

Arsenal to Armenia

ries as Australia (now improving but still behind the rest of Australian sport), New Zealand, India, South Africa, Canada, and The United States of America as in Britain or the rest of the world.

In North America where the Canadians and Americans have developed their own sports such as basketball, baseball, grid-iron football and ice-hockey, other British sports such as rugby and cricket are virtually unknown to millions of sports fanatics. Football (soccer) is widely played at the minor level today, but it still ranks way down on the list of spectator sports.

Now to get away from the idea that football, (which I will now reluctantly revert to the North American terminology of "soccer", thus avoiding confusion between Football and the grid iron stuff!) is a modern immigrant into the North American culture, it was actually played in the 17th century. In fact the American colonies were the first overseas territories of the British Empire to play soccer like games; in fact just 2 centuries later, the United States was the first sovereign country outside Great Britain to establish a soccer club and one of the first to form a national governing body. The club was the Oneida Football Club (near to Boston) in 1862. The first recorded games under rules which related to today's soccer rules was played on 6th November 1869 at New Brunswick, between the universities of Princeton, Columbia, Yale and Rutgers in New York. In 1867 a set of rules were written based on those established by the Football Association in London in 1863.

So soccer in North America is not a new sport!

The American Football Association, the first governing body of soccer in the United States was formed in 1884, becoming the third to be formed outside the British Isles.

A rival the American Football Association, was started some years later and this eventually led to the formation of the United States Football Association (now the United States Soccer Federation) in 1913 and also affiliated to FIFA the same year. One year prior to this the Canadian Football Soccer Association (now the Canadian Soccer Association) was formed and also affiliated to the world body. While nations throughout Europe and South America formed national leagues, many before the turn of the 20th century no such national league was ever formed in the United States or Canada until 1967.

Some professional leagues had come and faded away over the years, due to lack of attendance and internal disagreements. Yet two, founded in the 1920's, managed to survive, The American Soccer League, formed in 1921 on the Eastern seaboard of the United States, and the National Soccer League, formed in 1926 in Eastern Canada.

Both leagues had their individual difficulties, folding and reforming, but survived to form a coast to coast league across North America when the rival National Professional Soccer League and the United Soccer Association were formed, leading a merger which resulted in the North American Soccer League.

The United States Association, referred to as The In Laws, decided in 1967 to import entire club teams to represent its 12 cities:

Wolverhampton Wanderers played as the Los Angeles Wolves.
Sunderland played as the Vancouver Royals.
Stoke City played as the Cleveland Stokers.
Hibernian played as the Toronto City.
Aberdeen played as the Washington Whips
Dundee United played as the Dallas Tornado.
Glentoran (Belfast) played as the Detroit Cougars.
Shamrock Rovers played as the Boston Rovers.
Bangu (Rio de Janeiro) played as the Houston Stars.
Cagliari (Italy) played as the Chicago Mustangs.
ADO Den Hague (Holland) played as the Golden Gate Gales.
Cerro (Uruguay) played as New York Skyliners.

The National Professional Soccer League, known as The Outlaws, recruited players from all over the world to man its 10 cities:

Baltimore Bays
Philadelphia Spartans
New York Generals
Atlanta Chiefs
Pittsburg Phantoms
Oakland Clippers
St Louis Stars
Chicago Spurs
Toronto Falcons
Los Angeles Toros.

However, by the time the season was over, attendances in both leagues were well below what the owners had hoped for and was a cause of great concern and rethinking. The answer was obvious, if everything was to survive, the two leagues would have to bury the hatchet and merge. This did happen, but not overnight. The new North American Soccer League was born in December 1967.

Now the new format of soccer could go full steam ahead, the fans would no longer be confused by two leagues doing the same thing and the owners hoped that fans would turn out in their thousands. This did not happen, long before the season was over many of the clubs were in serious financial difficulties. This happened even though on two occasions, during that season, the league had a great boost with the arrival of the great team Santos appearing and also playing 8 games against various league teams. Members of Santos included players such as Carlos Alberto, Clodoaldo, Claudio, Oberdan, Rilo, Joel, Toninho, Lima, Silva, Pele, and Abel. Attendances shot up during this period, rave reviews from the media, but things returned to normal after this period.

One by one, clubs left the scene, and at the end of the season only 5 teams remained out of the 17 that started the 1968 season. All the playing records of the 1967 and 1968 season even disappeared.

Over the next few seasons, little by little season by season, the NASL clawed its way back onto the scene. But it was not until 1975 that the league gained a new image overnight. Pele was persuaded to come out of retirement. The North American players had a lot to prove and some of the many imports were either over the hill or just over for the paid holiday.

One of the main factors that caused difficulties with the success of soccer was the media. Most newspaper sports departments had so much popular sport to deal with, the thought of dealing with a new sport they knew little or nothing about, meant that the media coverage soccer received was so poor. Even genuine fans who tried to follow the game were left frustrated.

March 1985 was when the NASL officially died, having been born 19 years earlier and had continued through the lean years, reaching its ultimate goal in the latter part of the 70's.

This is the period of the late 70's I was fortunate to be involved with.

Chapter Ten

"There are a terrible lot of lies going around the world, and the worst of it is half of them are true."
WINSTON CHURCHILL

It was now officially time to meet up with the full Whitecaps squad, although over the previous number of days, I had been meeting them. I had met most of the English players in England at their medicals.

Vancouver Whitecaps

    1968   Commenced as Vancouver Royals, but lasted only 1 season.
    1974   Resurrected as Vancouver Whitecaps
    1984   Club folded
    1985   Resurrected as Vancouver 86ers.
    2001   Reverted back to Vancouver Whitecaps

Ground   Empire Stadium. Built for the Empire games in 1954. which featured the traumatic Marathon finish of Jim Peters of England. Also of the fantastic Race between fellow record holders of the mile Roger Banister and John Landy, where Landy looked over his right shoulder as Banister passed him on the left to win. A statue depicting this event was to be seen at the main entrance to the stadium.

    1983   moved into cavernous 62,000 BC Place Stadium
    1986   moved to 5,722 capacity Swangard Stadium.

Record Gate 32,250 versus New York Cosmos 1979

Mangers/Head Coach
    1977   John Best

1978/9   Tony Waiters
1980   Bob McNab
1980   Tony Waiters

Club Honours
1979   Winners North American Soccer League

1988,89,90,91   Canadian Soccer League Champions

Players
For the season 1979:-

Phil (Lofty) Parkes (Keeper)	Wolverhampton
Ray Lewington (Mid Field)	Chelsea
John Craven (Defender)	Plymouth/Coventry
Bob Lenarduzzi (Defender)	Canada
Roger Kenyon (Defender)	Everton
Buz Parsons (Mid Field))	Canada
Jon Sammels	Leicester/Arsenal
Trevor Wymark (Striker)	Ipswich
Bob Bolitho (Defender)	Canada
Kevin Hector (Striker)	Derby County
Peter Daniel (Defender)	Derby County
Dan Lenarduzzi (Mid Field)	Canada
Carl Valentine (Forward)	Oldham
Bruce Grobbelaar (Keeper)	Zimbabwee
Paul Nelson (Mid Field)	Canada

To Arrive later
Alan Ball (Mid Field)	Southampton/Arsenal
Willy Johnson (Forward)	West Brom

The training camp seemed to going well, at least it was good to start with a team that didn't have any injuries, although we did pick up a couple of small ones at the camp, but were able to start the season with a completely empty treatment room.

On our arrival back from the training camp, I was to travel the next day up to Kamloops to meet up with Jane. It was going to be my first experience of the famous Greyhound Coaches. That night was spent at the flat, but I couldn't sleep as I was expecting Harvey Wall Banger to start, but on inspecting the wall could see that Harvey had been fixed good and proper.

The NASL seasons fixtures were so different from the English fixture list, we were to fly everywhere, not for convenience but necessity. Our nearest fixture was at Edmonton, Alberta some 1,000 miles away.

Due to the amount of traveling expected, the whole league, consisting of 24 teams were divided into two Conferences and each Conference, 3 Divisions, Eastern, Central, Western, consisting of four teams. We were in The National Conference Western Division, (due to our geography).

The **NASL Alignment** looked like this:-

NATIONAL CONFERENCE
Eastern Division
Toronto Blizzard (Exhibition Stadium)
Rochester Lancers (Holleder Stadium)
New York Cosmos (Giants Stadium)
Washington Diplomats (RFK Stadium)

Central Division
Minnesota Kicks (Metropole Stadium)
Tulsa Roughnecks (Skelly Stadium)
Atlanta Chiefs (Atlanta-Fulerton County Stadium)
Dallas Tornado (Ownby Stadium)

Western Division
Vancouver Whitecaps (Empire Stadium)
Seattle Sounders (Kingdome)
Portland Timbers (Portland Civic Stadium)
Los Angeles Aztecs (Rose Bowl)

AMERICAN CONFERENCE
Eastern Division
New England Tea Men (Nickerson Field)
Philadelphia Fury (Veterans Stadium)
Tampa Bay Rowdies (Tampa Stadium)
Fort Lauderdale Strikers (Lockhart Stadium)

Central Division

Arsenal to Armenia

Detroit Express (Pontiac Silverdome)
Chicago sting (Wrigley/Soldier Field)
Memphis Rogues (Liberty Bowl)
Houston Hurricane (Astrodome)

Western Division
Edmonton Drillers (Commonwealth Stadium)
San Jose Earthquakers (Spartan Stadium)
California Surf (Anaheim Stadium)
San Diego Sockers (San Diego Stadium)

This will now give you an idea of the immense distances between teams.

1979 Schedual (Fixtures)

March 30th	Dallas (h)	8.00 pm
April 6th	Edmonton (h)	8.00pm
April 14th	Chicago (a)	2.30pm
April 21st	Portland (h)	8.00pm
April 27th	San Diego (a)	7.30pm
May 2nd	San Diego (h)	8.00pm
May 5th	San Jose (a)	8.00pm
May 11th	Rochester (h)	8.30pm
May 18th	Philadelphia(h)	8.00pm
May 30th	Edmonton (a)	7.30pm
June 2nd	Houston (h)	8.00pm
June 6th	Tulsa (a)	8.00pm
June 10th	Minnesota (a)	1.30pm
June 13th	California (a)	7.30pm
June 16th	New York (h)	8.00pm
June 24th	California (h)	8.00pm
June 27th	Atlanta (a)	7.30pm
June 30th	Ft Lauderdale(a)	8.00pm
July 4th	Toronto(a)	7.30pm
July 7th	Seattle (h)	8.00pm
July 11th	Los Angeles (h)	8.00pm
July 15th	New York (a)	7.30pm
July 18th	Washington (a)	8.00pm
July 21st	Toronto (h)	8.00pm
July 25th	Tulsa (h)	8.00pm

Dennis Loze

July 28th	Portland (a)	8.00pm
August 1st	Minnesota (h)	8.00pm
August 4th	Los Angeles (a)	7.30pm
August 8th	San Jose (h)	8.00pm
August 11th	Seattle (a)	7.30pm

This would be followed by the Division, Conference and NASL Soccer Bowl final.

In the league each team would play the other 3 teams twice, both home and away. The remainder of the fixtures was made up of games against teams of the other league conferences, playing once either home or away, giving a total of 30 games.

Now it starts to get more complicated.

For the playoffs, 16 of the 24 teams would qualify, consisting of the top 2 from each division, plus 2 wild cards from each conference, plus the third placed teams with the highest points. The semi final being the Conference Final and the NASL Final being between the two Conference winners.

During the league, 6pts would be awarded for a win, plus a bonus 1 point for each goal scored up to and including 3 goals. The losing team also qualified for this bonus, so a team losing 4-3 obtained 3 points and the winners 9 points.

As no game could end a draw, at the end of normal play (90mins) a further two halves consisting of 7½ mins. each were played, but the game could end when the first goal was scored. If there was no score at the end of the set extra time, then the NASL shootout was brought in. 5 players were chosen from each team. The ball was placed on the 35 yd line and the player must take their shot within 5 seconds. The player could shoot, dribble or anything legal within the rules of the game, to beat the keeper. The keepers movements are not restricted within the 5 sec, again within the normal rules of the game. If the score remained a tie after the prescribed 5 attempts, they continued to take alternative kicks until one had scored more than the other after an equal number of attempts.

So you can see that the season was packed, added to this the thousands of miles to be traveled and back to back games averaging a game every

3½ days. Added to this we had a small squad, putting added pressure on clearing up any injuries quickly. This will be evident as the season progressed.

One highlight of the season was seeing Jane actually attending every home match and not missing the televised away games. She even traveled to New York for the final against Tampa Bay. She really enjoyed not just the games but the close bond that was with the Whitecaps.
This was to be experienced in the first few days of being at Vancouver, when we were invited to the Supporters Club BBQ. We were welcomed by them like close friends, a contrast to England where you were either looked up to as an idol, or looked down upon as a nothing.

Jane said that day was a contrast to the Arsenal Supporters do, where people just wanted to look at you like a priceless jewel in a shop window, where as here they took to you for who you were.
She used to meet up for the home fixtures with a couple of ex-pats, Annie and Terry Carol an hour before kick off and have hamburgers etc. with no rush to get to your seats. A contrast to England again where it's all rush and push. After the games we all used to meet up at the players lounge and crack open a number of Labbats (we were sponsored by Labbats beer – so we had to support them). When all these had disappeared, it was off the find some other place, even if the games didn't finish until 9.45pm. It would be about 10.30pm or so before the first drink passed through your lips.

Chapter Eleven

∞

"Change is the law of life, and those who look only to the past or present are certain to miss the future."
J.F. KENNEDY

As I said, we had shaped into an excellent team, but we had had our share of difficulties over the season, and some other bizarre happenings, which will be revealed as we progress through the season.

The city of Vancouver is so beautiful, situated in the southwest corner of Canada in the province of British Columbia, at about 49° Latitude and 123° Longitude, next to the Pacific Ocean.

Vancouver is surrounded by water on three sides and overlooked by the Coast Range - mountains that rise abruptly to more than 1,500 m. Its climate is one of the mildest in Canada. Temperatures average 3°C in January and 18°C in July. Vancouver's average annual precipitation is 1,219 mm. Most rainfall occurs in winter.

With a population of about 600,000, Vancouver lies in a region of more than 2 million people. Vancouver is the largest city in the province of British Columbia and the third largest in Canada. It covers an area of 114 sq km.

The port of Vancouver is Canada's largest and most diversified port, trading more than $43 billion in goods with more than 90 trading economies annually. Port activities generate 62,200 jobs. The Port of Vancouver is North America's gateway for Asia-Pacific trade. Two of the Port of Vancouver's container docks are located in the city. The Fraser River has barge and log traffic serving forestry and other water related industries. Around 1,800 acres of industrial land provide an important range of support services, manufacturing and wholesale premises for businesses throughout the city and region.

Vancouver is a major tourist destination. In addition to the city's scenic location, visitors enjoy beautiful gardens and world-famous Stanley Park one of more than 180 city parks, and a combination of natural forest and parklands near the city centre.

Archaeological evidence shows that coastal Indians had settled the Vancouver area by 500 B.C. British naval captain George Vancouver explored the area in 1792. Vancouver was founded as a sawmill settlement called Granville in the 1870s. The city was incorporated in 1886 and renamed after Captain Vancouver.

However, one of main highlights for me was to see and be in the famous Empire Stadium, our home ground.

What made it such a fascination for me?

It goes way back to when I was 11years of age, with the names of great athletes such as Roger Banister, John Landy, and Jim Peters. The three of them competed in the British Empire and Commonwealth Games in August 1954, held at Vancouver, actually in the Empire Stadium.

Standing on the actual spot where these athletes continued to make world history.

Firstly Roger Banister and John Landy in the famous mile event, but the main interest started a number of months prior to that on the 6th May during a meeting between the British AAA and Oxford University at Iffley Road track in Oxford. It was watched by 3,000 spectators. The wind had picked up to 25 miles per hour (40 km/h) prior to the event Banister had said twice that he favoured not running, so as to conserve his energy to break the 4 minute barrier at a later date. But the winds dropped just before the race was scheduled to start and the race was back on. The main pace – makers, Chris Chateway and Chris Brasher , went on to establish their own great track history, but this time the light was on Banister. He won the race in a new world record of 3 min 59.4 sec. the first human to break the 4 minute barrier. The race was and still is called the "Miracle Mile" because some people doubted that a 4 minute mile was physically possible for man to achieve. The record, even though 4 minutes seemed to be the myth that was broken was broken again just 46 days later on the 21st June by Australian John Landy in Turku, Finland. The record now stood at 3min 58 secs.

The head to head was to happen at the Empire Stadium on August 7th. This was also to be the first time that these two athletes were to compete against each other. They were the only two athletes in the world to have broken through the magic 4 min barrier, with Landy being the record holder. Landy led for most of the race, building a lead of 10yrds in the 3rd of the 4 laps, but was overtaken on the last bend, with a winning time of 3min 58.8 and Landy 0.8sec behind. The crucial moment of that race was at the moment that Banister decided to pass Landy, Landy looked over his left shoulder to gauge Banisters position, with Bannister bursting pass Landy on his right, never relinquishing the lead. A larger than life bronze sculpture of the two men at this very moment was created by Vancouver sculptor Jack Harman in 1967 and placed at the entrance to the Empire Stadium. Even though the stadium was demolished the statue still stands there.

The second memorable race of the championship was that of the marathon in which the great Jim Peters was to compete. He had already gained a bronze medal for the 6 miles a few days earlier.

During the 1950s, Jim Peters played a major role in revolutionising the pace at which marathons were run, lowering the world's best time on four occasions. His greatest successes came in the Polytechnic or 'Poly' marathon, organised annually by the Polytechnic Harriers in England. Peters won the Poly marathon in four successive years from 1951 to 1954. In 1951, he won in a British record time of 2hr 29min 24sec. This run was far surpassed by his next three Poly marathons, all of which were won in a world's best time. In 1952 he clocked 2hr 20min 42.2 sec, followed in 1953 with a time of 2hr 18min 40.2sec, and finally a career best 2hr 17min 39.4 sec in 1954. Despite Peters having set fast times many minutes faster than his fellow competitors, his performances at major international championships were both sad and tragic. At the 1952 Helsinki Olympic Games he took the field out at a very fast pace and had a lead of 16 seconds at 10km. Soon after 25km he started developing severe cramps and although he fought on bravely, the cramps forced him to retire from the race after 30km while in 4th position. Unfortunately, he is most remembered for a race that he not only didn't win, but also failed to finish.

The marathon at the 1954 Commonwealth Games in Vancouver was held in oppressively hot and humid conditions. Seemingly ignoring the conditions, Peters led out at near world record pace.

Barely 20 minutes after Bannisters victory, as the temperature in the non- existent shade rose to 75F against the rather incongruous backdrop of the snow-veined Grouse Mountains, the 35- year-old Peters, favourite for the marathon gold medal, entered the sun-drenched arena, weaving and swaying from side to side.

Sixteen men had begun the race but only six were to return. Peters, along with his countryman Stan Cox, took an early lead, passing the five-mile mark in 28min 15sec. The race wore on up the steep Kingsway and through the Vancouver streets, deserted thanks to viewers watching on television or in the stadium, but before long it was plain that all was not well. Peters passed the 20-mile post in 1hr 48min but Cox, by now about 400 yards behind, was beginning to feel the effects of sunstroke. There was a heat haze over the roads and the melting tarmac began sticking to his rubber-soled shoes. Just before the 25-mile mark Cox became so groggy he crashed into a lamp-post but when he heard that Bannister had won the mile he got up and ran another 100 yards before the police led him away to a nearby ambulance. Peters, who had set a new world record earlier that year and had covered more than 5,000 miles in training, struggled up the last two hills but arrived at the stadium gates in a dangerously dehydrated condition with the last 385 yards around the track to run. Staggering and clawing his way along on all fours and falling at least six times, he took 11 minutes to cover the first 200 yards. Bannister, along with others at the track-side, could only watch, as they knew any attempt to assist Peters would disqualify him. Eventually though, after crossing the photo-finish line nearly 200 yards short of the actual finish line, he could go no further and with arms and legs still going through the motions of running he was carried off to hospital to join Cox, who was fighting for his life. That was the picture that had remained in my mind from a child , the picture of Jim not giving up, of fighting with every last bit of strength to finish what he started. Peters spent the next seven hours in an oxygen tent during which time no less than half a gallon of saline solution and dextrose was fed into him intravenously. As the treatment took effect, the two men began to recover. Joe McGhee, meanwhile, an RAF officer from Scotland, had fallen over five times during the race and called for an ambulance, but when he heard that Peters and Cox were out of the race he got up and finished the course to win. The psychological and physical reactions Peters suffered were so marked that he was advised by doctors to retire from athletics and he never ran again, although he always maintained he was robbed of the gold medal in Vancouver as the course was longer than the regulation 26 miles 385 yards. Those appeals fell on deaf ears, but the Duke of Edinburgh awarded him an honorary gold medal on Christmas Eve of the same year for his gallantry, and last year, to mark his 80th birthday, Peters was proud to receive the

Duke's good wishes once again. Born in Homerton, east London, but raised in Becontree in Essex, Peters was a useful schoolboy cricketer and footballer before taking up athletics. The outbreak of the Second World War interrupted his progress. Peters joining the RAMC, but afterwards, and by now a qualified optician, he returned to running, although he was disappointed to finish only ninth in the 10,000m at the 1948 Olympics in London. Approaching the age of 30, he was tempted to retire, but his coach persuaded him to take up marathon running and engaged him in a series of innovative training techniques focusing on speed and strength routines. In 1952 he set the first of four world records for the distance with a time of 2:20:42.2 but failed to finish at the Helsinki Olympics owing to cramp. The following year, however, with a running style that grew more and more exaggerated and led at times to blood seeping from his torso as his thumb-nail tore into his vest, he set two more world records and won four of the world's largest marathon races. Then, on 26 June the following year, with a time of 2:17:39.4 in the Polytechnic Marathon from Windsor to Chiswick, Peters became the first man to run under 2hr 20min for the marathon. In his later years Peters remained in touch with his club Essex Beagles and was a Rotary Club member near his home in Thorpe Bay in Essex. Prior to his death he had been fighting cancer for six years, and of those who witnessed his heroics in Vancouver or were among the millions to see it later on Movietone News, few would have been surprised that his final battle lasted so long. Adam Szreter James Peters, runner: born London 24 October 1918; married (one son, one daughter); died 9 January 1999.

We also have to remember that all this happened prior to the emergence of sports medicine, and the aspect of scientific training programmes. In fact Jims shoes were black plimsoles bought from Woolworths! Looking at the times he set, compared to the winning time of the London marathon where people were talking about the heat, Jim ran in hotter conditions than that, imagine what his time would have been if running in the 2007 London Marathon.

Well we were now facing the start of our season. Things had been progressing well and we looked like a good solid team. Also our numbers had been swollen by the arrival of good old Willy Johnston, who had arrived the night before our first game at home against Dallas. Typical of Willy he said that he would be fit for the first game, even though still being a bit jet lagged.

Willy had arrived with a blaze of media attention but not the sort of attention Willy had wanted. They had jumped on the story of his expulsion from the Scotland team during the 1978 World Cup, due to allegations of drug taking. I will cover some of this later, but after getting to know him you would come to the same conclusion of his innocence.

It was to be a disappointing result for us and also the fans, but it appears that the Whitecaps had only ever won one of their opening games in the past 5 seasons. Losing 2-1 in a shoot out was a lesson that we would learn from. Unfortunately Roger Kenyon picked up a hamstring injury which was to trouble him for most of the season, the legacy of the Astroturf.

Also the lack of treatment facilities would hinder the injuries recovery period. Barry Crocker came to the rescue, by obtaining an old shortwave machine which helped a lot.

Previously the Whitecaps had a qualified trainer, who dealt with knocks and bumps and the club used a Physiotherapist who was in private practice for the general treatment side. Therefore the facilities at the ground were very basic indeed, making Argyles look state of the art. It was going to be a bit of a battle regarding treatment facilities and to break through the previous hit and miss routine of treatments.

Roger was to miss out on our next game but Peter Daniel was always a person who would give you a full 100%. Due to the fact that we lost to Dallas the previous week, the attendance fell by some 6,000. It shows that the Canadians love to follow a winner, any Division in English League football would like the gates that we had and would continue to get. In fact, by the end of the season over 400,000 spectators would watch the home games at the Empire Stadium. Also we must remember that due to the vast distances traveled, 99% of that attendance would be Whitecaps supporters!

We were to defeat Edmonton 2-0 with goals through Cravo and King Kev, and we didn't need extra time. After this game, Bob McNab decided that his playing days were over and that he would concentrate on the coaching side.

Our first away match, was at Chicago with the experience of flying to the away matches plus the experience of American Customs! More about them later. Willy Johnston was the sort of lad to have on board. He would keep you in stitches with his antics, especially his interpretation of the invisible man with the use of sunglasses and a handkerchief.

Dennis Loze

The first evening in Chicago, was an experience especially seeing the city that had been portrayed in all the epic gangster films and stories of Al Capone., A few of us went out for a drink in one of the local bars, but no gangsters. It was the policy of Tony Waiters, one in which I believed, was that the senior players were allowed to drink (in moderation) the night before a game but they had to be in view of one or two of the management. The players respected this and it was never abused. We had a really good bunch of professionals who set a good example for the juniors.

On the morning of the game, Bob McNab and myself went to the ground with the playing strip and medical kit and to have a good look at the playing surface. Playing surfaces varied so much in this league. Some being Astroturf or grass, but it went further than that, with most being baseball pitches, so we had to cope with the diamond being across the pitch. At least the pitchers mound used to be flattened.

Wrigley Fields was the old stadium of the Chicago Cubs Baseball club, with the original wooden stands. A stadium steeped in history. The taxi which took us both to the stadium was an eye opener. The driver explained to us, that it was steel lined, which you could see, with a bulletproof windscreen and partition between driver and passenger, all Chicago taxis were the same. Perhaps Al Capone was still alive?

Later when we and the team were in the changing rooms, which was the Cubs changing room, with all their bits and bobs around, I had to take a bottle from Willy, which he had picked up from a windowsill labeled Salt Tablets, and explained to him that if it was necessary I had a stock, and you never know what was in that bottle. Unfortunately Willy had been sent home from the from the 78 World Cup for testing positive on a banded substance. What I had witnessed in that changing room was enough to prove that Willy was not guilty of taking anything planned to enhance his performance. He was too naive for anything like that.

The result went our way with a win with goals through Jon Sammels and King Kev, but Cravo didn´t finish the game due to a calf injury, also Roger Kenyon irritated the same injured hamstring

During the years of being involved in football, one of the things that people fail to understand is your responsibility is looking after the injuries both in their treatment and their prevention. When you are attending a game, your attention is not actually on the game itself but watching the players, seeing how they are moving in general play, heading, twisting, turning, passing, sprinting, shooting etc. So many times you miss goals being scored because your attention is on a particular player. Whilst researching for this book, I managed to get my hands on a number of the Whitecaps games on DVD. It is amazing whilst watching them and seeing incidents that you missed because of watching a particular players movement.

We arrived back in Vancouver knowing that we had 5 clear days before our next game at home against Portland. This was also a chance later to meet up with Don Megson, former Sheffield player, who was manager of Portland and also father of Gary Megson who was at Plymouth Argyle with me. Dons first words were "The chairman of Argyle is missing you!"

I mentioned earlier that I was going to meet up again with Huddy, who had by now walked out of Arsenal, because of his inability to get on with Terry Neil. In fact Huddy said that he realised that after his very first game with the Arsenal. This was in a pre season game at Vancouver, but it did show that players were coming to the NASL, not as in previous years, just to get a season of good money at the end of a career, but players who still had a lot to offer the game not just here in North America. We had the likes of Carl Valentine, Bruce Grobbelaar and Trevor Whymark.

Remember the weather interrupting a game at Plymouth, we were to experience situations like that. We were playing against Tulsa away during early June at 8.00pm, the weather was very hot and the humidity was very high indeed, so much so that you were drenched with sweat by just moving. In fact in the walls of the changing rooms, which were directly under the main stand, were streaming with water. The game commenced and you could see that it wasn't going to be one of our days, we quickly started to dominate the game, but nothing seemed to be happening in front of goal, but then the inevitable happened, yes, they scored. But then, we were aware of movement in the crowd. They were all distracted from the game, then people started to leave the main stand, orderly to start with, then more earnest movement started, mean while the game was still going on. The referee was called to the touchline, and then informed both sides that we were to return to our changing rooms and stay there until we heard more. So off we trouped, the heat was getting unbearable as the humidity was increasing, water was pouring off the changing room walls like a water fall, then it started to rain. After about 10mins, one of the officials came and said that the game was going to be abandoned due to tornados in the area in fact one was heading our way! We then met with the Tulsa officials and the stadium officials, and the game was re-scheduled for the next evening, which we won.

   I have attended games, which had been called off for snow, rain, frozen pitches but never for a tornado. The tornado in fact never touched us, but did so outside of Tulsa and caused a certain amount of damage. It was good also to know that the stand was built to withstand tornados!

   Another of those bizarre happenings came about during a game against Los Angeles at the Rosebowl in Pasadena. Trevor Whymark was struggling with a niggling hamstring injury, which later resulted in him being substituted. I had just been onto the pitch mainly to assess the condition of Trevor's injury and had left the pitch via the nearest touch line, which happened to be the opposite side from our team bench. As I was walking around the pitch, on my way back to the team bench and just as I was walking behind our own goal I was suddenly stopped by one of the ground security staff who wouldn't let me continue around the pitch as I wasn't wearing a security pass. Even after I had explained who I was and what had just happened, he said that he had seen that, but I still didn't have the right pass. At this stage I had a vision of me being ejected from the ground for not wearing the pass which we had never been issued with. So the only way was to completely ignore him, button up the lip (even though I really wanted to tell him what I thought of him) and walk straight past him, which worked so I could continue being part of the game. He never said a word to me as I brushed past him. I suppose he had carried out what he was told to do, but not what to do if someone completely ignored him.

Chapter Twelve

"For myself I am an optimist – it does not seem to be much use being anything else."
WINSTON CHURCHILL

The 5 days I had weren't enough to get Roger or Cravo up and moving, and with Bob not playing again, our defence looked weak, but only on paper as our lads would rally around and fill the gaps. This they did in style. Two super goals by Trevor brought our spectators to their feet. Our last two wins had brought our spectators back, all 23,137 of them!

Our next game was in 5 days at San Diego, Roger stayed behind to receive treatment at the Compensation Board where Barry worked, and Cravo who was recovering from his injury traveled with us, not to play, but for his presence. But it didn't work as we lost 1-0 against a poor side.

We were to get our revenge as this was a back to back fixture in 4 days time. With Cravo back in the line up, and 2 goals through King Kev, and Trevor. But again due to our bad defeat away, the fans stayed away, only 16, 985 turned up.

Things off the pitch were going fine, Jane and I were really enjoying our time in Canada meeting and making friends, and plenty of eating out at such a variety of restaurants. Jane had also managed to get a job with the Compensation Board again the Canadian work system was to swing into action. She was appointed as an Occupational Therapist, a post that had been advertised nationally, with no appropriate Canadian appointed. Jane applied and was given the post, but only for a six week period. The vacancy would be then advertised if no Canadian appointed, Jane would continue for another period of six weeks.

We got invited out for an evening with a former patient of Jane's, a smashing chap, Chuck and his family. They had a lovely house, to which Chuck had installed a "conversation pit." This was a large sunken area in their large lounge, which was about 5 foot deep and tiered so you sit around in a large circle to talk and drink. (A small auditorium) Chuck was a fanatic Whitecaps fan, so the topic was one way during the evening. Chuck had really prepared for us, in fact so much so that he had heard that the Brits drink warm beer so he had put a crate of beers out in the sun to warm. Fancy drinking warm lager! After I explained to him about Real Ale, we had a good laugh about it. Fortunately he had plenty of cold ones!

After our win against San Diego, we had two days before our game at San Jose, so we only had 1 day at home, before packing again. We had only picked up a few knocks and bumps, with only big Roger out injured.

Our game at San Jose brought us a 2-1 win with goals by King Kev and Peter Daniel (A Derby County double). On the down side, we lost Cravo with a torn Achilles Tendon, which we knew was going to take a while. In fact we put Cravo into plaster immediately on our return.

Fortunately, Roger was returning back to form and we had a week to work with him and Cravo before our next game.

Willy caused a bit of hilarity during a game, the pitch was a university American football pitch, and due to the fact that our football pitches are wider brought the sidelines very close and intimate with the spectators. Willy was lining up to take a corner, when he reached out and took a can of beer from one of the spectators and pretended to drink from it, I say pretend with tongue in cheek. This brought the spectators to their feet in laughter – yes they did understand the humour!

One of our favourite eating places in Vancouver was "Mother Tuckers", this was an eating experience. As much as you could eat for a set price. The salad bar was the biggest I had and have ever seen. No wonder the North Americans and the Americans are big. We also used to go to "B.B Beltons", a quieter place than mother Tuckers. The food was excellent, and the wine used to be poured out into the biggest glasses you have ever seen. We used to go there a lot with Annie Carol, so in the end we just called it Annies glasses. Even now when we see large wine glasses Jane and I look at each other and say "Annies glasses."

Arsenal to Armenia

Our next home game was against Rochester and Roger had come through the weeks work and joined the back 4. This game was a bit of a battle, but we managed to pull out a win with a goal by Carl in extra time. Roger come through it OK.

Cravo was now in a walking plaster, so we were able to work on maintaining his fitness, to which he responded like a true professional. We were now home for six days, which was good breathing space, before our next home game. We were doing most of the training at the Empire stadium, as we were working on the theory that if we were due to play on grass, we trained on grass, if Astroturf then we would do the vast majority of work of Astroturf, thus giving the body, especially the muscle time to accommodate to the change in playing surface.

The game against Philadelphia brought us another win, this time a 2-0 victory with goals from King Kev and Trevor. It also brought us into contact with Ballie who had joined Philadelphia a week previously and the other King, King Elvis himself Frank Worthington. It was great the next morning in my small treatment room, to have Frank and Alan who had picked up little injuries and had asked me to run the ruler over them. So with them and Roger, we had a Brit dominated morning, before they flew out in the afternoon. We were not due to play again for 10 days, so it was good to have another breather.

During this break Jane and I had a great evening up at Grouse Mountain. We had gone up to Grouse with Barry and his wife Gail, during the skiing season, to see the skiing. This trip was to be smashing, as we drove to the same spot, but then traveled up by ski lift to the top. What a view, looking down on to Vancouver and the surrounding area, and as the evening drew in the lights of the city came on, beautiful! Also the food in the restaurant was tremendous. An evening to remember.

Our next game was a short flight to our neighbouring Canadian club of Edmonton. A good victory of 3-1 with all three goals coming from King Kev. Not much time for celebrations as we were back to Vancouver ready to play against Houston in two days. It was good to get a double over Edmonton.

However, this quick turn around didn´t work, as we went down 1-0 in a game we should have wrapped up. On the positive side we didn´t pick up any serious knocks and with the Tulsa game in 4 days time, plus the flight, it didn't leave us much time.

Dennis Loze

My position at the club was similar to that of in England, but with some additions. Normally the work is 6½ days a week, the ½ being Sunday morning. This was thrown right up in the air here due to the amount of travel plus back to back games, so the demand was high. Added to this was looking after all the kit during the journey, plus working with the office regarding flight times, accommodation, car hire and paying for all this through the club credit card. I also held all the paper work regarding work permits, visas, etc. and especially the problem of Bruce Grobellaars paperwork. (covered later). All this added to the main reason for the job, treatment of injuries, kept me busy!

So with a quick turn around, it was Tulsa - bound. Now you can travel with me as I head out on the road for a 3 game trip Tulsa on the 7th, Minnesota on the 9th, and California on the 13th.

Firstly getting all the players at the airport on time, most traveled under their own steam. All the senior players had cars (under their contracts with the club) so they had no excuse for not getting there on time. The rest, including Bruce, Carl, Paul Nelson, and the more junior players (if required) and myself would travel in the club van, along with all the kit.

We would be dropped off at the airport, then try to get the players to carry the kit into the terminal which wasn't an easy task (fine if we had junior pros and they just did it). Once or twice we arrived, with Brucie forgetting his passport and once even his boots!

Then on to the check-in desk, with all the passports and tickets. All sounds good so far, but you have to know who wants to sit with whom, window or aisle. Hand out the boarding cards, inform what time, where, etc. then meeting up with the American immigration and customs, all within the departures terminal. Every trip into America, had the same ritual. One or two of the players and always Bruce, would be stopped and I would have to produce the work permits, visas etc. Bruce was always a target, because his passport was different from ours and being Rhodesian (Now Zimbabwean), whilst gazing into the reflective sunglasses of the official (why do they always seem to wear them). Then through the American customs, which was OK for the players, but me, a different story! I had my briefcase with all the players, and staff documentation, plus my medical bag, with all medications, prescription drugs etc. It was this that on every trip caused interest, even though I use to prepare the official paper work, with everything listed, amount, dosage, number of pills etc. this was the point of special interest. Me a drug smuggler, with everything listed, "Yes sir, I have a list here of cocaine, heroin, etc.!" But you cannot win and it was always the same official on duty every time we traveled. On one trip after about 15mins he allowed me to go through into the departure lounge, only to catch up with me, and ask to see the bag again, just as our plane was announced. This didn't deter him. Then, to my amazement, just passing through the departure gate, he stopped me again, asked for my paperwork, and opened the case. By the time he had finished, I just made it on to the plane by seconds before the gate closed.

Safely aboard! We also used to have traveling with us, a couple of the lads from the office PR dept, plus either one or two of the press. One of these was Ian Mechard, who worked for one of the local Vancouver radio CJOR 60. Ian was a smashing chap. We would share many a breakfast, whilst staying in hotels (players aren't breakfast people), Ian used to have some very weird concoctions for breakfast, well they were to me, one of his favourites was Strawberry Waffles! I mean, for breakfast!! On one away trip poor Ian fell to the attention of immigration, coming back from one of our games from New York. He used to have with him all his recording equipment and they made him unpack everything, even to the point of refusing him entry into his own country. This being way before the twin towers bombing! I would hate to do my role now.

We flew from Vancouver to Chicago, then on to Tulsa. It was in Chicago airport that the next incident happened. If you haven't been to Chicago O'Hare airport, let me tell you that it is huge. Here we are with 18 playing staff, 2 PR staff, 2 media and Tony, Bob and myself. Who is looking for the next Boarding Gate? Me. No one else is interested, just following me. I have always wondered about the intelligence of some footballers! As we were walking along, Jon Sammels, caught up with me. He had noticed the flock of sheep following me, and said "Dennis, head for the Gents" you guessed right, they followed me. All stood there with blank faces, just looking around, I am certain to this day that most of them still didn't understand!

Arrival at Tulsa airport, the next part of official duties for me, was getting the self drive rental cars which had been pre booked, getting the keys and locating the cars, plus all the bags of equipment and players allocated. The driving used to fall on a couple of the Canadian lads, Buzz Parsons and Bob Bolitho and who else, yes me! So another addition to the job description. Then, to locate the hotel off we would go in convoy. At the hotel it was me who used to register the players each player used to have his own "roomy" (room mate), I would find that the players would, if not stopped, rush off to find their rooms and leave all their bags, plus kit bags etc in the foyer. Our budget would not run to paying for the hotel staff in taking the bags up, and the players wouldn't think about paying them. Think of 30 odd bags, plus 4 large kit bags at approx 3 dollars a bag; Gloria in the office would have a fit!

Yes, our budget was a very strict one, which would cause a lot of problems at the end of the season.

So that was our normal away trip, just one extra thing, the kit had to be washed, who had to organise that? Yes, you have guessed right again.

Our game at Tulsa was mentioned earlier, regarding the tornado and rearranged for the next day. This meant a very quick turn around and straight to the airport from the game, so that previous arrangements would not be altered. At least we had points under our belt from with a 2-1 win with goals from Ray Lewington and Carl. The journey to the game at Minnasota was uneventful, and the game turned out to be a bad one for us as we went down 1-0 to a poor side.

Off to California without big Roger, as he had aggravated his hamstring again. 2½ games in as many days, was too much, also 1½ games on Astroturf and then quickly to grass. The muscles just could not acclimatise to the change.

The game at California was a nightmare for us, with having to pull Trevor Whymark into the back four. Trevor really showed true professionalism and took on the task. This would be a position that he would have to get used to for a number of games. We still lacked that something. When would it happen? It just didn't happen in this match, on a very bumpy and uneven pitch we went down 3-2 in a shootout. The journey back was a very quiet one, with only 1 win out of 3, - not good.

Chapter Thirteen

∞

"Strength does not come from physical capacity. It comes from an indomitable will."
MAHATMA GANDHI

Our playing staff were to receive a tremendous boast with the arrival of the man himself, Alan Ball. It is with great sadness as at this very moment news has just come through of Ballies death at the age of 61. I will now take this opportunity of paying my own tribute to this great player, a great and true professional and man of England through and through, a great family man who was so proud of his family, who in turn were so proud of him as a father. Ballie also played a great supportive role to his wife Ann through her battle with cancer. I know of this battle first hand as Jane and I are going through the same.

Two things remain in my mind about Ballie. One is when he told me that when he stood on a football pitch wearing the England shirt, with the band is playing the National Anthem, all the money in the whole world could not buy that moment.

The second is that of a true professional and family man. He had a toe injury and I drove out to his house, saving him coming to the ground. When I arrived at the house, there was Ballie sitting on a rocking chair, foot up on a pillow, cigar in one hand an a glass of wine in the other and his family all sitting around him. That moment was to remain with me. Young Jimmy (Alan's son, who was just a little whipper snapper) (Cornish for young lad) was so proud of his name, that if and when you asked him his name, he would shout out "Jimmy Ball!" with pride. The first thing Ballie said when I got there was, "Get Dennis a glass and one of my cigars." We sat and drank, whilst smoking our cigars. No money in the world could buy **that** moment.

Dennis Loze

On and off the pitch Ballie was to weave his magic. Players responded to his passion for the game of football. It used to be great to see him and the fun loving Willy keeping everyone amused on our long flights.

Our next game was at home to California and this time we had a week in which to get over the heavy schedule we had had. Up to this time we had played 15, won 10, but we needed a good run as we had lost games that we should have won. So having Ballie around was going to be good news.

In fact only 20, 814 turned up that night, but they were there to see Ballie weave his magic on and off the ball. It was a game we won 2-1 with Willy and Ballie getting the goals.

We were suddenly back on the road 2 days after the California game, to play 3 games over 7 days, including travel time.

Our first stop was Atlanta and the heat, a game we won with reasonable ease, with goals from Kevin (2) and Ballie. We moved on to Fort Lauderdale with a spring in our step, a two day lay over. Fortunately we had only picked up a few knocks and bumps. However on our first morning there Jon Sammels had some chest pains, and after examining him and carrying out some tests, nothing particular was showing up. To be on the safe side I managed to get him seen at the nearest Hospital with a top cardiac specialist. Again, on examination, Jon was given a full bill of health, but we decided to rest him for the first game against Atlanta.

The visit to the hospital was an eye opener, as just as I was going to register Jon in at reception, the first question they asked was how was I going to pay, so out came my credit card and I was a few thousand dollars worse off in the next few seconds. A bit different to England.

The rest of the team hadn't picked up any serious injuries so it was just the patching up process before, hopefully, seeing George Best.

That night George had done one of his famous disappearing acts, so missed a good battle between the two maestros. The game ended in a win for Fort Lauderdale 3-2, after a shoot out. Our goals were scored by Trevor and Poss.

It was straight off to Toronto the next day, so we could get a couple of days rest, before meeting Toronto at the famous Blue Jays Baseball park.

Arsenal to Armenia

The players were tired after the traveling and games, so only light training was carried out so as to get the aches and pains out of the way and some more patching up done. But all in all we were up for the next game. Whilst at Toronto, I was hoping to take a trip to see the famous Niagara Falls, but couldn't persuade any of the players or staff to come, so it was a trip I never carried out, and one that I still regret, as my Father had told me so much about the falls, when he worked in Canada and America in the 1920's.

Our last game of the road trip was a disappointment losing 2-1 with a goal from Carl. This game was a game that we should have stitched up early on, but things didn't run for us.
The return home wasn't as successful as we had hoped with just 1 win out of 3, but at least we hadn't picked up any long term injuries.

We had 11 games left and needed to start to put a good series together, We were lying 2nd in our group, but still had a lot to do to prove if we were able to get into the Conference final and the Soccer Bowl, which was not beyond our capability.

Cravo's knee seemed to be settling down very well and we were able to continue with his fitness. He was a good old war horse and would really punish himself to get his heart and lungs working. Roger was still not ready but things were starting to look better, only needing a couple more weeks of hard work to get him ready.

Our next home game was 3 days after we landed back in Vancouver from our 3 game road trip, so it was hard work for the players and the coaching staff of Bob and Tony. Motivation was what we needed. Our 3-1 win over Seattle was just what we needed, with goals from Bally (2) and Trevor. The gate was low at 20,041 but we had had an indifferent road trip. This win was encouraging as we had lost Willy who had picked up a hamstring niggle the day before the game.
We had 4 days before our next home game against Los Angeles and the famous Johan Cruyff.

The good news was that Willy had shaken off the niggle and was fit to play, with Pete Daniel and Trevor Wymark ready to do a fantastic job in the middle of the back four. We were prepared, with 28,764 supporters screaming their heads off. The atmosphere was tremendous, Cruyff did the damage with a single goal which was enough to bring them victory. We still couldn't string our wins together and we were due to face the Cosmos in New York in 4 days time.

Was this game to be our turning point?

Chapter Fourteen

"Let no man pull you low enough to hate him."
MARTIN LUTHER KING JNR.

On the pitch we were continuing to shape into a very, very good team, but admittedly we were still guilty of not capitalising on it. Soon we were going to be tested again by the well known and respected New York Cosmos, who seemed to dominate the whole championship year after year (with Pele playing his last game for them in 1977) the existing National Conference winners. We were due to play them home and away in the league.

The Cosmos came to us for the first of these league games, into the cauldron of the Empire Stadium, which was packed to the rafters with 32,372 fans, with extra stands added behind each goal. Even in the players tunnel you could just taste the atmosphere, players standing shoulder to shoulder with their opposite numbers. Casual talk was going on until the strong voice of Cravo, which made the walls vibrate, shouted "Don't talk to them, we are going to ******* well stuff them, they are the enemy".

Well that match was a corker and we did stuff them 4-1 even though they had such players as, Carlos Alberta, Marinho, Giogio Chinaglia, Dennis Tuert and so on, but the great Franz Beckenbauer was out injured. This result gave us a great boost, and made the Vancouver fans realise that something special was going to happen this year.

A month later we were playing them again, this time at the great Giants Stadium. We were welcomed to the ground by large banners stating that we were entering Cosmos country, plus Beckenbauer was playing his first game since the injury. The crowd was 48,753, mostly New Yorkers

Dennis Loze

as only a handful of Whitecap spectators had managed the 8,000 mile round trip. It was a game in which we were again to show them what we were made of, and coming out 4-2 winners. This game was to contain a 20 min stoppage of a bizarre nature. The Cosmos crowd had taken a dislike to Lofty Parkes, because of two things. Lofty was the top goalkeeper in the league and he was good at winding the crowd up by blowing kisses to them and by taking his time with goal kicks etc. This frustration of the crowd spread to the opposition, as Lofty was having, yet again, one of his spectacular games. The players, in their way were trying to unsettle him enough to get him sent off. After one of Loftys saves he was suddenly surrounded by a number of Cosmos players, with our players getting involved in the situation. The game came to a standstill, with the referee trying to sort things out. Suddenly from across the pitch from us, the Cosmos bench emptied as coaches, players, Pele and his henchmen headed for our goalmouth. All we could think of was that Lofty was going to get involved and be sent off, so me being the fastest, sprinted to get Lofty out of the way. I got there before the onslaught, with my 5ft 7ins protecting 6ft 4ins Lofty. Suddenly they arrived, being led by Pele who was dressed in a sparkling disco black suit and his henchmen each side of him. There was so much anger in his eyes as the tried to get at Lofty I managed to get my hands on Peles jacket and was pushing him away, with Phil shouting "Let me at him." If you knew Phil he was a real gentle giant. Finally the whole thing settled with no bookings etc. It was amazing to see then that Kevin Hector and Bally were both sitting in the centre circle having a chat, as if saying "We've seen it all before."

So the final result was 4-2 to us with goals from Bob Lenaduzzi, Ray Lewi, Kevin and an own goal.

I have recently been looking at a book which Jane bought me, "Game of two halves" by Tim Glynne Jones in which there is photograph of Pele in what would seem a very un-Pele-like stance or reaction. It is a photograph of the Santos and Brazil legend He is throwing a punch at Masiero of Internazionale as the two sides brawl in June, 1963. So it had happened before!

The saying that we heard once on Vancouver local radio comes to mind "*I went to a fight the other night and a hockey game broke out.*" Is a well used saying regarding the game of ice hockey, if you know anything about ice hockey you will know that it is not unusual to see a punch up

Arsenal to Armenia

on the ice, also at times seeing the two benches, of opposing players and staff pour onto the ice, in a mass brawl. That is what we saw at New York.

Yes that double over the Cosmos made us realise that we could go all the way and win not only the Conference but the Soccer Bowl!

However 3 days after our fantastic win at New York saw us losing away to Washington 2-1 with Ballie scoring. The last two games saw Cravo stretching his legs, and showing good signs of recovery, but we didn't want to force things. Also we were to be without Zac who had a sprained ankle and games were going to be coming thick and fast so we needed all our players right.

Just 3 days after our game at Washington saw us back Vancouver to play against Toronto. We were able to make amends for our defeat at Toronto by putting on the pressure to a 3-0 win with goals from Jon, Trevor and Ballie.

Our next game was in 3 days time at home against Tulsa. We were able to do a double over them which now added to our points. Our 1-0 win from a Trevor goal, gave us a record of played 25 won 16, scoring 46 and conceding 28 so things were now beginning to look good.

Playing for Tulsa was a young Derby County player, who was later to be transferred to Preston North End, Don O'Riordan, a lad who I would link up with a few years time.

We seemed to be in a groove of a game every 3 days and with the traveling involved could have put a strain on to our players, but now they seem to be getting used to it and reveling in the hectic schedual. So off to Portland and a game we were to win in overtime 3-2 with goals from Bob Lennarduzzi, Trevor and Bally. Also, seeing the full return of Cravo gave us all a boost. Unfortunately Trevor picked up a knock which would sideline him for the next couple of games, so we seemed to gain one and lose one. We had now won our last 3 games on the trot.

We returned home to face Minnesota in, yes 3 days. Could we avenge our defeat at Minesota, a game we should have won. In front of 24,656 expectant supporters we were able to give them what they wanted, a 1-0 win with a goal from Bob Lenarduzzi.

With only 3 more league games to play, we were lying top of our division, but with the Los Angeles Aztecs close behind.

We were due to play them in 3 days time in Los Angeles. This was what you would call a six pointer (more under NASL rules). We rested Cravo, although he was on the bench. Zac was nearly right and he also sat on the bench. But the afternoon of the game disaster struck with big Phil going down with a stomach bug, so Bruce Grobellaar stepped in for his first NASL game, Tony had to get changed as cover keeper.

This unfortunately could be put down as a Brucie nightmare as two goals sneeked past his near post and if you know anything about football, you will know the anguish if a keeper concedes a goal at his near post. We went down 2-0. We just couldn't continue our winning streak from 4 to 5 on the trot. Also, it meant that Los Angeles were a head of us in the league!

Our next two games were to be home against San Jose and away to Seattle. To win the league we had to win both games, as Los Angeles had completed their fixtures.

We gained a 1-0 win over San Jose after extra time with a goal from Trevor. This also saw Cravo, Roger and Zac completing the game.

The next day saw us traveling to play against Seattle within 24 hrs, but the tiredness was quickly forgotten as we won 2-1 through goals by Buzz Parsons and Bally.

We were though to the conference final and we had won our league, with stats of played 30 and won 20, lost 10, goals against 34, goals for 54 points 172.

Our first game was a double header against Dallas on the 15th and 18th August, Dallas had come 2nd in the Central Division, behind Minnesota. The first game away from home, we won 3-2 with goals from Ray, Zac, and Buz. Roger sat on the bench for this one, but Cravo was back to his old self, taking no prisoners. During the time I had known Cravo, at Plymouth and now the Whitecaps I had only witnessed him pulling out of one situation. It was when we were at Miami just before playing against Fort Lauderdale. A crowd of us had driven into Miami, and gone into a pub for a few ales. We couldn't have picked a more sleezy place if we had tried. After a few Cravo said he was going to the gents, but was not going by himself, so you can see how dodgy a place it was. He was escourted by a number of us, who were all dying for a leak, but too scared to say anything.

I also have just received news that unfortunately Cravo died a number of years ago at the age of 49. A Plymouth Argyle programme, when Cravo and I were there, featured Cravo in the Player Profile. One of the questions asked was "What is your personal ambition?" – Cravos answer was "A long and happy life!"

We were now due to play another double header against Los Angeles on the 22nd and 25th August. We lost the away game after a shootout 3-2 with both goals from Carl.

Now back to Empire Stadium in front of 32,375 crowd, we won the game by an own goal. But by NASL rules we had won a game apiece so we had to go into the mini game. Only 3 mins had gone and Kevin Hector nodded a cross from Carl Valentine into the net. We had done it. We were through to the NASL semi final, the crowd went crazy, tears in every ones eyes. A quote from a newspaper columnist Eric Whitehead summed it all up *"I can only account personally for a mere 32 years in this business, but I'll venture to say that for sheer joyous exuberance and fun of being there – which is supposed to be what sport is all about – this town has never had a night to match it."* So after we had run out of Labbats beer it was off downtown, we eventually got into a disco and more beers. The noise was nearly as bad as that in the Stadium, but I remember looking at Jane who was sitting beside me and she had fallen fast asleep. Spectating is a tiring job!

We were now due to play the semi - final or Conference semi - final in 4 days time, and then we heard that we were due to play the Cosmos both home and away, we had stuffed them twice, could we do it again.
New York Cosmos had a very tough time getting past Alan Hinton and his Tulsa Roughnecks. Tulsa won their home leg 3-0. But Cosmos won their home game 3-0 leveling the games and then won 3-1 in the mini game.

So we were due to face our old adversaries again in 4 days time at home.

Chapter Fifteen

∞

"When the eagles are silent, the parrots begin to jabber."
WINSTON CHURCHILL

Yes we had had the upper hand over the Cosmos during the season by having a home and away victories, but now these games had a greater reward, the final of the NASL.

I had managed to get all the knocks and bumps out of the way and also at long last both Roger and Cravo seemed to have got rid of their long term injuries. We were all set for the arrival of the league megastars. Many people were saying that this National Conference final would be in effect the NASL championship even Franz Beckenbauer said "The Whitecaps and Cosmos are the two best teams in the league, whoever wins this, will win the championship."

The box office was hectic with every ticket sold within hours of them being put on sale and thousands of fans being disappointed. It was agreed that the game would be televised so that British Columbian spectators could follow the game. (It was being televised in America by another network.)

With a capacity crowd of 32,875 plus the thousands watching on TV, were to see us completely outplay them. We won 2-0 with goals from Willie and Trevor Whymark. The game still had the nasty side, with the Cosmos player Andranik Eskandarian being sent off for a tackle on Kevin Hector. Also, after the game, Carlos Alberta, the former Brazilian captain was suspended for the next game for an incident with an official in the tunnel.

So it was back to New York for the next leg in 3 days time, things were a bit hectic in those couple of days. The media in Canada and America are a lot different from those in England. They seem to have complete licence to do what they want to do. I was in our treatment room, which was only big enough for two treatment couches, with Cravo and Roger, when the door burst open and in squeezed a camera crew and a sports presenter of the local Vancouver TV network. To me this was an invasion of the privacy of both Roger and of Cravo, so the hands that had grabbed hold of Pele pushed the whole crew outside. They responded by saying that the club had given them permission to televise the treatment etc. I told them in no certain terms that if they wanted to know anything about the injuries, they were to go through me, which would be a waste of time as they wouldn't get anything out of me. This did cause a bit of consternation at the office, which was feed back to me by the Club Director of Operations (the North Americans do love their titles). They received the same reply from me. Was this going to rebound back to me in the near future?

So it was back to Cosmos Country and 76,000 hostile New Yorkers!

Just like in all our games, which were geared for American and Canadian Television (taking into account the time zones – 4hrs difference between Vancouver and New York) it was an afternoon kick off of 2.30pm.in 90degrees temperature.

This was to turn into one of those bizarre games, with New York having to win this game, plus a subsequent mini game.

Within 10 mins Georgio Chinaglia gave them the start that they wanted, but we replied with a cracking shot by Trevor that thundered off the post. The pressure was kept up by us and a floating free kick by Bally was slotted over the line by no other than Cravo who had bored his way through the defence. Then, just before halftime, Georgio got his second. The changing room was as normal at half time. We had the players to do it and we knew we could do it.

We responded with a headed goal from non other than Willie. The game ended in a 2-2 draw

But the 30min session again brought no goals – so yet another shoot-out was necessary!

But we had played the 90 minutes which ended in a draw. Under European rules we would been the winners as we won the first leg, plus our away goals, but in the NASL, the game cannot end in a draw, so the extra time was played, and then the shoot out, which The Cosmos won.

Under NASL ruling, we had won one game and Cosmos one game, so it was a draw (yes I know we had scored more goals) so we had to play again. Now the absurdity was to move up a gear, the third game would be played, yes, the same day. One bit of sense was that it would consist of two halves of 15mins.

Back to the 6-15pm. kick off, this game ended in a 1-1 score line, then into a non scoring over time (extra time). It was then into the shoot out, and all was even when came down to Derek Posse. If he scored we were into the final against Tampa Bay. Poss just took two paces and with amazing coolness in a real pressure situation, and incredible precision, chipped the advancing keeper. We were through. The 76,000 New Yorkers were stunned. The only noise was from us and a few hundred fans who had traveled the 4,000 miles to the game. It was now nearly 7.30pm. some 5 hrs since the initial game started!

Yes through to the NASL Soccer Bowl against Tampa Bay, who defeated San Diego the following day. The date was set, 1 week time at New York Giants Stadium on the 8th September versus Tampa Bay Rowdies.

All our players were given a full bill of health, luxury!

The trip home was great, pressure was off and we were into the final. Work was to be done, but with a final on the horizon, the final which was what the whole season was about. For the first time in soccer history Canada was to have a team with the potential of winning the coveted accolade of having a North American champion within its borders.
Vancouver had already done that for Canada, with the Canouks winning the Stanley Cup in Ice Hockey, a few seasons previous, so not only was Vancouver up for this NASL final, but the whole of Canada was behind us.

I had a couple of afternoons of relaxation. I had a few months ago accepted a few hours of work at a Kids Sports Camp, to talk about sports injuries.

The camp was being run by Brian Budd, a former Canadian Soccer player, who had also won the World Superstars.
One highlight of the time spent at the Sports camp was meeting and spending time with the great Canadian athlete Debbie Brill. During my

time involved in athletics I had met numerous world athletes, but Debbie was a person who intrigued me. She was a young vibrant high jumper who had taken ladies high jumping to a new level. In England I had met up with a high jumper of great renown, Barbara Inkpen, but Debbie was something different.

Debbie revolutionised the sport with her reverse jumping style known as the "Brill Bend." She was the first North American woman to jump break the 6'0" barrier, and just months after giving birth to her son Neil she cleared 1.99m to break the World Indoor Record. She was named BC's Athlete of the Decade in 1980.

Debbie burst into international prominence in 1969 by winning at the Pan Pacific Games in Japan. From there it was on to three Olympic Games (1972-8th, 1976-DNK, 1984-5th), four Commonwealth (1970-gold, 1978-silver, 1982-gold, 1986-5th), three Pan American (1971-gold, 1974-4th, 1979-silver), and two World Cup Games (1972-bronze, 1979-gold).

Debbie has won over 65 national and international championships. It was at the 1979 World Cup in Montreal that Debbie had a psychological and technical breakthrough in her approach and confidently became World Champion. A controversial, enduring athlete and a unique woman, she became an Officer of the Order of Canada in 1983 and has been the recipient of many awards. In 1986, with James Lawton, Brill wrote her autobiography "Jump", her insight into the joy of jumping and the struggles of being a modern woman athlete.

The hours spent there were tremendous, seeing so much enthusiasm for young people, aged 10 to 15 years. It is so different from what I had experienced a couple of years ago, in fact in 2006. I had been asked by the FA to help a young lady called Sarah who was doing a University Degree at Plymouth University and for part of her thesis was conducting a survey on Football Treatment within local football clubs in Cornwall.

For part of the survey we were asked by the Cornish FA to involve a Local Community School who had the title of Sports Community College. We were using a class of 15 teenagers who were studying sport as a subject at GCSE level. What a contrast, no enthusiasm, each session we had with them, we had to deal with lack of co-operation, poor communication skills and an air of apathy. A real contrast to what I had experienced in Canada.

Chapter Sixteen

"Now this is not the end. It is not even the beginning of the end. But it is, perhaps the end of the beginning."
WINSTON CHURCHILL

We were due in New York a couple of days before the final. We had the Press to deal with and the TV. Also we were to have a NASL formal dinner with Eunice Kennedy Shriver as guest speaker.

She was the sister of former USA President John assassinated 1963 and brother Robert assassinated 1968. Eunice was the strength and muscle behind the development of the Special Olympics.

It was at the formal dinner that I was to meet up with a person I had treated at Chessington some 4 years previous. That person was John Gorman, who at that time was a player at Tottenham Hotspurs. John had a serious knee injury, and he came to us for rehab. All this had been arranged through the "old boy net work", with Mike Varney (ex Chessington) who was Physiotherapist with Spurs.

John was with us for a couple of months and in the last couple of weeks actually played for the Chessington Unit side. If only the opposition knew!

John was later to become No.2 to Glen Hoddle in the England set up.

For the formal dinner both teams we on the head table, with us coming in from one side of the room and Tampa from the opposite side, like gladiators. As soon as we spotted each other, it was just like my meeting with Huddy, with formalities pushed aside.

The game was soon to be upon us.

Arsenal to Armenia

We knew that the day before the game our wives were coming out and staying in a hotel a few streets away from us and that arrangements were being made at club level, that after the final, we would be exchanging rooms etc., so allowing husbands and wives to be together. Sounded good on paper! When someone in North America says "No Problem!" don't believe them, expect problems.

The morning of the game arrived, so did problems. The players wanted a meeting prior to the normal team meeting, which was a bit strange. Also as I was walking through the hotel reception area, the Manager said that we should vacate our rooms by 11 o'clock as the NASL hadn't booked us in for that night, I tried to explain to him the bookings that I had been given and also of the wives and Hotel swapping, all of which came as a surprise the him. I sought out Tony and explained things to him, and left it at that.

It was now time to go to the meeting room for the team meeting, by this time Barry Crocker had arrived on the same flight as the wives and supporters. As the both of us entered the meeting room, there on the blackboard was the team selection, it was one of those situations, where you didn't know whether to laugh or cry.

What had happened was that the Whitecaps Owners were having difficulties regarding the bonus of the team reaching the final. John Best, the Whitecaps President, had kept a very tight hold on the purse strings, hence the cars and not buses that we had been using all the season. The players had got together to hammer this out. Things were close to the players not even playing, but the wise head of Ballie came to the rescue by stating that it is not often you as a player have the opportunity to play in a final, so take hold of the opportunity and play, and sort it out later.

On the blackboard was the team selection, which had names like:

Tony as goalkeeper
Bob McNab defender
Me on the right wing
Barry as striker
The rest, young apprentices and junior pros.

But things after the final would show that the Whitecaps as a club were not expecting or ready for the great season we had had, or for the outcome of the final.

We arrived at the Giants Stadium which seemed to be surrounded by hundreds of Whitecaps supporters, who had traveled from the west coast of Canada to east coast of America.

On entering our changing room, we were met by a large banner which read "You are now in Whitecap Country", which had been put up by the American lads looking after the changing room. This was a great touch as the slogan usually reads "Cosmos Country."

I can remember aspects of the game, which has been refreshed by watching a DVD of the game, but I will be using the words of Jeff Cross a superb person and Vancouver Sports journalist.

(See appendix 3 acknowledgements)

"So when September 8 rolled around, the Whitecaps were more than ready. They were chafing at the bit, anxious to get into the final stretch run to the championship.

And what a final run it turned out to be.

Tampa Bay had steam rollered into their second straight Soccer Bowl with victories over Detroit Express, Philadelphia Fury and San Diego Sockers. The American Conference championships would definitely have something to say about the destination of the 1979 championship.

"Because we defeated the Cosmos, some people might believe we're virtually home free," said Waiters. "Nothing could be further from the truth. Regardless of who is the opposition, this is the final – one game everyone wants to be in, and wants to win. It's the game of the year. How can anyone not give it everything he's got?"

And the Whitecaps gave everything they had.

The record books will show it as a narrow 2-1 victory. In retrospect, the Vancouver team was in trouble only for a few minutes late in the game when Rowdies pressed relentlessly for a hoped-for equalizer, only to be foiled by two of the most magnificent saves Lofty Parkes has ever had to make. Tamp Bay stars Rodney Marsh and Oscar Fabbiani wrung their hands as Parkes flung himself sideways to block the two scoring efforts.

The Soccer Bowl is a time of nerves. It calls for unswerving selflessness, putting all doubt aside, and the demonstration of character that poet Bayard Taylor described.

Arsenal to Armenia

And on the day, it was the Whitecaps who did just that.

From the moment when, with just 12mins 37 secs gone in the game, rangy Trevor Whymark split the Tampa defence, shrugged off a spirited challenge by burly Barry Kitchener, and hammered a left foot shot from 19 yards past goalie Zelijko Bilecki, the Whitecaps were in charge.

Rowdies' goal bore a charmed life moments later, when a Whymark free kick rocketed back into play off the goalpost with Bilecki beaten. And from the rebound, Hector shot again, only to see his shot hit the crossbar.

This was Pressure.

Accepting the reprieve, the Rowdies moved downfield and Jan Van der Veen managed to get long enough to flash a 16 yard shot past Parkes, to tie the score. But it was to be the Rowdies only moment of joy.

That brilliant midfield general Alan Ball who was later to be named the Most Valuable Player of the Playoffs, prodded, pushed and eventually pierced the dour Tampa defence.

His razor-sharp pass found Whymark standing at the edge of the penalty area, and from 18 yards, the shy striker blasted another drive past Bilecki, this time with the right foot.

A slight deflection off the leg of Kitchener along the way had no effect. "It was going in anyway." Said the elated Whymark.

That was the clincher. Rowdies threw everything into attack, but the resolute defence of John Craven and Roger Kenyon never yielded an inch, and the acrobatic brilliance of Parkes handled the occasional shots that got through.

"Just the greatest thing that's ever happened to me." Said the 6-four goalkeeper after Whitecaps had accepted the Soccer Bowl trophy from Dr. Henry Kissinger. He and his weary team mates had taken a lap of honour before the 50,699 spectators who were still left in the Giants Stadium, and had watched Tony waiters race up into the stands to show the trophy to the solid phalanx of Vancouver fans at one end of the Stadium.

Now they were sprawled in the locker room while what seemed like every sportswriter and sportscaster in New York tried to get an exclusive interview with somebody.

Across the room, Alan Ball, Most Valauable Player (not money but skill value) was downplaying his award and pointing to the sweep of awards won by the Whitecaps – Trevor Whymark the offensive (attacking) of the game for his two goals, John Craven the defensive player of the game for his rock like work in the Vancouver rearguard which shut down the Rowdies chief threats, Marsh and Fabbiani."

"We won today because we didn't attempt anything we weren't capable of doing," said Ball quietly. "This is a team, not a collection of stars. A team."

I will return to Jeff Cross and his report later. Yes it was a fantastic situation that we had found ourselves in, I could now have a hair cut, as I hadn't had one since our good run had started. (Could do with that hair now!)

After we had all changed and finished off all the drinks in the changing rooms, players and staff wanted to meet up with our wives and families. So we all piled into the waiting coach, still surrounded by excited fans.

Where we were being taken we didn't know or possibly didn't care. We all wanted to eat and drink to celebrate our great victory and also winning the championship.

After which seemed an eternity, we entered a dusty road way and ended up at a large wooden building or bar, nothing fancy and a buffet of not very inspiring food. It was then back to the hotel. On entering the hotel we were met by the sight of all our bags in a big pile in the reception, with the news that we were not booked in for that night. So a massive ring around was called for, I must admit that I was fuming. What a fiasco or stronger words to that effect! Eventually with everybody staying in separate hotels, the whole magic had gone.

An early start the next day to fly back to Vancouver from Kennedy airport. I can still see, in the departure lounge, the cup surrounded by paper coffee cups and players and wives just sprawled everywhere. Our plane was called and as we started to the gate, the cup was forgotten until a shout broke the silence "The cup!"

The flight back was a quiet one, but the crew and airline were terrific. We were treated with Champagne etc. Yes, someone was organised, and it hadn't been us.

Arsenal to Armenia

As we cleared the airplane and were escorted through Vancouver airport, suddenly the noise of people in arrivals was building to a crescendo, and the airport staff were lining the corridors and cheering and shouting. As the doors of the Arrivals opened, a mass of people were just literally packed into the baggage claim. Some had even climbed up the baggage chute to have a better view. Jane and I were suddenly embraced by friends Annie and Terry Carol. Then onto the bus to the outskirts of downtown Vancouver. Again, people were everywhere, shouting and cheering. We then transferred to a convoy of open 4x4s for our drive to the centre of Robson Strassa, Vancouver.

Again thousands of people lined the streets, people in trees, up lamp posts, hanging out of buildings. It is estimated that over 100,000 people were there. It seemed to me that, that number of people were hanging from one building, so intense was the atmosphere.

I will now leave it to Jeff Cross and the continuation of his report:-

"And as a team they returned to Vancouver – to face the most ecstatic gathering the city has ever seen.

There have been many varied accounts of the size of the hometown reception, by folks who had watched all the New York drama on television and glowed with pride at the exploits of their team and their players.

The best estimate is that there were 100,000 at Vancouver International Airport, along the motorcade route into the city and in the centre of town itself when the procession ground to a halt. Certainly there appeared to be at least that many. But numbers are irrelevant.

This was a spontaneous outpouring of affection for a team of athletes who had brought honor to themselves, to their city, and to their profession."

"I expected a reception, but this is beyond my wildest dreams," said Bobby Lenarduzzi, the hometown boy who grew up just a stones throw from Empire Stadium".

Chapter Seventeen

"Change is the law of life. And those who look only to the past or present are certain to miss the future."
J.F. KENNEDY

The next couple of weeks were to be an anticlimax, with some if not most of the England boys and families returning to England.

During this period, we had a great night out at the Supporters Club do, they really made up for what the club failed to do.

Jane and I had found a great bungalow to rent, and had moved from our apartment, in a great location and were really looking forward to living in it and becoming settled.

Things didn't seem to be going well with the Whitecaps as a whole a lot of unsettled feelings seemed to be going around, I was hoping to get my contract settled for the forthcoming season, but again this air of unease was sensed. We returned to England in November and stayed with my brother in North Devon, as our house in Plymouth was still rented out.

After a number of attempts to get hold of anyone at the club, I was getting a feeling of being used, or was it me being paranoid?

We then went up to Derbyshire and spent some time with Jane's family in Matlock. Whilst there, I went to see a game of football between Matlock Town and Burton Albion. In the Albion side were two familiar faces, namely Zac Hector and Peter Daniel. I had time after the game to have a few words with them, but found out that both of them were not required by the Whitecaps for the following season, but even worse that, George Taylor the Physio from West Brom, had been signed by the Whitecaps and I had heard nothing at all!

Seemed like good communication skills or just man management?

Arsenal to Armenia

So here we were, back in England, a house we couldn't move into, both of us without jobs and a rented house with all our possessions in Canada. A few sleepless nights and long solitary walks to get rid of frustration and disappointment was on the agenda for the next number of weeks.

We eventually had some better news, that the people who had rented our house in Plymouth were moving out, so we would have somewhere to live.

After a trip down to Devon, Jane managed to obtain her previous position at the young Disabled Unit and I managed to get a position as sole Rehab. specialist at Moorhaven Psychiatric Hospital. Jane then returned to Canada to clear up things there. We were fortunate that Jane's bother Martyn and his wife Ro, would be going over for a holiday and would help her.

I remember so well meeting Jane on her return to Heathrow I could see nothing of her from behind a trolley which was heaped up with cases, bags, suit carriers etc., how she managed to get all these things through was amazing. We often talk about it now, especially having been charged "excess baggage" a few times since.

We soon settled back into our house, during which decorating was the name of the game. We also got our dog back from my father who had been looking after her.

The work at Moorhaven was different from Sports Medicine, but working with mentally disturbed patients wasn't much different from working with some of the characters in football.

We met up again with George Foster who was still at Argyle, and went to a couple of matches, but the interest had gone for me. We also went to a couple of the Argyle lottery evenings, which were good but not the same when you were out of the circle. We went to one in St. Austell, where a strange thing happened. We had had a few beers and I went through to the gents. I was there, standing in my cubicle minding my own business, when a chap next to me said that he knew me, but I didn't recognise him so paid little or no attention. He then repeated the statement and said that he knew that I used to be with Argyle. He then insisted that I looked at his ankle as he had hurt it playing football. My advice was to seek the diagnosis from a sober physio!

Dennis Loze

There he was sitting on the floor of a gents toilet with his shoes and socks off insisting that I had a look, I thought what has happened, from treating players of international status, to a lad in a gents toilet in St Austell!

A couple of months later I had the opportunity to take up a post with promotion at the Victoria Hospital in Blackpool, with Jane as Head Occupational Therapist in the same hospital. We sold up and moved up North and bought a house in St. Annes on Sea, a 15 minute drive from work.

The work was good but not challenging enough, but we also had the opportunity to meet up with Brian and Wendy Taylor as Brian was now playing for Preston North End.

One evening Brian rang me to say that North End were looking for a Physiotherapist and that he had already been to see Tommy Docherty and talked to him about me and for me to contact the club.

So following on from Brian's information of Preston requiring a person to look after North Ends medical side of the team, I contacted the infamous Tommy Docherty, who was the current manager.

He invited me to meet him for a general chat. This seemed to go well, then during our talk he had a phone call from Manchester City, regarding them releasing Tommy Booth, I got up to leave, but Tommy said if your going to be part of the management you sit still. His negotiating skills were brilliant I will not go into any aspect of the dialogue, but suffice it to say that Tommy was pleased, so pleased that another phone call to the club secretary was to bring in a bottle of wine. Our final discussion was over a glass of wine.

He wanted me to join them but money was tight and this would have to be agreed by the then Club Chairman Alan Jones. Our talk came to football in general and he was very open about his time at Manchester United and the issue regarding Mary and Laurie Brown, to which I stepped in and said that I knew both Mary and Laurie. In fact that I had just returned from a conference and I had shared a room with Laurie. This again eased things and again Tommy was very open about the issue. One of my passing comments was that I had only been married a few years so keep your hands off and the glasses were topped up.

Arsenal to Armenia

It was a further 3 weeks before I heard anything. The chairman wanted me to meet up with Barry Case, a local Orthopaedic Surgeon who looked after North Ends medical side of things and then I finally joined North End.

The history of North End is tremendous, but I was joining just a skeleton of the famous "Invincibles."

Preston North End can be traced back to 1863, but at that time it was also linked with cricket and the first game of football was 15 years away. At this time cricket was the only organised game to note in the town. The game was played near to the Ribble estuary at Ashton, but a split amongst the club members caused a move to Moor Park and the club name of North End was simply as an indication of the clubs base being at the north end of the town. Then in 1875 they took a lease on a field near to Moor Park at Deepdale, a field that was to be the home of the finest team of its era. Playing cricket and dabbling in other games such as lacrosse and rounders were not financially viable and so in 1877 members turned to rugby. Unfortunately, this venture was a failure since the club could not compete with the already well established Preston Grasshoppers. On the 5th October 1878 North End played its first game under association rules against Eagley, at Deepdale and lost 1-0.

In 1884 following a draw against Upton Park at Deepdale a protest was made to the FA regarding the eligibility of some of the Preston players, but the basic reason was that Preston was paying players. Preston was then expelled from the FA cup competition, but then commenced an historic move to have professionalism legalised, steared by William Suddell. The success Suddell brought to Deepdale, was illustrated by the fact that from 22nd August 1885 to April 1886, North End were undefeated and during the season won 59 out of 64 matches, scoring 318 goals and conceded only 60. The Invinciples were born.

The following season 1888/89 not only were they founder members of the Football League but they won the FA cup and were the first team to achieve the double.

Preston North End
    1875   First recorded experimental football match against Eagley.
    1880   Founded
    1885   Became a professional club
    1888   Founder member of the English Football League

Dennis Loze

Club Nickname
   Lilywhites

Previous Grounds
   1875   Moved to Deepdale from Moorpark (then cricket/athletic club)

Record Attendance
   42,684 versus Arsenal 1938.

League Scoring Record
   37 Ted Harper 1932-33 Division Two.

Most League Appearances
   447 Alan Kelly 1961-75

Club History

1888	Founder member of the English Football League
1889, 1890	League Championship
1889, 1938	FA Cup winners
1941	War Cup winners
1888, 1922, 1937, 1954, 1964	FA Cup Finalist
1891, 1892, 1893, 1906, 1953, 1958	Division 1 Runners up
1904, 1913, 1951, 2000*	Division 2 Champions
1971, 1996*	Division 3 Champions

* In 1991 the former Division 1 broke away from the Football League and former Division 2, 3, and 4 became Divisions 1, 2, 3 respectively.

Star Mention

The name Preston North End cannot be mentioned without the name of Tom Finney or should I say Sir Tom. After the war and until his retirement in 1960 the skill of Tom was the most important aspect of football at Deepdale. His genius and gentlemanly conduct was and still is, an example for all footballers to follow and brought great credit, not just to the maestro but also to his home town of Preston.

Arsenal to Armenia

Managers prior to me joining North End.

1981	Tommy Docherty (Manager at the time of my move to PNE)
1977-81	Nobby Stiles
1975-77	Harry Caterrick
1973-75	Bobby Charlton
1970-73	Alan Ball Snr
1961-68	Jimmy Milne
1956-61	Cliff Britton
1954-56	Frank Hill
1953-54	Scot Symon
1949-53	Will Scott
1946-49	Selection committee led by J.I. Taylor
1939-46	2nd world war (rearranged leagues)
1937-39	Management committee
1936-37	T. Muirhead Manager/Secretary
1932-36	4 man committee
1931-32	Lincoln Hyde
1930-31	Lincoln Hyde/Alex Gibson
1927-30	Alex Gibson
1925-27	Frank Richards
1924-25	Jimmy Lawrence/Frank Richards
1922-23	Jimmy Lawrence
1919-22	Vincent Hayes Manager/Secretary
1915-19	1st world war rearranged leagues
1888-1915	Management committee

Managers during my time at North End

1981	Tommy Docherty
1981	Alan Kelly (Caretaker)
1981-83	Gordon Lee
1983	Alan Kelly (Caretaker)
1983-85	Alan Kelly
1985-86	Tommy Booth
1986	Brian Kidd
1986	Jon Clarke (Caretaker)
1986 (1990)	John McGrath

Chapter Eighteen

"The time to repair the roof is when the sun is shining."
J.F.KENNEDY

The first day at North End was a bit of a shock. Things were not going very well on the pitch, also there seemed to be a lot of unrest amongst the players. Some senior pros who were out of favour had to use the away team changing room. (For those who are not familiar with internal workings of a club, is that during training sessions the home team changing room is for the first team squad, and senior pros., the away team changing room used by junior pros and apprentices). So something was amiss.

Meeting up with the rest of the management staff; namely

Ken Shillito   Assistant Manager
Alan Kelly   Reserve team coach
Alan Spavin   Youth Development

It was time to meet and get to know some of the players.

Brian Taylor (full back/midfield), who I already knew from our Plymouth Argyle days. He joined North End during the season of 78/79 and left in 81/82. After making 99 league and cup appearances.

Andy McAteer (full back), a local lad, who joined North End in 79/80 and left in 88/89, after making 292 league and cup appearances.

Peter Lichfield (goal keeper) who joined North End in 81/82 and left in 84/85 after making 134 league and cup apearances.

Arsenal to Armenia

Don O´Riordan (defence/midfield) (Played for Tulsa in the NASL when I was with Vancouver). Joined North End 78/79 and left in 82/83 after making 171 league and cup appearances.

John Anderson (defence) who joined North End 79/80 and left 81/82, after making 50 league and cup appearances, plus gaining 5 caps for Eire.

Steve Doyle (midfield), joined North End 74/75 and left 81/82, after making 205 league and cup appearances.

Mike Farrelly (defence) joined North End 81/82 and left 84/85 after making 87 league and cup appearances.

Mark Walsh (midfield) another local lad, who joined North End 81/82 and left 83/84 after making 77 league and cup appearances.

Simon Westwell (defence) another local lad, who joined North End 80/81 and left 82/83 after making 76 league and cup appearances.

Peter (Leo) Sayer (forward) joined North End 80/81 and left 83/84 after making 47 league and cup appearances. (10 Welsh caps prior to joining PNE)

Paul McGee (forward) joined North End 79/80 and left 81/82 after making 68 league and cup appearances, plus gained 6 caps for Eire.

Graham Houston (forward) another local lad, joined North End 79/80 and left 85/86 after making 113 league and cup appearances.

Jimmy Bell (defender) joined and left North End in 1981/82 after making 1 cup appearance.

Alex Bruce (forward) initially joined North End in 71/72 and left 73/74 after making 59 league and cup appearances (scoring 21 goals-joined Newcastle United). Rejoined North End 75/76 and left in 82/83 after making 323 league and cup appearances, scoring 149 goals.

Gordon Coleman (midfield) joined North End in 73/74 and left 82/83, after making 281 league and cup appearances.

Steve Elliott (forward) joined North End in 78/79 left 83/84, after making 213 appearances, scoring 78 goals.

Graham Bell (midfield) joined North End in 78/79 left 82/83, after making 128 league and cup appearances.

Willie Naughton (forward) joined North End in 79/80 left 84/85 making 167 league and cup appearances.

Signed at the commencement of the season or during the season I first joined North End:

Jonathon Clarke (mid field) left North End 86/87, making 129 appearances, plus a period of caretaker manager.

Tommy Booth (defender) left North End 84/85, making 94 league and cup appearances, plus a period as manager.

Gary Buckley (forward) left North End 82/83 making 29 league and cup appearances
John Kelly (forward) left North End 84/85 making 136 league and cup appearances.

Barry Dunn (midfield) left North End 84/85 making 11 league and cup appearances.

Martin Hodge (goal keeper) joined on loan in 81/82 and again 82/83 making 44 league appearances.

Apprentices
Stuart Wilcock
Neil Hanson
Stuart Flanagan
Chris Hunter (forward), who went on to sign professional for North End in 82/83 and left 84/85 after making 3 league appearances.
Seems a big squad, but most of the players were coming and going during this season, all will be revealed later on.

Not only were things going wrong in the changing rooms, but the play on the pitch wasn't up to much either.

Arsenal to Armenia

To be honest the club hadn't fully recovered from the prior season, which saw North End being demoted from the 2nd Division to the 3rd, which was a bitter blow and ultimately cost Nobby Stiles his job as manager. You couldn't help feeling sorry for Nobby, the former Manchester United and England star, as the lack of money available to strengthen his side at crucial periods was what cost him his job.

During that season a figure of in excess of £333,000 was required to bring the ground up to the safety standards, to which the club received a grant of £210.00. This was helped also by the sale of Mick Robinson to Brighton.

With the arrival of Tommy, during the summer, brought an air of expectation to the town. As an ex Preston player he played 346 league and cup games between the seasons of 1949/50 to 1957/8, plus 22 caps and captain of Scotland, before being transferred to Arsenal.

Also it was the club centenary year, but to celebrate this in the 3rd Division, with money low and morale low, was it too big an asking.

This air of expectation was short lived. By the end of September, North End had played 8, won 1, lost 3 and drawn 4.

As in the previous chapter with Tommy's phone call to Manchester City, brought at the beginning of October the arrival of four signings, Tommy Booth and Gary Buckley from City and John Kelly and Barry Dunn, This steadied things a bit but the 6 games in October brought only 1 win 2 loses and 3 draws. One of these games at home against Burnley on the 20th October was chosen as the game to celebrate Preston North Ends Centenary celebration. This was the game where I met up with Barry Case the Orthopaedic consultant and gained an insight into the medical set up at North End, and yes, this was as bad as things on the pitch. The game, by the way ended in a 1-1 draw and was North Ends first goal for 430 mins of play.

I joined North End at the very end of October. The number of injuries I faced wasn't like the Plymouth situation, but the medical procedure was classic of the medical regime of football during that period in time. The poem by Richie Hessian "Bucket and Sponge" quoted earlier in the book was very evident here.

The first thing that had to be done was to get a Medical Record File for each payer from the FA. Fortunately they were supplied with no questions asked, thanks to good old Derek from the office. There wasn't a medical record for any of the players, or a format established for the referral to Barry Case, or to the club Doctor for general problems.

Normally a local Doctor was used for general problems. This was an honourary position and also didn't ensure that the Doctor had any experience in dealing with sports injuries. This was also the case with some of the specialist used.

I remember a case at Plymouth. We were involved in an away fixture and one of our players had a cut shin which required stitching at the end of the game. The Doctor eventually arrived, smelling of alcohol. After three attempts to get the first stitch in, I stepped in and applied butterfly stitches and compression bandage. I didn't report this situation although possibly I should have, but as a GP he probably hadn't had a great experience in stitching and the drink aspect might have cost him his profession. I know he realised his mistake by the time I left him!

The players at North End would also soon realise the importance I put on physical rehabilitation and fitness, which hadn't happened before.

I remember one day I had the lads up in the weight training room. Some I had on specific individual exercises which related to their injury and the others I had on a general fitness circuit. It was all action and in came Barry Case. His comment was "Now people will see and understand why I wanted someone like you here dealing with the injuries," which was a great complement.

Our first game was at Lincoln, who had Lenny Lawrence as manager (previous manager at Argyle) which we did manage to win, was this a good omen?

No!

By the end of November we had played a further 3 league games and FA cup 1st round, and lost them all, so the Directors sacked Tommy and Alan Kelly stepped in as caretaker, was this de-ja-vu of Plymouth? Kel didn't have much time to change things as a week later Gordon Lee was appointed, bringing in Geoff Naulty as his assistant, with Kel now looking after the reserves and youth team.

Morale amongst the players was mixed as not everyone like changes, especially in management, but this did gradually improve. I would like to think that I had helped in this situation. Treatment rooms were at this time looked upon as a place for the weak ones with injuries being seen as letting the team down, and should be treated as such, very similar to Plymouth. This I had to change, again starting with bringing the injured in at the same time as the rest of the squad, so they met up, changed at the same time, left the treatment room doors open so we were all visible (obviously not when dealing with a confidential situation). Graham Bell and I came up with the idea of the word wheel (as in some of the newspaper; the Mail especially). This was to stimulate the players and to keep the brain active (hard with some of them I know!). One of the walls in the treatment room was of formica, so could be used as a white board. The letters were written up on the wall, and you had to try and make up as many words as you could. Players used to come in before and after training to participate again the injured met with the rest of the squad. We ran a prize for the winners and forfeit for the losers.

As in a lot of clubs the treatment room seemed to be taboo, as though you would catch something if you were seen near it. This attitude came from the management down. This taboo had to be changed if injuries were to be spotted at an early stage, so it was encouraging all early signs and symptoms to be reported to me before training commenced. This proved to a great success, not only in spotting early injuries and dispelling the taboo, but also, players with longer term injuries still felt part of the squad as they were still in contact with other players.

Partnership with Tommy Doc, was short lived, let's see what Gordon could offer!

Gordon came with all the credentials:
(born 13 July 1934, Cannock, Staffordshire)
Playing career

Gordon was a full back who began at Hednesford Town and joined Aston Villa in October 1955.

- Aston Villa (1958-64) 118 league appearances 2 goals.
- Shrewsbury Town (1966) 2 League appearances.

Management career

- Port Vale (1968-74) He succeeded Sir Stanley Matthews and gained promotion to the 3rd division at the first attempt.
- Blackburn Rovers (1974-1975) He led them to promotion to the 2nd Division.
- Newcastle United (1975-1977) Led them to the final of the 1975-6 League Cup
- Everton (1977-81) In the first season they finished 9th and reached the League Cup final and the FA Cup semi final. The next 2 seasons finished 3rd and 4th, but the 1979-80 season didn't start too well. He had brought in players who would prove later to be successful players Peter Reid, Kevin Ratcliffe, Graeme Sharp, Steve McMahon. Although he was well respected by the players, he was still sacked in May 1981.
- *After North End.*
- *Manager Coach in Iceland*
- *Leicester City (1991) As caretaker. Although this was for a short period, he saved the club from relegation to the 3rd division.*

Geoff Nulty, also had the playing credentials, but would he become a good number two.

Born 13th Feb 1949. Prescot, Lancashire.

- Stoke City
- Burnley 1968 to 1974. Played 110 games, scored 20 goals.
- Newcastle 1974 to 1978. Played 101 games, scored 11 goals.
- Everton 1978 to 1980. Played 28 games, scored 2 goals.

A serious knee injury in 1980 forced his early retirement.

Gordon was a smashing chap, in fact too nice a fellow for the politics of football. Actually, he was a very naive person where everything had to be black or white, grey areas didn't count. I remember a couple of incidents which will help you to understand what I mean. One day in the treatment room, some of the lads and I were discussing the England team and picking who we thought was the best starting eleven. Gordon came in and joined in the discussion. Suddenly Gordon went off at a tangent (something he did on a regular basis) and started not talking about players and how good they were, but about their actual names. His point was that he couldn't understand players who played for their country and didn't have that national name, e.g. why Malcolm MacDonald with a Scottish name, was allowed to play for England! The lads faces and eyes suddenly went blank. How could you better that one?

On another occasion, we were discussing athletics and the star at that time was obviously Carl Lewis with his amazing talent. Again Gordon came and added his pennyworth by saying "Yes, but he cannot swim!" Gordon really meant that with people having a black skin, their body fat was different so that swimming was difficult for them. So you can see Gordon was a one off.

Geoff with his first step into the management sphere was different. He tried to come over as the intellectual one, (not saying that he wasn't). Geoff again was a smashing person, but the lads didn't really take to him because of this image he tried to put over.

Gordon added to our squad by getting Martin Hodge on loan from Everton, Gordon had bought Martin from Plymouth during his period as manager at Goodison.

We then lost Tommy Booth who sustained a knee injury, resulting in ligament damage and torn meniscus (cartilage). This would put him out for the rest of the season and the start of the following one. Tommy was a real great pro. who worked really hard with me to get himself back onto the pitch again.

Martin did strengthen the defence up, like any good keeper and didn't hold back in giving his defence a good b********g, when needed. Results started to come our way and we did mange to salvage something and finished 14th in the table.

But as at Plymouth what was the next season going to bring?

Chapter Nineteen

"It is not enough that we do our best, sometimes we have to do what is right."
WINSTON CHURCHILL

I take this opportunity to introduce a few of the behind the scenes' people:-

Jimmy Milne, whose pipe you could smell a mile away it was a real good pipe tobacco smell.

Jimmy joined Preston in 1932 from Dundee United as a player. He left in 1946 and became Player/Manager for Wigan and then Morecambe in the Lancs combination league. Then in the late 40's coach/trainer to Doncaster Rovers.

He soon returned to Deepdale as trainer and was also manger from 1961 – 68. He then stayed on at the club as scout, bringing in players such as Mark Lawrenson, Tony Morley, Archie Gemmell and Howard Kendal.

Jimmy, during my time, helped out in all ways, such as DIY repairs to lockers, painting, helping with the laundry, doing the ironing, but was still a great encourager to players, especially when things were going wrong. A perfect gent, who lived all this time just a few doors away from the ground.

Mrs.C who used to iron all the kit.

Harry Hubbick joined Preston with Alan Ball snr. Harry was a player at Bolton Wanderers. Harry was the club trainer, who now into his late 70s still did his little bit of training every day.

Harry was the club trainer, until the Doc. moved him to kit manager.

Arsenal to Armenia

Then we had Peter McCallion as groundsman (wonder what country Gordon would have him playing for?). His assistant was Jim Fraser whose pride and joy was a Lada. He used to have to take a lot of stick from the lads for that. (but I would come to respect the Lada during the years that I was going to spend in Armenia.).

There were also the volunteer staff of Joe Cheetham, who was "Mr Fixit", with Jimmy Milne being "Mr. DIY" and Wally Hilton who always had a painting brush in his hand.

Another person who must get a mention is George "Snowy" Higham. He used to look after the changing room and players needs on match day. Snowy was a local lorry driver, who always seem to either start or finish his deliveries at Deepdale, so he was a very popular visitor. Every year he used to go on a sponsored diet for charity and spend the rest of the year putting it all back on again.

Also behind the scenes was Ray Linford who became our volunteer coach driver.

North End was a very friendly Club, but somewhat lacked the professionalism of the club it was in the past. In fact you were very aware of the smell of death lingering in the building.

The season of 82/83 saw a few changes with Keith Leeming taking over as Chairman from a very popular Alan Jones. This would also herald a farcical change or rearrangement of the Board Members.
Next was the loss of our training ground at Willow Farm. Willow farm had been part of North Ends history since the mid 40's. The farm was bought by North End in the early 50's, with changing rooms etc. being added. Then in 1973 bought under a compulsory purchase order, due to New Town plans, by Central Lancashire Development Corporation for a total of £138,000. The club continued to use the facilities until the lease expired. Then the club had use of Courtauld's sports ground, which it never lived up to Willow farm. Another nail in the coffin.

We also lost the services of John Anderson and Steve Doyle, two young players with great prospects. John had gained 5 caps for Eire, but we knew that they had to go because of wages. Alan Kelly worked well for the pair of them, with Ando going to Newcastle and Doyley to Huddersfield. Ando was to make 283 appearances for Newcastle between 82/83 and 1987.

Both on free transfers!

Brian Taylor was also axed, again at the end of his contract, - freed to save a wage.

Brian was a very astute person, who was well prepared for when his time in football was up. He had gone into partnership with my ex brother-in-law John. They set up a large printing firm in Preston, John being a printer by profession. This successful partnership continued until Brian's death from Motor Neurone Disease.

Gordon now pulled in his contacts and managed to get Alan Gowling to join us on a match basis, Alan played a total of 40 games for us that season in attack and defence. He was a great person to have around, because of his professionalism and experience playing top level football for Manchester United and Newcastle United. Alan was a very intelligent player (his degree in Economics probably helped) but was not endowed with the glamour looks. I remember during a home fixture Alan had a smack in the face and went down. I went on to see him and managed to get his hands from his face. His lips were cut and he was bleeding from his nose, but nothing serious. So my comment to Alan was that everything was OK and it hadn't altered his good looks!

Even with Alan's ability we had only 4 wins out of the first 20 games. Jim Arnold was brought in on loan from Everton as keeper for half a dozen games, which helped us to get a couple of draws.

As well as things not going too well on the pitch, it was being matched off it too.

It seemed to happen every month, that when I went to Derek in the office for my pay cheque (direct debits weren't done), each time Derek would apologise that the cheques were waiting for the Directors to sign. Sometimes it would run into a week before mine was ready. Cash flow difficulty was obvious.

A local businessman had stepped in to help North End out of this problem in the form of Barney Campbell. Barney was a great chap with a matching personality. His son Glen was on our books as reserve keeper. Barney was to step in as Managing Director. His main brief was to get us out of the cash flow crisis that were in.

Arsenal to Armenia

I had a meeting with Barney and suggested a way around treatment expenditures. That I would become self employed, thus saving them National Insurance and tax and I would treat the players in the morning and afternoon, and then late afternoon and evening use the treatment room as a private clinic. This would also give them another saving as I took a cut in salary. Barney accepted the deal. I changed the treatment room around and brought in new pieces of equipment and developed a modern treatment room.

One of the other things that Barney brought about was that the number of directors would increase to a "Guinness Book Records" **18.**

With each director putting into the pot £2,500 a long way from our modern game of the Glaziers of United etc.

My working hours were now turning into very long ones, so to ease the problem, I would not cover the away games and would only come in on the Sunday morning of an away fixture.

The clubs spirits were lifted a little by way of the FA Cup. We were drawn against non league Shepshed Charterhouse at home and got a good 5-1 win, and we got a home draw against our neighbours, Blackpool. The league form continued to depress us all, including the fans and relegation was a distinct possibility. We had a good 2-1 win over Blackpool it brought over 14,000 through the turnstiles, which more than quadrupled our normal gate. We were drawn against Leeds United at Leeds. We managed 1 win from our next 5 games before our venture to Eland Road. Not the most encouraging foundation. Leeds stuffed us 3-0, so it was back to the league survival I remember one aspect of this game so well. Tommy Booth had to be subbed because of a knee injury. On our way back to our bench, so many coins were hurled at us that if I had been brave enough to pick them up I could have become a North End Director!

Things changed for us again with the arrival yet again of Martin Hodge, as well as Paul Lodge also from Everton.
This resulted in us only losing 1 game out of last 13 games, and finished a respectable 16th in the table.

We had picked up a number of short and longish term injuries during the season, but morale amongst them was kept high. One of the other things that I used to do with the players who were in their later stage of rehabilitation, before rejoining the playing squad, was that at the end of each session, which was carried out on the nearby park, was chip the cross bar. It was a case of having the ball placed on the edge of the penalty area and each of us would take it in turns to chip the ball so that it clipped the cross bar. This was something that I had been doing for a number of years so my aim had become very good, which use to annoy the lads. The loser was the player with the least number of successes out of 10 attempts; they would have to treat each of the group to a Mars Bar. Poor Leo (Pete) Sayer's pocket used to come in for a hammering, but his reply was that he was paid to put the ball in the net, not to clip the cross bar.

Now the shop which relieved the losers pocket must get a mention. It was a little corner shop opposite the players entrance, The lady's name has slipped my memory at this stage, but to go into the shop was an experience never to be forgotten. She had a couple of cats, who seemed to get everywhere in the shop, walking and sleeping and goodness knows what else. It was always cold in the building, so she used to come to the counter in her pinnie and clutching a hot water bottle. However the piece-de-resistance was her wig, I know it wrong to laugh but you found it hard to keep a straight face, as each time it was on at a different angle and sometimes back to front. You never bought anything that wasn't in a wrapper, but it had been known that some have purchased, eaten, and survived a meat pie!

I must also mention, before moving on to the following season, that the Directors had got hold of a bus, thus cutting down the costs of our away trips. A local firm had also said that they would carry out the servicing of it as part of a good deal. Sounds good, but you had to get the full benefit you had to experience a journey in it. For one, no heat could or ever would get beyond the engine so you had to be wrapped up even on a warm day. With more ice on the inside of the windows than the outside, if the cold didn't kill you, the carbon monoxide would. As for a comfortable ride, well you can guess, what Jeremy Clarkson of Top Gear would have to say!

We even had one of the Directors driving it at one stage, but then it fell mostly to Ray Linford.

Why did I leave Arsenal?

Chapter Twenty

∞

"Our lives begin to end the day we become silent about things that matter."
MARTIN LUTHER KING JR.

The move into private practice was just starting to work out, but to advance any further I had to move into my own premises. North End was fine, but it had its restrictions.

After a lot of searching I found premises near to the town centre, next door to a local pub, "Coconut Grove" on Lancaster Road.

I had a reception room, two treatment rooms, an office and a room which I was going to convert into a rehabilitation gymnasium plus the usual toilets etc.

I had a contract with the Amateur Swimming Association to look after their swimmers, mainly the Northern Squad, based at Wigan Wasps at the International Pool, Wigan.

Swimmers like the Osgerby twins, Ann and Janet, June Croft and Nick Hodgson.

Ann Osgerby 1980and 84 Olympics Butterfly, gaining a silver in the 1980 medley relay.
Janet 1980 Olympics Butterfly.
June Croft 1980 Olympics Freestyle. Silver medal 4x100 Medlay. 1984 Olympics 400 Freestyle Bronze.
Commonwealth games 1982 100 Freestyle Gold, 200 Freestyle Gold. 100 Freestyle Bronze
Nick Hodgson 1986 Olympics 200 Butterfly. 1984 Commonwealth games Bronze medal

Liking up with the Wasps was an experience, as I was going to witness real dedication by the swimmers, the coaches and the swimmers parents.

You must remember at this time, swimmers were not on any form of sponsorships. The training sessions were something that left me totally exhausted and I was only watching. To think that the swimmers were working or still at school, but still put in two long training sessions each day.

I also worked with Blackpool Borough Rugby League Club, I was starting to get very busy, but dealing with local lads and lasses who couldn't really afford treatment so I was a soft touch, so money wasn't matching the hours put in, but early days yet.

I must tell you more about Blackpool Borough Rugby League Club.
A Blackpool club were members of the Northern Union Lancashire Second Competition in 1898/99. The first unsuccessful application for a Blackpool team to join the Rugby League was made by a in December 1950. Blackpool Borough were accepted into the Rugby League for the 1954/55 season.

Borough played at Blackpool St Anne's Road Greyhound Stadium but larger fixtures were played at Blackpool FC's Bloomfield Road Stadium. Their record attendance was 12,015 on 10 September 1955 when they drew with the New Zealand tourists 24-24 at Bloomfield Road. Blackpool Greyhound Stadium was sold for housing and in April 1962 Blackpool Borough Council granted a 21-year lease on a new ground - Borough Park - on the former gas works and coach park site at Rigby Road and Princess Street.

In 1978-79, Blackpool won promotion to the First Division for the first and only time by finishing fourth in the Second Division. However the next season, they finished bottom and were relegated back to the Second Division.

In April 1982 Borough were put into liquidation less than nine months after being taken over by a Cardiff businessman. A new company, Savoy Sports and Leisure Ltd, then bought the club and a new Blackpool Borough RLFC was formed on 4 August 1982 and accepted into the Rugby League for the new season.

It was during this 1982 season that a bizarre situation arose. It was to be a normal training evening, but on arrival all the changing rooms etc were locked up and sealed. John Chadwick who was Club Secretary gave me a shout to come and see him in his office. Again going into his office I could see that everything had been sealed, filing cabinets, drawers and even the drinks cabinet. He gave me the news that he club had gone into

Arsenal to Armenia

liquidation. I would have to put in a claim for the consultancy fees that were owed to me but under the terms of the liquidation, it was doubtful that I would get the full amount or even anything, so hence the money was just lost. John then produced a bottle of Whisky that had not been spotted by the Liquidators. So we sat and emptied the bottle, to me it was the most expensive drink I had ever had.

Was the same thing going to happen to me at North End!

Blackpool did continue to in Rugby League, but in 1987 became Chorley RFC, and further split happened again in 1990 saw the forming of Blackpool Panthers who still exist today. With John Chadwick as Chairman.

The season at North End started without some players players such as Alec Bruce transferred to Wigan, Gordon Coleman to Bury, Graham Bell to Carlise, Gary Buckle to Chorley, Simon Westwell to Chorley, Martin Hodge back to Everton and Alan Gowling who retired.

I was still seeing the players at North End but carrying out the treatments at my new Clinic at Lancaster Road.

The season started like a dream with the first 7 games resulting in no defeats. With 3 wins and 4 draws in league and cup, but this was later followed by 8 consecutive defeats. Nothing seemed to be going right for us, although injuries were at a minimum, but we just didn't seem to be able to conjure anything up.

It was during this run of bad play that the next bizarre thing happened. We were playing against Wigan at home and although we did manage to score twice, Wigan managed three which put us in a difficult position. We had just returned to the dressing room, and the players were sat down waiting for Gordon to say something when the door burst open. Despite Snowy always manning the door, the complete unknown in football happened, one of the newer Directors burst in and started to blast the players! Words like "you are not worth your wages, I'm going to see that your wages are stopped for the month, until things start to............" He never finished his sentence. Poor Gordon just stood with mouth open completely lost for words, Geoff turned his back and faced the wall, so something had to be done, …… yes me again I rushed forward saying that he was completely out of order and I didn't care who he was, no-one comes in the dressing room after a game until the manager has finished. If you have something to say, do it in the boardroom and not here. With that I pushed him out of the door and slammed it shut.

We had silence until Gordon started on the players, but not the slagging off that they had just experienced.

Nothing was ever said again about the incident, but I am sure one of the more experienced directors put the new one right in dressing room etiquette.

Things continued to go wrong on the pitch, no matter what Gordon tried. I remember one Friday, I had just finished working with some of the lads on the track (around the pitch) and was going back up the tunnel as Gordon was walking out of it. He looked as if he could do with some company so I walked out on the pitch with him we were soon joined by Pete, the groundsman. We were chatting in general also about the home game the next day, and Gordon asked what the weather forecast was like, as it would be good if we had a real heavy frost and have the match called off. Pete replied that the forecast was in fact below freezing during the night, but that the pitch is bone dry, so the frost wouldn't go deep enough into the ground to cause a postponement.

I got to the ground about 12.00 on the Saturday and walked out on the pitch to see Pete and a small group of people looking at the Fulwood end penalty area. On looking at it there was large icy areas everywhere and the frozen ice had penetrated deep into soil. The game was called off. Who threw buckets and buckets of water onto the pitch, because that is what it looked like, we will never know.

But it did give us a week to prepare for the next game.

I have just finished reading Brian Cloughs book "Walking on Water". He said that on home games he himself used to come back to the Forest ground at night and turn the sprinklers on, as he knew that a heavy pitch suited his team better. But on one occasion he fell asleep and areas of the pitch looked like it had been hit by a monsoon.

My private clinic was ticking over, but the hours were long and appointments seemed very spread out, then a help came along in the shape of the Lancashire FA. They had contacted me and asked to me run a number of lectures on sports injuries and not just confined to Lancashire, but Liverpool, Manchester and Cumbria.

This was great, because although it took me away from the clinic, I could then condense the treatment times.

This was followed by the Yorkshire FA asking me to do the same, but this I had to turn down as it meant more time away, but I did cover the West Yorkshire area.

Arsenal to Armenia

My name was getting around, but nothing permanent was opening up. The lecturing and teaching was right up my street, and I took to it like a duck to water. It also took my mind off the difficulties at North End.

The results continued to be spasmodic, resulting in Gordon and Geoff being in early December sacked, with Kel to step in again as caretaker manger.

This was followed by yet another financial problem at North End, which would affect me!

One of the directors came to see me with the news that they could not afford to pay my retainer, but they still wanted me to look after the treatment of the injured players. Out came his calculator and the next bit was farcical, this director ran a car sales business. He entered in my retainer, then asked what I charged per session at my clinic, to which I reminded him that a treatment session at the clinic is an average half hour, whereas a session at the ground and my clinic as before, was what was needed, may be up to 4 hrs. So he plucked a figure out of thin air and entered that in to his calculator. After pushing a few buttons he was pleased that it would save the club money. However I could see the situation differently, I agreed in principle and that a contract would be drawn up on the figure agreed. After he had gone I mentally worked it out as they would in fact be paying me more and if I had a minimum of 3 players injured per day through out the season, North End would owe me a lot of money. The figure was then readjusted but not too much.

So from now on the players would report to me at my clinic, I would contact the club and Kell, and bill the club monthly.

It was hard to be away from the club as I missed the everyday contact with all the players and staff, but that I had to contend with.

During the pre season, Gordon had brought in a few new faces, David Jones ex-Everton who had been playing in Hong Kong, Geoff Twentyman from non league Chorley, Mark Jones, David's brother from non league and Peter Houghton from Wigan. Also during the season some of the ex apprentices were to make their first team debut.

At this time, the Referees Association contacted me through Roy Hart, a Preston based referee assessor. He would like me to talk to the referees and linesman (before assistant referees had been thought of) on fitness. This took me around the North of England and to the Referees annual conference at Aston Villa and the NEC.

Kel had a job on his hands, but he had the right pedigree to have a real good go at it. The first two games brought about the normal outcome when a new manager is put in charge, two victories.

But things were a very mixed bag regarding results. Even though Kel used a permutation of players, and some of the young pros. Injuries too tended to be a very mixed bag, Tommy Booth seemed to be picking a number of injuries. Was it his body reacting from a long career? However he was the type of person you couldn't write off. Despite receiving a nasty head injury at Bristol which resulted in an overnight stay at Hospital, he still continued after a recommended lay off. Although medical advice was to call it a day, he continued, but spasmodically. Andy McAteer also picked up a difficult ankle and Achilles injury which was to give him problems, especially when the famous Deepdale turf was exchanged for astro turf in 1986. But more of that later.

More news regarding the clubs financial difficulties were to be announced that North End would cease to be in evidence at the end of the season, unless a further rescue package to the sum of £250,000 was to be found. This was obviously a blow to the public and spectators, but those within the club had the feeling that we were not on the right side of solvency.

Even an ex player, Alec Ashworth auctioned his 1964 FA Cup Final shirt. A final played against West Ham, which was a great game ending in an injury time goal, giving West Ham a 3-2 victory. A game in which North End was at one time leading 2-1. This result brought their season to a "nearly season" as they also finished 3rd in the table, missing out on promotion to the 1st Division.

Now, 20 years on, facing the ultimate embarrassment of disappearing from the Football League, a league that Preston was one of the founder members.

A financial rescue package was brought about by the Preston Town Council who decided to purchase Deepdale Stadium, which automatically cleared the immediate debts.

Results were very much up and down, but we still managed to finish 16th for the 2nd season running.

Arsenal to Armenia

Our Wedding Day

Whitecaps Supporters BBQ

Dennis Loze

Vancouver Whitecaps 1979 - N.A.S.L. Champions

Left to right.
(Back row) Me, Bob McNab, Willie Johnson, John Craven, Trevor Whymark, Lofty Parkes, Roger Kenyon, Bruce Grobbellar, Dan Lenarduzzi, Carl Shearer, Bob Lenarduzzi, Peter Daniel, Tony Waiters.
(Front row) Bob Bolitho, Steve Neeson, Derek Possee, Paul Nelson, Carl Valentine, Jon Sammels, Buz Parsons, Ray Lewington, Drew Ferguson, Gerry Gray, Kevin Hector.
(Alan Ball to sign later)

Arsenal to Armenia

Stunning Jane (right) with friend Annie

Match day (right to left) Tony Waiters, Bob McNab and yours truly.

Dennis Loze

*Willy having a rest during the final, with me helping him!
Trevor Whymark and Kevin Hector looking on.*

Good Season! Yours truly with Barry Crocker.

Arsenal to Armenia

With NASL cup and Ray Lewington

*Supporters do on return to Vancouver.
Right to left Ray lewington, Carl Shearer, Bob McNab and myself.*

Dennis Loze

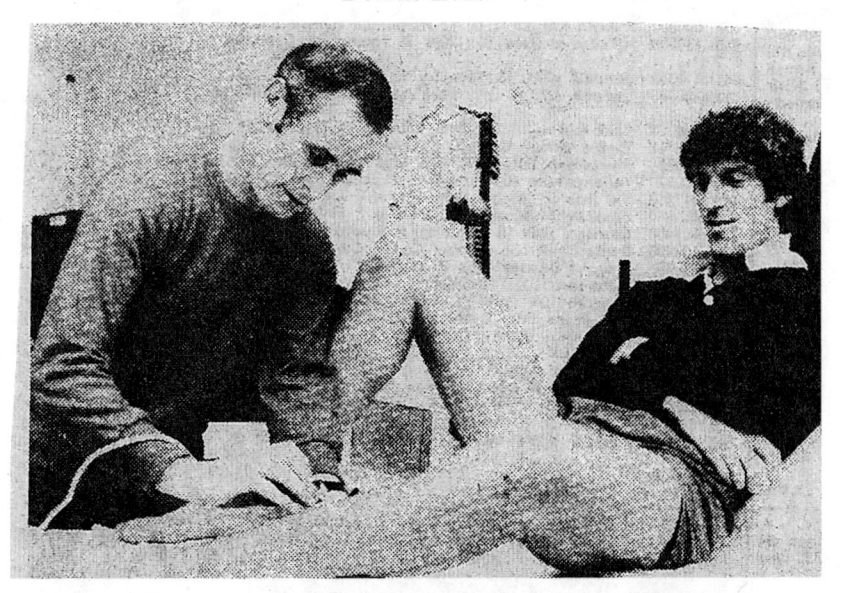

Treatment on Tommy Booth at Preston North End

Back Row: (Left to Right) Don O'Riordan, Jonathan Clark, Steve Elliott, Peter Litchfield, Glen Campbell, Willie Naughton, Mike Farrelly, Tommy Booth. Middle Row: Andy McAteer, Simon Westwell, Mark Walsh, Alex Bruce, Gordon Coleman, Gary Hough, Neil Hanson. Front Row: Graham Houston, Chris Hunter, Gary Buckley, Gordon Lee (Manger), Peter Sayer, Graham Bell, John Kelly.

Chapter Twenty One

"The Empires of the future are the Empires of the mind."
WINSTON CHURCHILL

The season started with the loss of a number of players, who had come to the end of their contracts, and to save money not resigned by the club for the coming season.

Steve Elliot although the previous season played in every league and cup game and was the leading goal scorer, transferred to Luton. Pete "Leo" Sayer was a really smashing lad, who seemed to spend his evenings at Tiggis in Preston (an Italian restaurant) consuming plenty of garlic. I used to ban Leo from eating at Tiggis if he was injured, as the smell of garlic seemed to ooze from his pores. He transferred to Chester. Paul Lodge went to join Bolton, local lad Mark Walsh transferred to Exeter, Joe Hinnigan to Gillingham and a couple of the young pros David Bleasdale to Cork City. With Stuart Cameron, and Telfer not retained

With no money for really entering the transfer market, Kel managed to pick up a number of free transfers, some at the beginning of the season others as the season progressed..

Our own family excitement was the birth of our daughter Morgana in the September. I also had taken on the role of Honorary Editor of the Medical Society that I belonged to; this brought Brian Taylor onto the scene as we used his printing firm to produce the magazine. Little did I know at the time that things within my marriage would start to get sour, mainly due to my link as Hon. Editor.

Results at North End were again spasmodic, as we just couldn't seem to get a good run. David Johnson, the former Everton and England player, was brought in, plus a young local lad Nigel Greenwood, Simon Gibson, Jeff Whelands was brought in as loan keeper, due to Peter Litchfield leaving. The keeper role would be taken on later by young Glen Campbell (the son of director Barney Campbell). Then with the addition Terry Gray, these additions only temporarily lifted things.

Then I suffered sledge hammer blow to myself and to the finances of home life. With a young daughter, Jane had returned to work on a part time basis as Community Occupational Therapist.

North End said that they could no longer afford to pay me and they would rely on the aged Kit man Harry Hubbick.

I met up with Kel and said that I would still fit the players in for treatment on an ad-hoc basis, but they would have to fit into my appointment schedule. I had a phone call from Kel a couple of weeks later asking me to pop into the ground to see him; what a lovely surprise awaited me. The players and staff had bought me a cut glass decanter and glasses as a leaving present and to show their gratitude. These are still in my glass cabinet and have airings on special occasions only, as they mean so much to me.

Two weeks later Kel resigned from his position as manager and Tommy Booth was installed as caretaker manager.

Now I was only in contact with the players on a appointment basis only, so contact with the club was lost, plus the revenue it brought. What would come along now?

One of the things that I didn't see coming was an affair with Pat a female therapist from Yorkshire! People say that affairs don't happen overnight, that there has to be a tendency for wandering first, but this was not the case, Jane and I had been very happy, especially now that Morgana was with us, but it did happen.

I also had made contact with the Leyland Health and Fitness Centre which was being managed by Dave Hewson and his colleague Martin, both graduates from Crewe and Alsager. This was brought about by Ann Osgerby, who was receiving treatment for the swimmers greatest nightmare, wear and tear of the shoulder joint. Ann was working part time at the Centre.

My overheads at the Lancaster Road Clinic were becoming an important issue, especially now with the loss of North End fees, plus my added expenditure of my Yorkshire trips! I had a good chat with Dave who was interested in me moving my clinic to the Fitness Centre, thus reducing my overheads and also giving the Fitness Centre a cutting edge over the surrounding Centres.

So the decision was made I worked out my lease at Lancaster Road, and moved my equipment etc. to Leyland.

Meanwhile at North End, even though results were still poor, Tommy had been appointed full time manager. To assist in helping him to change things around, he had appointed Brian Kidd as assistant manager.

Losses seem to be the main feature on the result sheet, but injuries seemed to be not helping. They had Graham Houston and Dale Rudge both out with dislocated shoulders, which didn't help matters.

The season seemed to end like a damp squid with North End finishing 23rd in the League and relegated to the 4th Division – once Proud Preston was now Pitiful Preston.

At least moving my practice to Leyland was turning out to be more successful than expected. Dave, the manager and Martin, his assistant were both excellent guys with a good professionalism and good sense of humour, whose thoughts on both health and fitness were very much on the same lines as my own.

This was evident with the Body Programme, a computerised fitness analysis system which was developed by them. It worked in well with the Sports Injury Clinic.

It was still long hours, with late evening appointments and my West Yorkshire attraction and trips, was putting a strain on my family life. On the up side, the social life surrounding football, which involved lots of drinking, especially after matches and early into the week were taken away from me, except when meeting up with Brian Taylor! It was always a laugh (well we thought so!) visiting them or should I say leaving them. Brian and I used to be in good flow, a fresh drink always seem to coincide with Jane wanting to go. The number of times that Jane has got into the car and be driving away without me, always slowing enough for me to get to the car, only for her to drive away again.

When Brian and I were both at Argyle, Wendy was expecting Peter, their first child. We invited them over for the evening and for fun covered our chairs and settee with polythene saying to Wendy that it was in case her waters broke! A couple of days later Peter was born. The day before

Morgana, our daughter was born, Brian and Wendy invited us over for the evening, and they did the same trick. It worked as in the early hrs of the next morning, Morgana was born. So now you know what to do.

With the lads at North End I had always had a good relationship, and I was good at my job, so respect was there, but as I said previously, the position of club physiotherapist although a management position, you were closer to the players than the rest of the staff and this was also socially.

Gary Buckley was a great lad, but he used to have problems keeping up drink wise. So many times after a game we would be getting a few pints down our throats and Gary never refused a drink, he equally would get them in, but if you looked behind him, his full glasses would gradually increase in number.

Good watering holes, used to be the Witheys, especially before they refurbished it, and the Black Bull.

The new season started at North End in the 4th Division. Would it mean a quick return to the 3rd or would the misfortunes of previous seasons continue? Only time would tell.

News came through to me that Barney Campbell had recruited physiotherapy services in the form of two ladies who were just commencing a Private Practice, and were willing to take on North End as well!

I was busy enough, still working with the Wigan Wasps, the FA. the Referees Association and also expanding the Fitness Analysis programme. I still wasn't happy with how things in the practice were heading, as no single aspect seemed to click, I was still being pulled all over the place. One of the aspects I would love to expand and concentrate on was the fitness analysis and lecturing. Something would happen, but what? Also the pull towards West Yorkshire was becoming stronger!

Meanwhile at home, Morgana was continuing to be a super child and loved company which Jane provided for her through a local St. Annes Mums and Toddlers group, and a music group for young babies and toddlers, also playing with friends children. Unbeknown to us at the time, the Mums and Toddlers group would play a significant part in the future of the Loze family.

At North End the misfortunes continued, although a number of free transfers had been brought in to halt the decline.

Arsenal to Armenia

Leaving the club are:-

Paul McGee, Paul had in fact been on loan to Burnley. This had been in dispute during the time of Gordon Lee, so for a short time Paul came back, but now things had finally been settled.

Willie Naughton to Walsall
Pete Litchfield to Bradford City
Mike Farrelly to Altrincham
Jon Kelly to Chester City
Glen Campbell to Southport
David Jones to Southport
Chris Hunter to Chorley
Pete Houghton to Chester City
Andy Murphy
Paul Wilkins to Barrow
Jeff Wealands loan period finished (Manchester Untd)

Brought in:-
Nigel Keen from Barrow
Wayne Foster from Bolton Wanderers
John Thomas from Lincoln City
Mick Martin from Rotherham
Brian Chippendale from Burnley
Vernon Allatt from Crewe Alexander
Bob McNeil from Lincoln City
Shaun Reid on loan from Rochdale
Robert Cooper loan from Leicester City
Phil Harrington loan from Blackpool
Danny Ibbotson no contract
Mel Tottoh no contract
Also from apprentices/youth:-
Mark Rodgers
Alan Kelly Jnr.
Andy Pilling
Nigel Jemson

In December Tommy resigned. Results hadn't been good, in fact out of 28 games played (both league and cup) it was won 7 drawn 6 lost 15. Injuries had been difficult, even local non league players had been temporarily drafted in to ease the situation. So Kiddo was placed in charge, this coincided with the resignation of the physiotherapists. In his first week Kiddo contacted me if I could spare a couple of hours a day to help him regarding looking after the injury backlog and continue with the club. I could have turned him down, but he and the club were in a bad enough position as it was, so I returned for a couple of hours each morning and would attend the home fixtures only.

In fact I was looking forward to working with Kiddo as he had an extremely successful playing career and this was being matched by his success in non league coaching/management. Would this partnership out last the previous partnerships – only time would tell?

The atmosphere hadn't really changed at the club, players were happy enough, but they were there to play football, no matter who for, or who with, so the actual players morale was good. The day to day banter amongst the players and also amongst the staff was good, but the overall atmosphere within the club itself was still there. North End wasn't a sleeping giant waiting re awakening, but more like the giant that had been mortally wounded and the hospital bulletin was critical.

Results weren't coming our way. Was it that some of the players weren't good enough even for the 4th Division – but this wasn't really my problem – but it all added to the atmosphere.

My time with Kiddo wasn't going to last long as after the next 12 games the results were:- Won 1, Drawn 3, Lost 8. It seemed that no matter what he tried just didn't work, even the gates were down to an average of 3,000. Then in March Kiddo resigned and Jon Clarke was appointed caretaker manager.

Clarkie hadn't been playing for a while due to an operation to his groin, so this was added pressure to him, but he grabbed hold of the challenge with both hands. We actually spent some time discussing North Ends future, plus what was happening on the pitch and what should be happening.

The players responded to his enthusiasm and we won the next 4 games. We now had young Alan Kelly in goal, who was not just following in his fathers footsteps, but also in his older brother's who was in goal for Newcastle Utd. What a family!

Young Alan as a young lad was always popping into the ground. His smile and laughter were very infectious and nothing ever seemed to bother him. He used to play with a local side, Fulwood Amateurs. In fact

Arsenal to Armenia

I think he virtually played in every position and goalkeeping seemed to be a million miles away. The people at Fulwood Amateurs were fabulous Alan Kelly Snr. was one of the founder members.

Meanwhile back with North End, we lost the next two games, and slipped back down to next to bottom. Could the remaining games have the right results to save North End from disappearing from the football league?

The season ended with North End finishing in 23rd place, escaping the bottom place, which was filled by Torquay Utd. Having to reapply for re-election was the final shame for this once Proud Preston. Celebrations were very muted, as I think the embarrassment was too great. But Clarkie had done a great job in keeping us up and I think personally that he reacted with great promise in having the position suddenly thrust upon him when we were actually dead and buried. He worked hard and had gained the respect of the players around him. Taking all this into account, he should have been offered the job full time but things are never predictable in life, let alone in the world of football.

Chapter Twenty Two

∽

"Hate the sin, love the sinner."
MAHATMA GANDHI

The off season saw Peter McCallion being busy moving thousands of tons of soil, prior to the laying down of the new plastic surface. A decision that was made by the directors, to make the ground more accessible for other sports and the community;(also easing the finances of the club!)

At home, Gavin my son, came to live with us in St. Annes. He had just finished his GCSE's and was studying for his A levels. He had shown an interest in sports especially cycling, and was naturally interested in the fitness analysis side of my practice. I introduced him to a small fitness clinic in St. Annes I had been asked by the owner, who had been struck down by an illness, to oversee the daily working of the clinic, so bringing Gavin in was helpful for both of us.

Also I had been asked through the DTI (Department of Trade and Industry) to do a series of talks on Stress and Exercise with the National Savings Group based in Glasgow, Durham, St. Annes and London. This I really enjoyed doing and obviously meeting different people, but the different aspects of my work were stretching me, notably long working hours, giving me less and less time at home.

Gavin was really enjoying the work at St. Annes, especially the fitness analysis aspect, so much so that he later attended Crewe and Alsager studying Sports Science. Part way through the course he realised that most of the other students had no real interest in sport, so he changed his course to that of Sports Psychology. This he completed and took a research and lecturing position at Edinburgh University. He is now working within the Sports Psychology and fitness field as an independent consultant.

Pre-season started at North End with the appointment of John McGrath, who had experience of management in the lower divisions with Port Vale and Chester. John had a very successful career as a player especially with Southampton. So with that experience he looked right for North End, also bringing in Walter Joyce and Les Chapman as coaches. Clarkie would continue as a player.

Players to leave:-
- Graham Houston to Burnley
- Geoff Twentyman to Bristol Rovers
- Mark Jones to Southport
- Dale Rudge to Djon (Norway)
- Terry Gray to Gooletown
- Mark Walsh to Exeter
- Simon Gibson to Rochdale
- Andy Pilling to Wigan
- John Platt to Stalybridge Celtic
- Ian Stevens to Stockport
- Nigel Keen to Enfield
- Wayne Foster to Hearts (Wayne actually appeared for Hearts in European Cup)
- Danny Ibbotson to Morecambe
- Mel Tottah to Accrington Stanley
- Mick Martin to Newcastle as coach.
- Brian Chippendale to Farsley Celtic
- Mark Rodgers to Stenhousemuir
- Shaun Reid returned from loan to Rochdale
- Robert Cooper returned from loan to Leicester
- Phil Harrington returned from loan to Blackpool

So with the new pitch laid, new players brought in with the added advantage of them knowing the new surface the new season looked promising.

Players brought in:-
    David Brown from Bury
    Peter Bulmer from Ryle
    Alex Jones from Oldham
    Sam Allardyce from Bolton Wanderers
    Oshor Wiliams from Port Vale
    Ronnie Hildersley from Rochdale
    Mike Bennett from Cambridge
    Steve Taylor from Rochdale
    Gary Swann from Hull
    Steve Saunders
    Steve Wilkes from Wigan
    David Miller from Tranmere
    Paul Williams Nuneaton
    Frank Worthington (late signing) from Nuneaton
    Peter Zelem from Wolverhampton
    Shane Beeby
    Paul Booth

On first meeting John McGrath, I was unsure if I could work with him, after all I had only stepped in to help Kiddo and North End out of a difficult position.

My first impression was confirmed just before the season commenced - this was my own personal feeling and nothing against John at all. (Who actually died in 1998) The final decision was made after a disagreement over a couple of issues. One was that I had experience of the injury problems brought about by artificial surfaces, and how in Vancouver we had overcome a number of the problems, but it was like talking to a brick wall. The other was that, John seemed to be a user of players to achieve what he wanted, so players tended to be like pawns. So I popped along to see Derek who was now Club Secretary, and informed him that I couldn't give my time to help out North End and gave my reason.

Arsenal to Armenia

The only time I have been back to North End since was for Brian Taylor's funeral.

Now at least I could concentrate on the private practice, although I would miss the day to day activity at the club. Would it be the last time working in football? Only time would tell.

Chapter Twenty Three

"Personally I'm always ready to learn, I do not always like being taught."
WINSTON CHURCHILL

Over the next couple of months it seemed strange not to have football on my mind – but it did give me again time to reflect on my future. The West Yorkshire attraction had become top priority and both my work and family life was suffering because of it.

A happening to Jane had caused me to build up an even greater barrier between us. The Mums and Toddlers group which Morgana and Jane were attending was in fact run by the local Baptist Church, which had caused a bit of hilarity on my part, by saying to Jane "Look out for the Bible bashing." She had made friends with a number of Mums, but in particular Liz with her son Richard (same age as Morgana) They were a super family, and some times we used to meet up with them and Liz's husband Dave.

Jane later started to attend the Church each Sunday, with Morgana. A particular Sunday she came back home with a beaming smile on her face. She said that the service had particularly touched her and she had become a Christian!

This was like the final act for me, Jane was now wide open to my anger, frustration and humiliation – so home life was pushed even further away by me.

Work did continue, linking up with a number of local sports club. A number of Rugby League players from Wigan were members of the Fitness Centre, and I was seeing a few of them regarding injury problems. The FA and Referees lecturing, plus the DTI work continued, but with no great financial rewards, but I did enjoy the work and meeting up with different people. The thing was I was still looking for the one thing that would give me the break through, and not seemingly having fingers in so many pies. Weeks and months seemed to be flying by, with nothing really happening.

Out of the blue it did happen but not in the way that I had ever expected or imagined happening to me. I had met up with a number of the families from the Mums and Toddlers group and a few of them attended St. Annes Baptist Church (where Jane and Morgana were going), but I couldn't seem to get close to the men as they weren't the type of person I was use to being with; they weren't real men!

One man in particular I did find it easy to be with and to talk to was Gus, who in fact was and still is an evangelist. No he didn't hit me over the head with the Bible – something I think that I had expected. Gus, his wife Wendy and children Jamie and Holly were and still are a lovely family.

On a particular Sunday Gus was preaching, he had just returned home from Poland, so I went with Jane, because it was Gus. Nothing in the service meant anything to me, in fact deep down I didn't want to be there!

During Gus's talk, which I must admit I wasn't actually listening to, my mind as telling me to get up and walk out, but my legs weren't listening to my brain. Suddenly I just broke down in tears, yes men do cry, although I can never ever remember crying before. Looking around me I could see members of Janes Mum and Toddler group and the Ladies Bible Study group that Jane had been attending. I later found out that they had been praying for me for the past year.

Did it change me, yes, I could see people differently I had more apathy for the people I met, also I realised my love for Jane. I had even caught hold of Janes hand, whilst I was crying, which was the first time I had done that over the past number of years.

Work continued, but life did seem different. Sport was still a big thing in my life and I wanted to continue working in the sporting world, the day to day activity within that world would still remain within me.

One day at work I received a phone call from Don MacKay who was manager of Blackburn Rovers asking me to come over and see him. Don had taken over as Manager after leaving Coventry City, he was a former goalkeeper for Forfar Athletic and then Dundee United.

Dennis Loze

I had been to the Rovers ground once before, a pre season game with North End, so it was good to have a good look around with a guided tour by Don.

Over a pot of tea in the club restaurant, we came down to real reason for me being there. Don wanted me to take over as Club Physiotherapist, on a full time contract. I was impressed that football still wanted me, the journey to Blackburn only added a few miles on to my existing journey to Leyland, Don also seemed to be a very genuine person. The stumbling block was finance, it seemed that all clubs were struggling financially, I didn't want a fortune, but the offer was far short of my minimum. The Chairman joined the meeting, and added that he would supply me with a car. Seeing that I already had one, this didn't make up the short fall. The previous person was unqualified so the wages were low, they wanted an experienced qualified person, but with no wage increase. Unfortunately I had to turn the offer down, even though I was very tempted with the job offer, but not the financial one. I must be learning, as before I would have jumped at the job offer, as money would take second place.

What would crop up now – I still wanted to be working with people, particularly a mans environment.

I also knew that my West Yorkshire trips would have to stop, this was hard as my affair was a very meaningful part of my life – but I knew now that it was wrong for me and the effect on both families was wrong. So I had to make the decision, which did come about.

A couple of days after the Blackburn offer I had another phone call – meeting up with men in a mans environment, real men. The call was from the Chaplain of Kirkham Prison. He wanted to meet with me as he wanted some Christian men to come and meet up with the inmates at Kirkham, and my name had been mentioned! He didn't want prison visitors, but people who would work alongside him. I knew that this wouldn't involve any finance, but I knew that this was right, meeting up and working with real men, men that society didn't want on the streets!

I remember that I had said that the church didn't have real men!

I must admit that I like a number of people who say "Lock them all up, make it hard for them, and throw away the key" how would I come to terms with these thoughts. This was taken care of on my very first visit. Kirkham prison is an open prison, with men serving shorter sentences, plus those who had served longer sentences at another prison, but were coming to the end of their sentences. It is situated on the main

Blackpool to Preston road, a road I had driven on everyday of the past number of years, and never really taken notice of it. It as a former RAF camp, with wooden huts and some main brick buildings, so it was just like some of the RAF camps I had been on.

On arrival to the Prison gate, and going through all the formal security checks, I was free to go and meet up with Jeff the Chaplain. Jeff was an Anglican Minister attached to the Prison Service, he had been working for them for a number of years. After a formal chat about what he required of me, and what you can and can't do, it was time to go and meet up with some of the men.

One of the many things that you do not do is to ask what they are in for? If they want to tell you they will – thus you haven't built up any prejudices. Also is to restrict the information you give them regarding your family, work or where you live – this is only to safe guard yourself.

Any prejudices I previously had went out of the window, these where men, just like me – they had done wrong – so had I – they had got caught – I hadn't. OK you may say that they have done things that are a lot worse than I had done – fair enough – but we had all done something wrong!

They were men, with lives, with families, some married with young children, a wife who has to cope with husbands being locked away, husbands who will only see their families on official visits, individuality taken away from them.

I could drive out of the gate and go home – they couldn't, would I swap? No! Would they swap? Yes!

Almost most of the men had some interest in sport – so we had a common interest. I started visiting on a Wednesday afternoon and again on a Friday evening, soon this would develop into 3-4 times a week, for a couple of hours at a time.

On one visit Jeff asked if Jane and I would like to spend an evening at his home in Lytham with his wife and son. It was during this evening that he said that the Prison Chaplaincy were crying out for people like me, it would mean going to Theological College and being ordained into the Anglican church. This was something that I hadn't considered, and would mean a lot of thought and prayer. The thought of wearing a dress and being called father, didn't really appeal to me, but……

During this time I had made a decision to end the West Yorkshire attachment, the visits had been dwindling, it was a hard decision but when made, to my amazement life was a lot easier.

I knew my life was going to change drastically, although I was still holding on to one of my biggest interest, sport. So the next opportunity to appear surprised me.

The owners of Leyland Health and fitness Centre were looking for a new manager as Dave had left to concentrate on the Body Programme. They asked me if I would help them regarding advertising, sorting out a short list and to be involved in the interviewing etc. When the applications came in, no one really jumped out, a few had experience of running the Gym floor, but not in overall management. It was after the first interview that one of the owners, who was part of the interview team, asked me if I could manage the centre for them. This was a shock but was something that I knew I could do, also the salary would help. So the practice was gradually run down including all my lecture contacts, so I could concentrate on the centre.

I had made the owners aware of the fact that I was considering Theological College but hadn't made a decision yet, this they agreed to.

We appointed a young man as Gym manger for the mens sessions, and promoted Rowenna who was a senior member of staff, for the ladies sessions. I would now be working more reqular hours, so giving me more time at home, and to do the prison visits, plus the salary, the first for a number of years.

Chapter Twenty Four

"In the end, we will remember not the words of our enemies, but the silence of our friends."
MARTIN LUTHER KING JNR.

Soon Jane and I came to a decision that the Anglican Church wasn't for me, but I would like to move into some form of Christian work – especially where adults, men in particular were concerned. I was talking to Gus and Wendy about what we felt was right regarding the Chaplaincy, and Gus asked if I had considered going to Capernwray Bible School as a student, which was non denominational. We had been to Capernwray for the family holiday weeks and enjoyed the setting, teaching and everything about it. Capernwray is set in north Lancashire, just north of Lancaster, near Carnforth (where the classic film "Brief Encounter" was filmed.) So I applied for a place in the following year. The salary that I was receiving would also cover the fees.

The work at the centre kept me busy, plus the prison work which was very rewarding, not just for the men but I was learning so much about myself. I was building up a good relationship with a number of them and when one of the lads was being discharged he made a speech. In it he gave me a great feeling as he was thanking a number of people who had helped him. Of me he said that he and the rest of his colleagues looked upon me as a fellow prisoner and that I was spending so much time there, he wondered what pad (cell) I was in!

Soon we were to receive the news regarding Jane and her cancer, which I wrote about in Chapter 1. She had found a lump in her right breast, which our local GP acted very quickly to indeed. Within days we had an appointment with the Oncologist at the Blackpool Victoria Hospital, who said he would take a biopsy and contact us, but not to worry! In a few days Jane had the phone call saying that the consultant wanted to see her the next day. This was the news I received from Jane when I got home.

When we saw him the next day the news wasn't what we wanted, or expected to hear. They arranged for Jane to have the lump removed completely and then to attend Christies in Manchester for radiotherapy treatment.

The Christies treatment would coincide with me being at Capernwary which is residential, but on contacting them they allowed for me to come home at weekends and I could catch up on aspects that I may miss.

So I could take Jane to Christies on Sunday evening and then pick her up on the following Friday evening, which would work out extremely well. Janes Mum came over from Derbyshire to look after Morgana, who now was at school in St. Annes.

The weekend would also give us time together and also to pop into Kirkham Prison on the Sunday before going on to Manchester. Even when Janes treatment finished Capernwray still allowed me home at weekends.

I honestly do not know how I would have coped with Janes illness - and I know to some of you it may sound like a cliché – but both Jane and I knew that without experiencing the love of Christ during that time and ever since, we would have gone under.

Whilst at Capernwray I had a desire to work with people with inner city problems, the focus kept pointing to Plymouth and the problem there. So I contacted Crossroads a Christian organisation who were involved in such work, in Devonport. Again nothing seemed to fit together, but the pull was definitely to the West Country. My father had died recently and left his house to my brother and myself and the house was only 20 miles from Plymouth. So we took the bull by the horns and I left Capernwary, put our house on the market and moved back down to Cornwall. Jane in the meantime had obtained a community post at Devonport, and me……what would be waiting?

Jane had been given the all clear from Christies, the quick action of our GP, and Blackpool Victoria Hospital, had been tremendous and a mention must be made of the expertise of Christies, had made things much easier for us to deal with.

Arsenal to Armenia

We had only been in Calstock a short period, when a person I knew who also was a shareholder of Plymouth Argyle told me that they were without a Physiotherapist and he had told Peter Shilton, who was manager at that time, that I had moved into the area.

I received a phone call from him and arranged a meeting. When I met up with him, we arranged that I would look after the injuries on a morning basis and I would also attend all games, just to help them out for a period in time. I had been there a week when I realised that being back in football wasn't for me, that I had done that, got the tee shirt and the video it was time to move on. So was it the end of football?

I still fancied inner city work, but still nothing seemed to open up for me, until on a particular Sunday realised that it is not only inner cities that have their problems but also towns and even villages. Our own village plus the surrounding ones had problems, where a number of young children from broken homes were having and causing problems, some other children who were having problems were not from broken homes, so I am not putting the blame purely into one court. Also a number of teenagers with the current "I'm bored, there's nothing to do." So Jane and I commenced a number of clubs, holiday clubs, after school clubs and a youth club. We were having approx 90% of the young ones attending.

We did encounter a lot of opposition to what we were doing simply because we were Christians, this was very hard to understand. We even had letters and articles in the local rag, warning parents to keep their children away from us.

We linked up with Operation Christmas Child, which indirectly help to show the people of our concern for young people.

Operation Christmas Child began on 10th October 1990, when Dave Cooke and his wife Jill, where watching a television broadcast about Romanian orphanages, from their home in Wrexham North Wales.

The Cookes asked this question: how can we help the real victims, the children, who live in these situations day after day? They realised they could offer something – the gift of love. Together, they filed a convoy of nine trucks with medical supplies, food, clothing and Christmas gifts for children, and drove to Romania. This marked the beginning of the world's largest children's Christmas programme.

Since that date, Operation Christmas Child have delivered gift filled shoe boxes to children in war torn countries, over 100 countries and over 50 million shoe boxes have brought a message of hope to those children.

The response to this work was great, and people who had become opposition to our work with the young even responded to Operation Christmas Child. We involved schools in the area, also Plymouth, local churches and organisation. We use to keep the boxes in our house prior to collection, we had boxes in the hall up the stairs our dining room used to so packed that we couldn't use it.

The work continue with the local children and youth clubs, plus starting a local church and the shoe boxes kept not just me but our family busy.

Then Jane found another lump in her right breast, not again!
After a biopsy at Derriford Hospital in Plymouth it was confirmed that the cancer had returned. It would now call for surgery in the removal of the breast, plus chemotherapy. This was as hard to take on board as the first time, but we had been through things before so it can be done again. The surgery was successful, fortunately the chemotherapy was going to be by tablet, so no hair loss, but with the normal effects of tiredness, sickness etc. Jane came through it so well, in fact local people could not believe what she had been through after she started back helping with the clubs.

Chapter Twenty Five

"It is not enough that we do our best, sometimes we have to do what is required."
WINSTON CHURCHILL

Jane's remarkable attitude towards her problems are and still do astound not just other people but me, she still smiles through it, but some people do not seem to appreciate what is going on behind that smile.

I remember a number of years later. Jane was having chemotherapy at Derriford Hospital and I was in the waiting area. A man came out from the treatment area, and a couple went up to him and said how well he was looking, to which his answer "How did you expect me to look?" That comment summed things up so much regarding cancer. People just don't know how to react around a person who has cancer. Either they don't know what to say or what it is. I still can't understand them.

Jane's recovery was excellent, which allowed her to go back to work at Devonport and also for our work to continue.

A few months later I was to receive a surprising request from Dave Cooke. A call which would in time change our lives. Operation Christmas Child was going to take a group of North Lancashire footballers and coaches to Armenia to set up coaching and playing sessions amongst the refugees, concentrating on children. They required someone to cover the medical aspect of the sessions. They were going for 10 days and leaving in 2 weeks time! Naturally I jumped at the opportunity but must admit that after putting the phone down the first thing I did was to find out where Armenia was!

I was to meet up with the rest of the squad at Manchester airport prior to boarding Armenian Airlines (at that time they were the only airline flying into the country) to Yerevan airport. Flying with Armenian Airlines was something that you had to experience before you could even start to understand!

As we finally circled over Yerevan prior to landing it was pitch black, not a light could be seen no street lights or even a house light. Armenia was still reeling from the effects of the fall of communism and also from the ongoing war with Azerbaijan over Nagorno Karabagh. Electricity was restricted or in some areas none existent, this went for water also.

Over the next 10 days we were to visit orphanages, refugee camps and the destroyed towns from the 1988 earthquake – with thousands of people living in temporary shelters/shacks/water containers. So much poverty and heartache – but we found the Armenian people to be proud and full of hospitality – being offered anything that they had or what they didn't have or couldn't afford.

During that 3rd day we were in the area of Zatoun on the outskirts of Yerevan. We had been there the day before to be with some refugee children. Most of the families lived in a deserted ex prison with no electricity, no water, no toilets in fact nothing. This particular day we had been working with the children in the morning and challenged to a game by the men for the afternoon. The pitch was what use to be a park, but now was like a bomb site. It was during the game that I heard a voice saying to me "Dennis you are going to come back here" I looked around the only ones near me were some of the children from the morning session, and I knew that they didn't know any English.

The next number of days flashed by, seeing the same situation wherever we went. So much to be done, so much help needed, but what could I do?

On arrival back home I just couldn't get what I had seen and heard out of my mind, especially the voice that spoke to me. Jane and I spent hours talking and praying about it.

A number of weeks later I contacted Dave Cooke to have a chat to him about Armenia. He said that he was in fact returning to Armenia in a couple of months to make arrangements for delivery of Christmas Shoeboxes etc., he said that why not come over with him and get some confirmation one way or another regarding going back to Armenia.

During the next couple of months we were extremely busy preparing for the summer holiday club, writing plays and scripts, painting scenery etc, but also trying to arrange finance for my trip and visa etc, so my mind was well and truly occupied.

Eventually the time came to face Armenian Airlines again, what would fall off this time – no I am not joking!

On arrival I spent a lot of time accompanying Dave on his visits to various Ministries etc as well as meeting up with the representatives of the Armenian Football Federation, they were very interested in using my qualifications and experience – could this be an opening – or was it just the Armenian culture.

One of the people I met was the young Mayor of Spitak which had been the epicenter of the 1988 earthquake and was totally destroyed. We had been there with the football camps, which I remember so much. The original football field had been used as a mortuary area, which since had been completely dug up, trying to erase the thought of what it represented. This mayor was in the process of clearing an area for a couple of football pitches, in fact he had people still clearing the area whilst we were working with the children. I remember so much setting up 5 aside post on a the dust packed soil, and looking up a seeing hordes of young children shouting and running down the hill side towards us, most with no shoes on, those who did have shoes, were hand me downs and too big for them. We had so many children that we couldn't carryout what we wanted to do, I remember having a group of about 20 children, and we just played silly children games.

This young Mayor was really trying to get the town rebuilt, not just the houses etc. but the people also. He had such a unique way of dealing with people. I was to experience this on my second visit. We were walking through a park area when we saw a young boy begging. He went up to him and said "You must come from one of the surrounding villages, but remember that we are all poor here but we don't beg. You are welcome here anytime, but please do not beg."

This young Mayor was to be involved in a very mysterious fatal car accident in December 1999.

It was a couple of afternoons later and we were at the Ministry of Social Welfare that I had confirmation of me coming back to Armenia. Whilst we were waiting for Dave to see the Minister, we were shown into a small office. I noticed that on one of the walls was a painting of a cross with the sun setting behind it. It seemed strange seeing that in a still very authoritarian government building.

Again I heard the same voice saying "Yes you are coming back, but as a family."

So on returning home, we had so much to talk about and do.

We didn't take long before we both said yes to going, so much to arrange such as:-

- How long are we going for
- How can we finance the trip
- How about education for Morgana
- How about accommodation

These were just 4 items on an ever growing list.

Finally things were in place Jane had secured a 6 month unpaid sabbatical. We used all our savings which included Morgana's education fund and gifts from family and friends. Notre Dame school were very supportive of Morgana being absent for a six month period – they also said the education she would get from seeing the workings within what had become a third world country would outweigh missing formal education. Our accommodation was hopefully being found by an Armenian church Pastor.

Jane's leave would run from January until July, so we would depart late January, we would soon find out that this time of the year wasn't a wise choice!

This would be Morgana's 1st experience of flying. She used to ask why it was that all her friends were going abroad for their holidays and they were flying, why not us? Yes, but not on Armenian Airlines!

After securing the house for the 6 months we were soon on the bus from Plymouth to Heathrow and then on to Yerevan.

We were to arrive in the early hours of the morning to a very snow bound airport. On entering the building it must have been as cold inside as outside. The building was very austere all the officials wrapped up in their military uniforms or in the standard long black coats, giving off a very unfriendly welcome. As we were waiting for our bags to arrive, which was nearly an hour, a little bit of panic started to set in. The Pastor who was arranging our accommodation was also picking us up, but as of yet no sign of him.

Eventually our bags arrived and so did our transport, I don't think I have been so pleased to see a person. The thoughts of what had I done to my family was going through my mind.

Then through customs, although we had to fill in forms on the plane regarding how much money were we taking in, if we had watches and what value, same for rings etc? This was repeated again, then after seeing an Armenian couple in front of us being given a rough time, we were allowed through. Then through to the arrivals entrance, where it was running the gauntlet of so many people grabbing hold of your bags and trolleys. This was so that they could take your bags to your car and receive payment. Unemployment was so high in Armenia, therefore people were desperate for money. As we stepped outside, the temperature was around -10°, colder than inside, but only just. We were pleased to climb into a warm Volga car.

Although we were still very tired you couldn't help but notice and feel the number of large potholes in the road plus the lack of lighting. – What was going through Morgana's mind – we would find out in a few days time!

We eventually came to a halt, looking through the blackness I could make out the shape of a typical soviet highrise building, not a light in sight. Fortunately, the driver had a torch and we entered the building. As the torch light flashed around you could see large icicles hanging from the roof, this building was colder than outside. The walls above the electricity boxes were blackened obviously by fire, the number of loose wires coming from these boxes gave you the reason. We were later to find out that these were called "left lines", illegal wiring to by pass the boxes so that people could get free electricity, but with obvious consequences "fires." We were later to see these left lines every where in all sorts of buildings, even Government ones.

To our surprise and fear, the lift was working! It was no larger than a coffin! We slowly progressed up to the 5th floor. I was so pleased to get out of the box, stairs for me next time. - Or would it be after I had seen the state of them the next day?

We were taken to a door which was opened by two girls. To our surprise we were to be sharing the flat with them.

They had a meal for us, but all we wanted to do was to get some sleep. The three of us were in one bedroom, which again was so cold, good job we had our Arctic sleeping bags with us. Not many clothes were taken off and we climbed into our bags. So much was going through my mind but sleep came quickly.

The next morning we awoke to find that the girls had gone to work. They both worked at the Pastors church. It gave us time to look around and find what was what. The flat had only one electric portable heater, no hot water, a gas cooker straight from the Ark. It used bottle gas and the bottle was next to the cooker! One ring and the oven worked, but we were later to be introduced to the "cooking stool".

Morgana took some convincing to climb out of bed, - don't blame her I was freezing.

We busied ourselves unpacking and Jane tried to find some food for us to eat. We went outside to see if we could see any shops, even though we knew nothing of the language. All I had learnt to say was hello, goodbye and count to 10. This is when we would see the state of the stairs, talk of concrete cancer, great chunks of the treads were missing and icicles and ice everywhere, on the landings the glass in the windows was missing so the cold winds were having a field day. So a toss up stairs or the coffin lift?

Our first day was an education but not really what we had hoped for. The girls didn't get in until 9 pm. Their working day was from 8am to 9pm! The girls got some food together and we all tucked in. One of the girls was Yerevik an Armenian girl who spoke no English, she was a very kind and pleasant natured girl, the second Monja a German girl who had come to Armenia for the same reason as we had. She spoke excellent English and was becoming very fluent in Armenian.

Chapter Twenty Six

∞

"We set sail on this new sea because there is knowledge to be gained."
J.F. KENNEDY

The next day we set out to brave the weather, although it was colder in than out. we eventually found a small street market, where bits and pieces were for sale, but regarding food, not a lot. Potatoes and onions seemed to be the most popular, and some carrots were spotted, then a street butcher. I will use the term butcher very loosely as he had some meat, a big wood axe, and a lump of wood (chopping block). We got some meat, to which we were very honoured as he put a piece of cardboard over the wood before cutting! We then had to find our way back again. On our way back we found a tin shop (shop made of galvanised iron) which sold bread. We were to find out that bread was the staple diet of the Armenians, but the bread would go stale after 24hrs, so it was a daily trip.

Night time came and the wild dogs woke up. Near to the flat was a large piece of waste land, where the dogs lived in packs. They slept during the day and hunted for waste food at night, this would disturb other dogs, hence good old howling and barking, so sleep was hard to come by.

It would soon be time to get our visas updated as 10 days was the max. I could get from England.

We had managed to get details of the location of the Ministry responsible, so off we walked, through the city and eventually walked into the building. A very cold building which seemed to consist of long corridors with brown doors leading off. To help us, none of the doors had numbers or signs, and what seemed like hundreds of people were just waiting, so we waited. Some uniformed officials would suddenly appear, unlock a door, and people would just pour in, then after a few moments the official would empty the office, lock the door and disappear. This seemed to happen to every brown doorway. I noticed a group of people standing outside one door and they had passports clutched in their hands. So we joined, passports in hands, only ours seemed to be UK, so we waited. Eventually a official arrived opened up, and we were ready, in we went with the mob and found ourselves about 5th in the queue, not bad for beginners, we were learning. Armenians do not queue, well they do but the queue does not signify the order you are to be seen, or when you arrived, just push.

Our turn, we managed to get over what we wanted, which really shouldn't have been anything else as that is what this office did, Visas, but all things are hard, within ministries or should I say they make it hard. Forms were signed and the passports put in the top drawer of the desk and we got told 3 days. We were to find out that everything is three days, which doesn't mean three days. I was given an amount to pay, but you didn't pay here you had to go to another building to pay. We got given a name of the building, another Ministry, but not where it was. So more walking, hunting, showing people the slip of paper with the ministry name on it. We got various directions, not all the same way, what we did get was the Armenian mannerism of frustration, which is the right index finger pointed into the air, and the wrist twisted in the air in an anti clockwise direction, and a click of the tongue which means No. We eventually got to this building which was the main Ministry of Internal Affairs, later we found out nick named Ministry of Toe Nail extraction, also that from the cells in the basement you could see Siberia (in other words, torture and then being sent to Siberia).

I eventually found a person who could speak English who took me inside, much to Jane and Morgana's dismay, but still failed to find the right office, we were then directed down the road to what looked like a social club for the ministry and paid money into a cupboard got a receipt, and back to the other Ministry to hand in the receipt, and go back in 3 days. The magical 3 days arrived and off again, queuing, waiting, standing and eventually got into the same office, same person, who went into the same top drawer, same desk, our passports, same paperwork. He then ushered us all outside the door, locked it and disappeared up the corridor with our passports. Approx 20 mins later returned, unlocked the door and I shouldered myself into the front of the queue, our passports handed over to us, visas inside. Hooray!

This would have to be repeated in 3 months time, but at least we knew the system!

Arsenal to Armenia

Over the days and weeks, we got to know Yerevan very well indeed as we walked everywhere, also getting used to the weather, holes in the pavements and roads, where we could buy various bits of food, but you had to act quickly, if you saw something for sale buy it as it wouldn't be there tomorrow may return in a month or so or never. Milk was a problem, even powdered milk, but again we found a shop that had some Danish Powdered milk. This lasted for about a month and then disappeared, so it was hunting again.

Our "potato man" got used to seeing us, and Jane had now got used to prices and Armenian numbers. He was amazed one day when he told us the price of 5 kilos of potatoes and Jane said No, and stated the price that she could get them for , so he charged us that price. From then on he called her "Teacher".

We were soon to find out what Morgana thought of Armenia. We had now been there 3 weeks and had met a number of Armenian families, who had been introduced to us by Monia and Arevik, who then had asked us to their homes, so we had a good picture now of Armenia and the situation they were in. Back to Morgana who said that if the Health and Safety Department were to visit Armenia, they would close the whole country down. She also wondered if "Watchdog" could do anything!

One of the ways Jane use to cook was the "cooking stool". This was a metal stool on four legs which stood about 1ft high, if you imagine an electric fire with the coiled wires, the top of the stool was like that, it was then plugged in and the wires would heat up and you could cook, plus get warmth, when the electric was working. A similar piece of equipment was used to heat the water, a coil of wire around a piece of wood at the end of the flex, which was dropped into the water and plugged in, the coil would get hot and heat your water. Perhaps Morgana was right.

As I said we were gradually meeting people but nothing seem to be happening regarding what we were meant to be doing with our time in Armenia. The pastor of the church was pushing us towards working for him in the church, but both Jane and I knew that this was not in the right direction.

We started to make friends with a smashing American lady Nazane whose grandfather was Armenian. She was working with the International Red Cross. One day she asked us if we would like to accompany her and a few of her friends who used to put some money in a kitty and buy some food for an orphanage. Each Saturday morning they used to take the food to this orphanage and feed the kids, i.e. watch them eat. So the following Saturday we piled into her 4 wheeler and headed out of town, past a military base, a large grave yard, the local refuge dump and onto the orphanage come school.

Eventually we arrived at an isolated building, surrounded by a high wall, 2 large rusting doors, gradually opened by an elderly man draped in a large overcoat who held them open and in we drove. Little did we know that this would be the first of many visits, which would not only change our lives or the children in this orphanage but have an effect upon thousands of children in the whole of Armenia!

As we entered the building, the coldness just hit you. It wasn't just the temperature that was cold, the whole building was so severe and bare and so quiet, were there any children?
We walked down along stone corridor and through double doors into a large room with long tables and benches, sat on these benches were children aged from 7 years to mid/late teens approx a 150 in total. Everything was so quiet, not a whisper, walking between the tables were 4-5 adults wrapped up against the cold who seemed to be warders or even prison guards, again no smiles.

We had brought peroskies, which were meat or potatoes in a pastry, a typical Armenian food, apples and what fruit we could find.
The children ate so fast and all the crumbs were not missed, but again in total silence as the "guards" looked on. Soon the food was eaten and some of the older ones started to sweep the floors and clean the tables. I couldn't stand still any longer, so I just sat amongst the little ones, who seemed amazed that an adult was sitting amongst them, then it was time to get them to laugh, but it seemed as soon as laughter started the "guards" gave the look of disapproval to the children. What an atmosphere. Soon it was time to leave.

That first visit was to be the topic of our family conversation for the next week until it was time for the following Saturday visit.

Jane spent most of the following week trying to arrange meetings at the Ministry of Social Welfare, and I made contact with the Armenian Football Federation to see what would happen there, so at least something was happening.

Arsenal to Armenia

Regarding Morgana, she had visited the orphanage with us, and had lots of questions to be answered. Also we were aware that she needed company of her age. We located an International School which was in walking distance of our flat, worth a try. So we arranged a visit. They were mostly American children, with Danish, Georgian, Armenian American, Swiss and English making up the remainder. The school Director and his wife were American, who had started up the school a few years earlier. Unfortunately it was fee paying, and I mean high fees, so this was completely out of our league, but the director and his wife, said that Morgana could spend lunch time there, so mixing with other children of her age and younger. This gave such a lifeline to us and of course her. Over a period of time, the lunch time included PE and games and music, in the longer term led to even more involvement, but that is in the future.

At first the Social Welfare seemed to be opening to something, but again we were to find out that the Armenian way was never to say no right away, especially where foreigners are involved as it may mean a lot of money. After a few weeks Jane realised that this was the case, as they wanted her to head up a fund raising format, which we knew was not what we had come here for.

My contact with the Football Federation seemed to be the same. They wanted me to run a series of lectures for local club doctors etc. on sports injuries etc. This I was willing to do, but I wanted hands on work also. Nothing seemed to be happening. I couldn't seem to nail the president and secretary down to any specific dates or times. Again, the same, keep them waiting!

We also visited the children's Rehabilitation Centre, which was situated outside of Yerevan towards the airport, which we found out was called Zvartnots. The rehab centre was well run, a lot of American money had been poured into it, a legacy of the earthquake. Jane and I were to make a number of visits, but that was all it seemed to be, foreigners visiting. This period was so frustrating!

Soon I was contacted by the Football Federation who wanted to see me regarding the lectures. At last something. I met the president and had a good talk with him and a time was arranged. He had to be away at a FIFA (International Football Association) meeting for 1 week and then we could get it all organized. So something was to happen or was it?

Yes something did happen, the Football Federation's President was dismissed by the Government for misuse of funds, or was it that some other's palms were not greased? So, back to square one. I had met Gevorg who worked for the Federation as Manager/overseer of the youth set up. I can't remember the full title. We hit it off well. He spoke very good English and had previously been a teacher and then with of the Armenian Customs. He lived in Yerevan with his wife and two boys. He asked me if I could help him out with the National under 18's who were having trials before selection of the National team. I said that I would, as nothing else seemed to be happening.

We had now been in Armenia for 5 weeks, and were getting to know the city of Yerevan well, as we walked everywhere. we hadn't ventured on to any other form of transport yet and also we knew where things were and wouldn't by transport. The weather was starting to warm up, temperatures in the low single figures at least it was + and not - . The main form of transport were the amazing minibuses which seemed to go everywhere. For the vast majority, it was amazing that they moved at all. What MOT? Petrol was a problem in the country. The main distribution was mafia controlled, but you would see men sitting at the kerb side with a bucket and a few jars full of petrol for sale. It wasn't pure petrol, but watered down so he would have more to sell. The results were all vehicles having black exhaust which made your eyes water, plus back firing which nearly had you diving for cover. I have seen a man (at this stage you never ever saw a female driving a car, or sitting in the front, a male country) pull up in his Lada car and buy a jam jar full of petrol.

I mentioned Lada as it seemed that 90% of the cars were Lada cars or 4x4 Lada Niva. The other 10% either, Mercedes or BMW - all new ones. Guess where the money was? Jane got so intriqued with the Lada that she has a photo album full of Ladas. These cars would be used for everything and anything.

It would be nothing to see a man driving a Lada, which was absolutely packed, and I mean packed to the roof with either cabbages or melons to sell. One day we saw a Lada pull up outside our flat. The driver got out and started shouting his sales pitch, then open his boot. Inside was a block of wood, an axe and yes, a load of unprotected meat, and then sales would start.

Our continued weekly trip to the orphanage, which was called Nubarashen 11.(Nubarashen was the name of the area, and 11 was just the number of the orphanage/school.) We were getting so close to the children and you could tell that Saturday was the highlight of their week, not just because of different food, but having someone who had fun with them and cared for them. Jane and I were starting to get emotionally attached to all of them and abhorred the conditions they were in, and also their daily routine. We used to spend hours talking and praying about the situation. If only we could get there more often, spend more time with them and show them fun and love, but we had no transport and we didn't know the language, just two small problems.

The Football Federation had started their trials, and were based in a small hotel off Republic Square, I used to go to the hotel twice a day and look at the lads who had recent or long term injuries. Most of them were 18/19 years of age, but some of the chronic injuries I saw, I would expect to find in a real seasoned professional footballer who has come to the end of his career. There was little or no knowledge of treatment of sports injuries, so minor injuries would soon become long term or chronic problems. As we got to know each other they used to call me Doctor Dennis. We were due to play our first International game versus neighbouring Georgia at home, then an inter - club knock out competition of 20 mins each way was to be held a number of miles away from the city in an area called Amovere. Then, two weeks later, as part of the under 18s European Cup, for games against France and then Portugal.

These trips would be an experience, but deep down all I wanted to do was to be at Nuberashen 11!

Dennis Loze

Family Loze a Sunday evening break via Sarah Sunset Tours. Armenia

Jane (in the pink) taking some children from Nubarashen 11, for a walk.

Little Armen showing how it is done.

Dennis Loze

*Introducing team work activity at Nubarashen 11.
In the background, a football match on the pitch we made.*

Introductions to finger painting at Nubarashen 11

At Gerhard Church (Armenia)

Chapter Twenty Seven

"All great things are simple, and many can be expressed in single words: Freedom, Justice, Honour, Duty, Mercy and Hope."
WINSTON CHURCHILL

Although for the next couple of weeks I would be in France and Portugal, but the real action would be happening back in Armenia.

Morgana had started to make some good friends at the International School, she was now attending for lunch time, Music PE and Art. The school directors were doing us very proud. Two of the families were the Smiths from America and the Wesths from Denmark. These two families would also become very good friends of ours also. Morgana was really showing the girls that not just boys could play football etc, and threw herself in all activities that the school put on. It was through her friendship that she found out that a small Sunday Christian meeting was held in the school.

The first meeting that Jane and Morgana went to would open up the doors to our future in Armenia, and be an answer to all our prayers and heartaches.

After the meeting Jane was introduced to the Drummond Smiths. Peter was Country Director of Mission East, a Danish aid Organisation, and Jikke his wife was Project Co-ordinator. The conversation came to Nubarashen 11 and our concerns over the children. To Janes amazement, they both were aware of the problems there. In fact they were to start a large refurbishment programme of the sanitary facilities. The next part of the conversation was to amaze even more. If we could come up with a programme for the children Mission East would provide transport, as they were going up there anyway and also a translator for the number of hours we were going to be there!

Arsenal to Armenia

This was the news that met me on returning from Portugal.

My trip to France and Portugal was interesting, and result wise not too bad, although the France trip was not what I was led to believe, but in fact an International knock out between under 21's of France, Poland, Jamaica, Italy, Russia and Morocco. We didn't do too badly playing 4 games winning 1, drawing 1 and loosing 2.

We had flown from Yerevan to Moscow and then Aeroflot from Moscow to Paris, then by train to St. Jean de Luz for the tournament. I had told the Football Federation that I would not need a visa etc. for Europe but as we were staying overnight in Moscow would require a visa for that part of the journey and also for the return journey, added to that on leaving Armenia, I would require a new one on my return to Armenia. The answer "No problem," watch this space.

The first sign of problems was at Moscow International Airport my passport was thoroughly examined stamped and let through, but then later the same person accompanied by a second person located me and went through the same procedure, but took no action.

After the France tournament it was back to a train journey through Spain and on to Lisbon, then by bus to Porto. We were going to be here for a couple of days before the game and then travel back the day after the game. So it was time for Gevorg and myself to try and get my visa sorted. We located the Russian Embassy and managed to fill in the necessary forms, but had to go into Lisbon itself to get the photographs taken. Job done, then back to the Embassy we had made an appointment to see the member of staff who would issue the visa. When we got back there we seem to be waiting for hours, when we were informed that it was a nice day and he had gone fishing! Then he was on leave for a number of days (Sounds familiar?), so we would have to brave it out and risk me not getting back into Armenia.

Our game against Portugal was a good game. We managed to hold them for a period of time but came out losers 3-1 with the second leg at home in a couple of weeks, a hard task but at least we had an away goal.

It was back on the train to Paris, where organisation failed. The plane we were to fly into Moscow had developed problems so we would be put up in a hotel until an alternative flight could be arranged. Gevorg and I took the opportunity to try the Russian Embassy in Paris. Success, one entry visa to Russia. We also had a couple of hours to see the Eiffel Tower and the Arc de Triumph, with the compulsory photos. Armenians when they take photographs of anything, they have got to be in the photograph. Possibly proof that it is their photo.

We got a Swiss Airlines flight to Moscow and I was legal this time but still had the Armenian entry to get through. This is where Gevorgs previous employment would come into action. As it happened I just walked through where the rest did their normal Armenian thing of not queuing so I wasn't seen.

Customs, where sometimes you are asked for your passport again, was easy as one of Gevorgs mates was on duty, so I could get home.

The weather was getting warmer but still a really cold wind. This I would experience the next day, Jane had yet again gone to the Ministry of Social Welfare and Morgana and I were sat in the spartan lounge. We were both sat at a table writing and warming ourselves over a heater that Nazine had loaned us, when the wind picked up and found many of the holes and gaps in the window frames etc. and blew the paperwork etc off the table. It was time to look for another flat.

The Ministry visit came to nothing, so we sat down and started putting together a programme and proposal to Mission East. Peter and Jikke had invited us all over for a meal and then we could discuss the project. On meeting both of them you could tell that we were to become friends and possibly future work colleges. We had a great evening, Morgana thought they were something special, so alright there too.

The proposal was accepted by Peter so the next thing was to meet up with the Director of Nubarashen 11 and get his approval, but seeing of the work that Mission East were going to do there and had already done we couldn't see him having any objections.

We were now 3 months into our 6 months, and we were discussing extending that by another 6 months, if we could get the adequate funds together. Our meeting with the Director went very well, both Peter and Jikke came along, and the proposal was accepted. We would go 3 afternoons a week, and work with a different age group per afternoon session. We also found out more about Nubarashen, which was technically an "orphanage" for children with "mental problems." The daily routine was education in the morning which included Armenian, Maths, History, PE, and Crafts, classes taken by teachers, the afternoon was for "homework" supervised by "educators". With meal times etc fitted in at the usual times. We would come during the "educators" sessions and have as much time as we liked, which would be 2.00pm – 5.00pm. Monday, Wednesday and Friday, this fitting in with Jikkes trips to supervise her refurbishment project.

We hadn't any equipment, but we decided to use recycled materials and to make all the necessary equipment, so that the staff could see that you didn't have to have specialised expensive equipment, which would suddenly develop legs and disappear any way!

Mission East also provide us with a translator, Armine, who would be with us for the 3 afternoons. Armine was a student at the University, so the money would come in useful for her.

For the first couple of sessions we spent most of the time seeing what actually went on during the afternoons. This was easily assessed as the result was nothing at all. The young ones would be put together in one room, with an older "student" over-seeing them. Not a noise would be heard, with a flickering black and white TV on a Russian station, and the children sat on the floor, for hours at a time. Any noise was met with a smack or a hit (obviously the older students had learnt by experience). It was nothing to notice a broken leg of a chair to be within easy reach! Whilst the "educators" sat in another room talking and drinking coffee. There was only one educator, who had a lovely attitude towards the children, the others could not be bothered.

We also spent time looking at the facilities available. There was a gym, or should I say years before there was a gym, now it was a cold room, with cracks in the walls and floors, with ancient gymnastic equipment. A room which hadn't been used for years. So we would have to use the long corridors when inside. Outside wasn't much better, with everything that used to work didn't any longer, and was beyond repair. The children were not encouraged to go outside, as it would take supervision. Most of the land had fruit trees, some tomatoes etc at the bottom of the garden a family of pigs. All of these provided by Mission East. Did the children benefit from any of these? Only time would tell.

At home, we spent time preparing sessions and the equipment for them. Also we had been informed of a flat for rent. We had a look at it and decided to go for it. With the hotter weather coming, it had a fridge, something Jane had been praying for. Mission East gave us a hand moving, plus Gevorg, so the move was done quickly and we at last had our own space.

Dennis Loze

It was only a couple of stops on the Metro, which was something we had now got familiar with. It was only one line from the north of Yerevan to the south and only cost 10 drams (about 2 pence). So Morgana could go by metro, or walk, most of the times to start with we use to go with her.

We settled into the flat, although it didn't have hot water or a working cooker, but Jane had now got used to the cooking stool and we had got confident with the unconventional water heating tool.

We were a lot more settled now especially being in a place of our own, and the rent was cheaper even though it was superior to our previous one. At weekends there was a market just outside our door and soon people began to recognise us and we made some good friends. Also our circle of friends was growing since we started to attend the Sunday meeting at the International School.

Nubarashen 11 was dominant in our lives, as we slowly started to develop our programme. The children responded so much to the games and activities we were teaching them. They were now learning how to play, laugh and show affection. We soon started to realise that the children were so different away from their minders. Also that their different problems or disabilities were not being addressed either medically or educationally. The attitude of the staff seemed to be that what they were doing was correct, and if the children do not benefit from it, it is their fault. We were also realising that we had approx. 2 months of our 6 months left. Were we to stay longer? So many questions, but we already knew the answer.

The weather had already started to get hot. Everyday was up in the 40's, so we had to vary our programme to suit the childrens exposure to the heat, space was at a premium. We used corridors, but not the classrooms as we wanted to get them away from their normal environment. An area which we decided to work on was infact outside, a flattened area, but very overgrown by weeds which were like cactus plants, so we got stuck in. It took a number of weeks to clear, mainly due to the heat, but eventually we had an area cleared of approx. 20 by 15 metres. Three of the older children Anna, Yelana and young Suren worked hard with us. It served as a true multi purpose area, which Suren could now play his beloved game of football. When we used to arrive at the gate in the Mission East Niva, our driver Sam, used to be very hesitant as most of the older children, on hear the car and come rushing to meet us, just as he was trying to drive in. His car was his pride and joy, so to let grubby hands and faces near his paintwork would be a disaster. Also Sam had been brought up under the Soviet belief that children with any form of disability were not really human, and also that you could catch so many different diseases from them. Sam was so worried about us as we used to greet the children with big hugs and kisses, that we might catch something. It was amazing to see in the future how he would slowly change, to think of the children as real children.

During the next couple of weeks we sat down with Peter and Jikke to discuss the future. They and Mission East were so pleased with the work that we were carrying out at Nubarashen 11, but they couldn't promise any increase in funding, and could only see them continuing to provide a translator and transport as before. We knew already that our answer was to be that we would be returning to England at he end of the 6 months, to have a break, but then returning to Armenia in the August for a further 6 months. How would we fund it? Our top priority was that we would be continuing the work in Armenia.

Chapter Twenty Eight

∽

"If a free society cannot help the many who are poor, it cannot save the few who are rich."
J.F KENNEDY

The next number of weeks just seemed to fly by. One of our new friends was Sarah, a lass from the North of England but with a Jenny Agutar speaking voice. Sarah was a qualified Midwife, who had previously worked in Afghanistan. She and a friend had now set up their own organisation "Family Care" in Armenia. Its main aim was to train medical staff in midwifery. Sarah was to become an extension of our family over the next number of years. She became famous for "Sarahs Sunset Tours." Many of a Saturday or Sunday afternoon, Sarah use to call and say that she was going out for a drive, and she would be calling for us right away. Maybe 2-4 hrs later Sarah used to arrive all full of apologies, so the intended trip was modified, hence Sunset Tours. Her trips out and the cups of Earl Grey tea and chocolate biscuits from our "Special Occassions" cupboard, Sarah was and still is a treasure as far as the Loze family is concerned.

Jane and I also spent a large percentage of our time other than at Nubarashen, planning the content of the next six months work. The running of the institution was the responsibility of the Ministry of Education and Science, under the department of Special Education. This was a small department consisting of one junior minister and 3 staff. Over the 3-4 years we were to spend some very frustrating and heated hours in discussion, not just with this department but further up the chain with the Deputy Minister of Education.

During the hours of planning we knew that we were only scratching the surface, and that something really big was going to happen how and when we didn't know, but who was going to create it, that we did know. Little did we know how big a thing was being created.

Soon it was time to fly back to England, but with coming back we could leave a lot of our stuff behind. Our friend Nazine from the International Red Cross was looking for short term accommodation, so we arranged with our landlady that she could take over the rent whilst we were away.

Armenian Airlines had the week of our flight decided that they were not flying to England. The nearest for us would be either Paris or Amsterdam. So Amsterdam it was, and then KLM to London. At least we would have some comfort on the KLM part of the flight.

Our arrival back to England and home was a culture shock in reverse. We were now exposed to a country of GREED, where people had so much but were never happy with it, being driven to satisfy themselves even at the expense of others. A Nation of self centred people, or was I becoming a grumpy old man? No, our country was on the decline!

When meeting up with people back in England, we soon realised that they weren't really interested in what we had experienced in the past 6 months. This was so hard to take. we weren't saying "Look what we have done!" It was as if people couldn't or did want to even start to understand, they were happy in their own little world. "Trespassers will be prosecuted" seemed to written on their chests. Yes I do know that people will give money on the particular flag day, lie in a bath of beans for 6 sponsored hours, but again its look what I have done.

Whilst I am the same subject, a true story comes to my mind. A preacher once stood up in church and said "Did you know that over 10 million children die of starvation every year?" This was met by silence. He then said "Did you know that over 10 million children die of starvation every year, what are you going about it?" Again the same silence. He said again "Did you know that over 10 million children die of starvation every year, what the **hell** are you doing about it?" This time a huge murmur buzzed about the building. The preacher said "What has upset you most. That 10 million children are dying each year of starvation, or that I have just said Hell?"

Our months break seemed to be slipping away, it was good to see family and close friends again, but we had so much to arrange. Jane couldn't get a further period of unpaid leave, so she had to resign from her position. Then Morganas place at Notre Dame had to be cancelled. For her continued education, I had managed to contact a College that did a correspondence course for GCSE, when the material arrived, we knew that our baggage would be overweight again (Jane did pride herself on having the airline red labels on our luggage with HEAVY printed on them, as long as we weren't charged for them. We managed to get a flight with Swiss Air, who had now commenced flying into Yerevan on its way to Turkmenistan, we could only afford single tickets. So we knew that our next 6 months was going to be harder as far as finance was concerned, but at least Jane knew where all the cheap markets etc were.

We also attended our local church whilst back in Cornwall, Grace Community Church in Looe, and met up with people from our house group, in particular Roger and Mary. Roger and Mary would become a strong prayerful and practical supporters of the work we were involved in. Another person who must get a mention is Lenny. Lenny, a very quiet Cornishman, who had been involved (and still is) in a re-building programme in Kosova. We could understand each others frustrations, and had great respect for each other, and the work that had been entrusted into our hands.

So it was back to Armenia, at least we knew exactly what was happening this time, and we could get straight back to work, and no weeks, months of waiting. We arrived at Yerevan airport to the welcoming smile of Sam, Mission East Driver. No matter what time of the day it was Sam always had a smile on his face. We were to be taken back to Mission East and stay in Peter and Jikkes flat as Kim, Mission East Managing Director and Peter had been discussing our project, with a very pleasing outcome.

Peter and Jikke were back in England, so we had the use of their flat until we arranged with Nazane to get our flat back.

The very next day, we had a copy of Kim and Peters correspondence. In it stated that Mission East would like us to be Mission East Aid Workers. Although they hadn't funding for the Project they would continue to pay for a translator and transport, also pay for our accommodation and be on their general aid workers payroll. This was brilliant news!

We contacted Nazane who said that she would move out as soon as we wanted, and that also she knew of a young couple who also liked the flat. So this gave us another option. Knarik who worked for Mission East said that she would look at different flats for us and sort out the negotiations. One of the options she came up with, was in the same block as Mission East. Peter and Jikke lived on the 3rd floor, and Mission East offices were on the 4th floor (at the top). The first floor flat was available (not far for work). So we went for it and moved in. It was small, with kitchen, bathroom, small dining room, lounge and two small bedrooms, a bonus was that as soon as the main gas supply was connected, we had gas central heating (very antiquated but!) As it happened our street was to be the very first street in the city that the gas was reconnected and within a month of us moving in. A gas cooker that worked, hot water from the tap, and a fridge - luxury! So by the time Peter and Jikke had returned, we were settled into the flat, and already working on the programme for Nubarashen 11.

We had decided that we had to know more about the children their history, diagnoses and reason for them being there. We would then assess each individual child so that an individual programme could be developed. As well as the group work we were already involved in.

We soon realized that we needed a different translator, Armine had been terrific, but she was still at University so could not really work the hours we needed, also we needed someone with a strong personality. Would we get the person to fit the bill?

Sarah came to our rescue in the form of Inna. One of Sarahs staff shared a flat with Inna, so she came with a personal recommendation. Even on her first day, we could see that Inna indeed was the person we needed. She was put in at the deep end. See Armenia did not recognise that any of their population had any disabilities. Yes there were people from the earthquake and from the recent and one going war, but people were not born with disabilities. On example of this was that Armine, our previous translator, had the worse eye sight, blind as a bat would spring to mind, but she would not wear spectacles. Because even the wearing of spectacles was seen as a disability, and disability and Armenia didn't exist.

So Inna didn't have much or indeed any idea f what she was going to see or hear, but she was terrific. Her command of English was terrific and she had our type of humour, her response to the children was just what we wanted. Plus we were soon aware that when we wanted to put forward a strong point to the Director or member of staff, Inna would translate not just what we said but also in the manner that we said it. So we offered her the position and we were so pleased she accepted. Inna is still working for Mission East in Armenia as Project Officer on the same education programme that we were involved with at the conception stage.

Chapter Twenty Nine

∽

"We need men who can dream of things that never were."
J.F.KENNEDY

We managed to get permission from the Director and the nurse to look at the medical records of all the children, or should I say what records that they did have. This was to turn into a mammoth task as the records were in a terrible state – with a large number of children with no records. Over the next number of weeks a picture was starting to evolve, and not a good one.

Soon we were to commence on our own assessment of all the children, using a programme of practical, educational and cognitive exercises. Our aim was from the results of the assessments and the medical reports to design an Individual Programme for each child, with the results being presented to the Ministry of Education and Science.

During the individual assessments we were to get to know more about the children, especially those who had little or no communication difficulties. We were also able to build up a picture regarding families, if they existed or not, and their location. In time Jane would take control of this side of the project and to the development of a Family Liaison position and the employment of a person with social welfare training, this training would be supplemented by further supplemented by Janes wealth of experience..

The results of our assessments confirmed our thoughts that at Nubarasahen 11 over 85% of the children should not have been there, that they had been falsely diagnosed so as to gain access. This may sound strange to you, but because of the very poor social and economic situation in Armenia, so many families could not afford to clothe and feed their families. So the parents would either save up the money or borrow it even to seek loans so that a local Doctor and Psychologist would falsely diagnose that the child or children had "mental problems" and therefore gain admittance into a "boarding school" where the child would be fed, watered and boarded. Over the next year these findings would be confirmed when we were "let loose" in the rest of the special schools. One of the main problems concerning education for children who were deemed as having "mental problems" was that they were immediately labeled as being unable to learn. Under the Soviet system a specialised person with the title of "Defectologist" was qualified to find educationally and physical defects in children, this would then completely prevent that particular child from any form of main stream education. Also the attitude of the staff employed in "special education" towards the children that they found in their schools or classrooms with no learning difficulties (accept for the diagnoses). Here were 85% of the children with no learning difficulties attending a school with 15% of children with learning difficulties (ranging from mild to moderate), but the staff would not recognise the difference. They were all classed as having "mental problems", therefore all treated the same. Nubarashen had 130 children, 15% of these we classed as having some learning difficulties, but 90% of those would be classed as having mild difficulties, and 5% moderate and 5% moderate to severe.

This a rough breakdown of our findings:-
- 130 children assessed (ages 7 years to 15 years).
- 90% of those assessed could not recognize any letters.
- 85% could not do a simple addition.
- 85% could not recognize colours or shapes.
- 94% did not know their age or date of birth.
- 85% could not tie their shoe laces
- And so on

So in fact no one was learning to their full potential.

All our findings were presented to the Ministry of Education and Science, who in typical ex Soviet thinking, tried to flannel us by asking us to put together a proposal etc. This would be an education in itself.

Peter, the Mission East Country Director and Jikke had become good friends of ours as well as work colleagues. Jikke was now pregnant and expecting twins, so Morgana was now in her element.

One week after work we had a big Mission East party, Christine who ran the medical programme in Southern Armenia was leaving. That is one thing that the Armenians do not need encouragement for and that is a party. We used our front yard, and in no time Sam had the Armenian Horazats under control. For those who don't know that is a BBQ with a flare, meat has to be tasted to appreciate what it is all about. Christine had been with Mission East for a few years, and now had decided that it was time to move on. Christine was French speaking Swiss, and had a lovely attitude to things. Morgana used to admire her, because she was the type of person who would look glamorous in a pair of torn jeans. We gave her a great send off, and of course Peter had to do his party treat, or sending the Armenian Champagne cork sailing over the buildings, and breaking his world record.

Our Sunday meetings had moved from the International School and was now being held in either Peter and Jikkes flat or ours, now with the twins on their way we all decided to hold them in our flat.

The School had now moved to newer premises in the north of Yerevan, the students who lived in the city traveled by a special bus service. Morgana still attended for the odd day or so per week. She ha a great number of friends at the school, and they all use to meet up on non school days. Her studies were going well and I am still full f admiration of how she managed her studies. The postal service was so hit and miss, letters to and from England seemed to fall in the 10 category. 10 days – 10 weeks – 10 months. So for a correspondence course it was difficult. But all her work seemed to be getting through.

Marine a young Armenian used to spend a number of hours with Morgana, mainly to help regarding her Maths, and also teaching her Armenian. Marine was from a super loving and caring family. Her family and Benjimen, her future husband, were very passionate Christians, and we loved them very much. Our previous church in St Annes had donated us some money which we used to purchase a number of Armenian Bibles. Both Marine and Benjimen, were going to Iran to see Benjimens family and they were going to smuggle the Bibles to Armenian Christians. They were successful.

The childrens project we renamed "Mosaic Project" as we looked upon the children as shattered pieces of colourful stone, but when put together formed a beautiful picture. Peter was of great support for us and the project. We used to arrange to keep an eye on each other during any Ministry meetings, which would stretch the patients of any saint, if either of us started to show any sign of loosing patients a sharp kick to the shins would signify "Take it easy."

Arsenal to Armenia

We eventually came up with the requested Ministry proposal, so we looked forward to our meeting with great expectations. During the meeting which went on for over an hour, we were again made to keep waiting, as the proposal that we were requested to come up with, wasn't in the Ministry format, we would have to re - do it using their format. When we requested a copy of the official format for us to see, we were told that they didn't have one to hand, but if we altered a few things on our proposal and brought it back for a further meeting in a weeks time. This kept happening week after week, we never did see the format. So in the end we just did things, and informed them of what we had done.

At Nubarashen 11 things were starting to get a little difficult not with the children but from a management level. In everything we did at the school, we tried to include the staff. But I think we were becoming too popular with the children, and showing up the staff, also we were finding out how the school ran, the short comings were so obvious.

The ministry wasn't being very supportive to the staff of their schools, the wages were never on time, even though they amounted to the equivalent of $10 per week, so motivation wasn't high on the staffs agenda. In a number of moths time we were to realise that the non payment of wages, depended on some directors.

A number of afternoons after a day at Nubarashen, we used to walk from our flat to the Smiths to collect Morgana. The Smiths has two daughters one about Morganas age and one younger. Bill worked for USAID and Anita ran the house and family including Bill. Anita was amazing she just seemed to know when things weren't going well with our work, the number of times she appeared at our door with a bag of doughnuts and announcing that the Lord had told her to come!

At the Smiths house we would just sink into their comfortable arm chairs and be waited on with Earl Grey and biscuits. The Americans don't do suffering!

The other families included the Wesths from Denmark. Michael was with the Danish Missionary Society working at the Armenian Seminary. The Wesths were blessed by having a great sense of humour and the gift of hospitality. Mona was very caring and sensitive, the daughters Marie and Kristen were a bit younger than Morgana, and they both went to the International School. We were to spend a lot of our free time in the company of the Wesths. Marie came over to England from Denmark to be at Morganas wedding.

Dennis Loze

Then there were the McFees, another American family, who both worked for USAID, they had two younger children Cameron and Miriam, Morgana used to baby/child sit and spend a number of hours entertaining Cameron. We are still in contact with Emily and Winston.

Chapter Thirty

∞

"An eye for an eye, makes the word blind"
MAHATMA GANDHI

At Nubarashen 11 we managed to obtain a small room for our own work. Really it was too small for any group work, but it as offered so we grabbed the opportunity, at least we could so small group work. We set about decorating from the drabness of the Soviet era into bright colours, Jane painted animals etc on the walls, it was now full of brightness and colour, the children loved it. When it was break-time our room used to be invaded by children who wanted to know when it was their turn for us to work with them.

Jane also used her knowledge of where you could purchase different things in Yerevan. Sam our driver used to be amazed with Jane, when she used to give him directions to various little shops. He used to say that he was born in Yerevan but that Jane knew her way around better than he did.

In the school there wasn't a clock of any description, so we purchased some wall clocks, (colourful ones) for each classroom and corridors. Jane also designed a large chart alongside the clock, showing the weather and the date. We then taught some of the older children how to change and update the charts.

From the limited information we obtained regarding the children from the school and medical records we were able to identify some birthdays and used to buy little cakes etc to celebrate. Jane was then to do a big family hunt and home visit programme. We discovered that a large percentage of the children came from an area south of Yerevan in an area called Zot, but didn't appear on any maps etc. So Jane and the recently appointed trainee Social worker set off on the hunt, leaving me to continue things at Nubarashen.

After a number of days Jane started to locate some of the families. The vast majority of the living conditions were terrible, due to extreme poverty. She was also to have confirmation that the children did receive false diagnoses so as to enable the children to be fed and watered. I accompanied Jane on a couple of family visits, she had located the mother of 2 of the children and had made arrangements to visit her the next day. We had to wait until she had finished her mornings work at the local market. She used to go out early in the evenings and collect wild herbs which grew in the mountains, and then most mornings try and sell them, but most people were in the same financial situation as she was, so money didn't come easy.

She eventually took us to her flat, which consisted of two rooms, with no furniture. In the sitting area was a plank of wood resting on two concrete blocks, which served as the only seating area. The Armenian hospitality kicked in as she insisted that we have coffee, all our refusal fell on deaf ears, as she went to her neighbours to beg or borrow coffee, she also came back with an apple which she sliced up for us to eat.

Every visit that Jane made was a mirror image. What could be done?

With all Janes findings we sat down with Peter and Jikke to see what we could come up with. One of the major points was the lack of contact between the children and the families. Te parents and children were in fact like strangers, Nubarashen 11 as technically a boarding schoolfor orphans with "mental problems". We hadn't come across any child without parents or a parent, in some case the families had simply signed their children over to the Ministry, so technically abandoning their children al bet legally.

Thus contact had to be reintroduced and continued, some families did see the children over the Summer time, but not during then year. A minority managed to see the children once every couple of months. An option was to hire a bus every month to bring the parents to see the children.

Looking at the financial side of the family, a possibility of investing in Vertigrows for the families, a vertigrow.is a unique system that specialises in vertical growing and vertical gardening to utilise space and energy in an efficient manner.

It uses hydroponics or "soil less" gardening and this basically means gardening without soil. Soil less medias that support the plant include such products as perlite, coconut fiber, vermiculite, peat moss mixes and sometimes bark or lava rock.

It can be used to grow so many basic produce.

Another option was to look at the fertility of the soil in the surrounding area, so that families could have a piece of land, similar to allotments.

The same obstacle arose its head "funding."

The allotment idea was squashed when we found out that the whole of the Zot area was on a large salt marsh, so nothing would grow. With all these options but no funding our ideas had to be temporarily shelved.

Meanwhile the Bosnia situation was a critical situation and Mission East had been informed by the Danish Government that they wanted Mission East to be involved in aid work there.

A survey was being carried out by Brussels based desk officers, regarding the development of a refugee camp, which was something new for Mission East.

Peter had received a request that either both Jane and myself or just me to be involved in the planning stages with the idea of me going to set p activities etc for the children and families. The idea with the refugee camp was to set it up as small villages, composing of people from the same areas, instead of everyone in a free for all. So this was added to our ever growing list.

Things at Nubarashen were continuing to be more and more difficult. It was now obvious that the Director didn't want us there. A decision had to be made, it is even now hard to put into words, the emotional effect is was having on us, even more so when we withdrew the project from Nubarashen.

What was going to happen now?

So back to the drawing board and continue with our ongoing proposal with the ministry of Education and Science. We still had very heavy hearts regarding Nubarashen, but as one door closes, another one opens. This did come true.

Dennis Loze

During our visit back to England and since, I had been exploring all aspects of Special education, and had made a number of contacts in Derbyshire Special Schools plus loads of educational materials to pour over. I knew all this wasn't going to go to waste.

We had gained so much information which we had poured into Nubarashen with such excellent results, all based on Play Therapy with the individual programme, based on findings from our assessments. So armed with all these results it was back to the Ministry. They said that there was nothing that they could do regarding the attitude of the Director of Nubarashen 11. There is a saying in Armenia that some people have a "roof over their heads." Which actually means that some people have or know people in high places, or have something over them? This was the case at Nubarashen 11.

But the Ministry were encouraging enough to want us to continue, we pushed that we would like to access to all the special schools in Armenia, to visit assess and to carry out a series of talks and practical sessions with the staff regarding Education through Play. They agreed in principle, but still required us to complete the proposal, which now had to include the latest changes – even though we were still awaiting the format!

As I said earlier when one door closes another one opens – but for how long could we keep it open?

We tried and tried to get a full list of special schools for children with "mental problems" from the Ministry but they either didn't have one or were just playing their old game. So it was a case of "detective work" and shoe leather. We finally ended up with a list of schools to visit

- In Northern Armenia   Gymri
                                          Gavar
                                          Hrazdan
- West and Mid Armenia   Abovian
                                            Armavir
                                            Zvartnots
                                            Nork
                                            Yerevan 5
                                            Yerevan 8
                                            Nubarashen 1

- Southern Armenia   Sisian

                                      Kapan

Also we were to visit a further 6 schools which turned not to fit into the category of special school.

So we visited each school as per list, spending a day looking and talking – then if seen appropriate to arrange a full days practical on Education through Play for all the staff. Some schools we had to do it over 2 days where the afternoon session was a repeat of the morning session so as to allow all the staff to partake.

It was amazing to see to see the real rigid formal teachers suddenly being transformed into a group who worked together with humour and fun, all the rigidness melted away. But could they do it in the classroom day after day and be willing or have the insight to want to change. The educational teaching system used by the staff within the special schools was a watered down mainstream system – teaching was the teacher out at the front talking – with little or no interaction with the children, they just sat. If the children didn't or couldn't learn it was their fault!

The conditions of the schools varied, but all were in a bad state of repair. Most of them had some children staying overnight – but not weekends – seemingly only Nubarashen 11 fell into that category.

Regarding the nature of the children, just based on pure observation, seem to fall into the category of poor social and economic situation similar to Nubarashen 11.

Our analysis of the past two months, which took us all over Armenia, carrying out both practical and Theoretical sessions and seeing the workings of the school and staff, was a resounding need for our work to continue. So armed with all our information it was back to the Ministry. They seemed to be impressed, or was that just my impression, but with some reservations. They balanced all things up and wanted us just to work in one school, and for them to monitor and evaluate the project. We knew that the monitoring and evaluation would never happen, firstly no way did they have the resources or the man power to do such a thing, secondly it was a bit of a stand-off, as ministries were use to organizations working in Armenia on the Humanitarian side but were challenged when it came to Development as it meant change. With situations like this Ministries normally kept their heads down and weather the storm, yes make things difficult, but get the benefits, and wait for the organisation to either lose patients, time, or money and move on, but we were going to do non of these. We were here to stay, we had committed a year and intended to see it through or until God told us otherwise.

After a long session at the ministry we persuaded the Ministry that we would initially work in two schools, but also to involve 3-4 other schools in training sessions, so as the project would be ready in 1 years time involve other schools.

The schools selected was Yerevan 8 which was in the centre of Yerevan just 15mins from our office, and Zvartnots which was west of Yerevan approx 1 hrs drive. So we were keeping as close to our schools as possible, but also taking in account the attitude of staff and directors. Although these two schools were selected we knew that we still had a lot of work to do in bringing a positive attitude amongst the staff.. Not just towards the project but to teach and convince them that children with learning difficulties can learn!

We were now due for our break so we decided to go back to the UK, leaving Inna and to continue gaining information of the schools the children and families. Whilst making arrangements for our flight back, British Airways announced that they were opening a flight from London to Tajekastan via Tablisi (Georgia) and YES Yerevan!

When we got to Yerevan Airport we were greeted by a young Armenian man dressed in a British Airways uniform, who said "Welcome Mission East." This was such a fantastic greeting, it appeared that he lived not far from us and the Mission East office and used to see us nearly every day going off to work. Yes what a great welcome.

Once on board, what luxury – we had had a very exhausting and emotional time with the ups and downs of the project, in fact I had lost over a stone in weight, yes what luxury but more was to come. Morgana had insisted on her independence not to sit with us but to be grown up and sit some way behind us.

Just after take off we were giving a bottle of wine each, and spares stuffed into the seat pockets, lovely "Chapel Down" white wine. This was followed by a snack and, whiskey and ginger for me and gin and Tonic for Jane, we were treated like Lord and Lady. Jane and I just looked each

Arsenal to Armenia

other and tears started to run down our cheeks, we knew that God was saying to us "Thank you." (As I write this tears are again running down my cheek.)

Our time in England was to be a busy one gaining information regarding special education and play therapy. We knew that our bags were going to be over weight for the light back, but the books etc kept piling up.

We also decided this time to let our house out, as we knew that we were going back to Armenia for the long haul. Morgana was happy with going back as she had made so many good friends. Also the International school liked having her around that just before we left they said that they had a study area that Morgana could use, and that she could attend everyday, and join in any of the joint activities.

Whilst back home it was good to meet up with our church house group, especially Roger and Mary also Norma and Denzil. Roger and Mary had both been treasures towards us, with letters and even phone calls to us – they were true faithful servants.

Our break was soon over and back to a wintery Armenia.

Chapter Thirty One

"I submit to you that if a man hasn't discovered something he will die for, he isn't fit to live."
MARTIN LUTHER KING

I am now reflecting over the periods in time that this book has taken you through. Like the title of the book from Arsenal to Armenia, we have in fact taken you from Arsenal and now into Armenia.

The Armenian part continued for a further 4 years, then I knew that I had taken the project as far as I could. We gained funding from the Danish Government to the tune of ¾ million American Dollars for a further 5 year project which continued on from the project that we were proud to have started. I have left the story at the commencement of our 2nd year in Armenia, but so much happened in the following years to be contained in this book. I might in time put pen to paper or fingers to computer to tell of this part of the story. It does end with the official blessing of the Armenian Parliament. And now children in Armenia who have learning difficulties whether moderate or severe are entitled to an individual education programme based on their learning abilities. So no longer are children falsely diagnosed, no longer are children treated like "animals" and pushed away from society. Even now it is still early days of changing peoples attitudes towards any form of disability.

I am writing this sat in our little Caseta in southern Spain. We came to live here just over a year ago. Jane is still battling against cancer, she now has bone cancer. The oncology care here is excellent, we have a great specialist in the local hospital. Jane has gone through so many treatments in England and here, her mobility at present has been restricted to a wheelchair and walking frame. Yes at times we find the battle hard, but have fun and laughter, and we can reflect upon our work in Armenia which started from nothing but has resulted in effecting a whole country.

Arsenal to Armenia

We are expecting our daughter Morgana, her husband Jon and our 5 month old granddaughter Niamh over to visit us in the next couple of weeks, and I can guarantee you that Armenia and Arsenal will enter the conversation

You may have noticed at the beginning of each chapter a famous quote, or saying. I will now finish this book with two more another quotes, the first for life in general:

"However, I consider my life worth nothing to me, if only I may finish the race and complete the task the Lord Jesus has given me – the task of testifying to the gospel of God's grace."
Paul (Acts 20:24)

"For whoever wants to save his own life will destroy it, but whoever destroys his life for my sake and the sake of the Good News will save it. Indeed, what will it benefit a person if he gains the whole world but forfeits his life?"
Jesus the Messiah (Mark 8 35-37)

N.B.
This book is dedicated to Jane for her continued love. She died two days after finishing the above section. The last two chapters remain as written, not proof read by Jane with her red pen.

Appendix

A

Derris Albert "Eddie" Hapgood (September 24, 1908 — April 20, 1973)

Born in Bristol, he started his career as an amateur (while employed as a milkman), before getting his big break at Kettering Town. He was signed by Herbert Chapman to Arsenal for £950 in 1927. Playing at left back, Hapgood went on to become captain of the Arsenal team which dominated English football in the 1930s, winning five League Championships and two FA Cups. He played 440 times in all.

Hapgood played for England 30 times, wearing the captain's armband 21 times. His first match as captain was the infamous "Battle of Highbury" on November 14, 1934, against Italy, who were then World Champions (England had declined to take part in the World Cup, so the match was billed a "true world champions" match). The match was notoriously dirty, with many players sustaining injuries, including Hapgood himself with a broken nose; England beat the Italians (who were effectively reduced to ten men for most of the match) 3-2.

Hapgood also captained England in an even more infamous match, against Germany in Berlin on May 14, 1938, where Hapgood and his players were made to give the Nazi salute before the match, under pressure from British diplomats. Hitler was not in attendance; England won the match 6-3.

The Second World War cut short Hapgood's career, but after the war he had stints managing Blackburn Rovers, and then Watford and Bath City. After that he left football completely, and spent his later years running a YMCA hostel in Harwell, Berkshire and in Weymouth, Dorset. He died in Leamington Spa on Good Friday 1973.

David Bone Nightingale Jack (April 3, 1899 - September 10, 1958)

The first footballer in the world to be transferred for more than £10,000.

An inside forward, born in Bolton, Jack started his career at his father's club, Plymouth Argyle in 1919, scoring 11 goals in 48 appearances. In 1920 he returned to the town of his birth, moving to Bolton Wanderers for £3,500. He spent eight seasons with the Trotters, forming a formidable partnership with Joe Smith. While at Bolton, he made history by being the first person to score a goal at Wembley Stadium, in the 1923 FA Cup final. A year later, he won his first England cap, the first of nine; he scored three times for his country.

He won the Cup again with Bolton in 1926. In 1928 he was signed by Herbert Chapman's Arsenal for £10,890 (nearly double the previous record); famously, Chapman negotiated the transfer with Bolton's representatives in a hotel bar, his tactic being to drink gin and tonics without any gin in them, while letting the other side drink as much as they possibly could.

Jack was a success at Highbury, becoming a regular straight away, and was the club's top scorer through the late 1920s and early 1930s. He won three League Championship titles and another FA Cup winners medal. By 1933-34 he was reaching the end of his career, and retired after winning his third league medal, in 1934. In all he scored 124 times in 208 matches for Arsenal, making him the ninth-best goalscorer in the club's history.

After retiring from playing, he went on to become manager of Southend United from May 1934 to August 1940, and then Middlesbrough from November 1944 to April 1952.

Alexander Wilson James (September 14, 1901 – June 1, 1953)

Born in Mossend, Lanarkshire, Alex James played as an inside forward, as a supporting player for the main strikers. He was famed for the excellent quality of his passing and supreme ball control, leading many modern-day comparisons with Arsenal forward Dennis Bergkamp. His rheumatism meant he wore "baggy" shorts to hide the long johns he wore to keep warm; the baggy appearance became his trademark.

James started his career with local youth clubs, before joining Raith Rovers in 1922. He spent three seasons at Starks Park, recording over a hundred League appearances, before moving to Preston North End in 1925. He spent four years at the

Second Division side, scoring 55 goals in 157 appearance, but towards the end of his stay there he fell into several disputes with the club's management, partly over wages – at the time, the Football League operated a maximum wage of £8 a week – and also because Preston refused to release James for international duty.

James left Preston for Herbert Chapman's Arsenal in 1929 for £8,750, making his debut against Leeds United on August 31, 1929. In order to circumvent the maximum wage rules, James' employment at Arsenal was supplemented by a £250-a-year "sports demonstrator" job at Selfridges, a London department store. After a forgettable first season, James settled into his role with Arsenal and became part of the dominant side of English football in 1930s; playing as Chapman's designated "midfield schemer", he took a little time to adjust to Arsenal's style of play, but he would become one of the club's all-time greats.

Playing so deep as a supporting player, he scored relatively few goals for Arsenal – only 27 in 261 appearances – but created many times that number. James's passing and vision supplied the ammunition that David Jack, Cliff Bastin, Ted Drake and Jack Lambert all gratefully put into the net. He won the First Division Championship four times (in 1931, 1933, 1934 and 1935), and the FA Cup twice – James scored the first goal of the 1930 final (which was Arsenal's first major trophy win), and captained Arsenal to their 1936 win over Sheffield United. Such was James' influence that in the one Cup final he missed – the 1932 final against Newcastle United – Arsenal lost 2-1, albeit thanks to a highly controversial goal from Newcastle's Jack Allen.

Despite his sparkling club form, he won just eight caps for Scotland. However, this included an appearance for the legendary 'Wembley Wizards' team that thrashed England 5-1 at Wembley in 1928, with James scoring twice.

Alex James retired from playing in 1937. During World War II he served in the Royal Artillery, and after the war he became a journalist. In 1949 he was invited back to Arsenal to coach the club's youth sides, before his sudden death four years later at the age of 51. James was inducted into the English Football Hall of Fame in 2005 in recognition of his contribution to the English game.

Arsenal to Armenia

Clifford Sydney Bastin (March 14, 1912 — December 4, 1991)

Born in Heavitree near Exeter, Bastin started his career at Exeter City, making his debut for the club in 1928, at the age of 16. Despite only playing 17 games (and scoring 6 goals), his talent was evident enough that he was signed a year later for £2,000 by Herbert Chapman's Arsenal, who went on to become dominant force in English football in the 1930s.

Bastin would play the rest of his career at Arsenal, scoring 178 goals in 395 games; he was Arsenal's all-time top goalscorer until 1997, when his total was surpassed by Ian Wright. In 2005 Thierry Henry passed both Bastin and Wright's totals, thus meaning Bastin is currently (as of October 2005) Arsenal's third-top goalscorer of all time. His record of 150 league goals for Arsenal stood for slightly longer, until it was equalled by Thierry Henry on January 14, 2006. Bastin's scoring feats are all the more remarkable considering he played on the left wing rather than as centre forward; the partnership he formed with Alex James was the source of many of his goals. Had his career not been interrupted by the Second World War it is likely that he would have scored many more goals for Arsenal.

Despite being so young, Bastin made an immediate impact and was a regular in the Arsenal side through the '30s, earning him the nickname "Boy Bastin". With the Gunners, Bastin won the FA Cup twice, in 1930 and 1936, and the Football League five times, in 1931, 1933, 1934, 1935 and 1938. Bastin also played for England 21 times, including a notorious match against Germany in Berlin in 1938, when the England team was ordered to give the Nazi salute before the match.

The Second World War intervened when Bastin was 27, thus cutting short what should have been the peak of his career. Bastin was excused military service, as he failed the army hearing test. Thus, during the war, he served as an ARP Warden, being stationed on top of Highbury stadium with Tom Whittaker. He also played matches in the war-time league (but, strangely, not internationals) to boost civilian morale. In 1941, Fascist Italy's propaganda broadcast on Rome Radio, contained a bizarre claim that Bastin had been captured in the Battle of Crete, and was being detained in Italy. The Italians were seemingly unaware that Bastin had played his entire career being almost entirely deaf.

Bastin had injured his right leg in the season before the war, which would go on to hamper his performances in wartime matches, and ultimately curtail his career. After the war was over, Bastin, by now in his thirties, would only play six more times before retiring in January 1947.

After retirement, Bastin returned to his native Exeter and ran a pub. He died in 1991 at the age of 79. A stand at St James Park, Exeter's home ground, is named in his honour.

Leslie Harry Compton (born Woodford, Essex September 12, 1912 - died Hendon, Middlesex 27 December 1984)

Compton spent his entire career at Arsenal, spanning 23 years, making him one of the club's longest-ever serving players. He joined the club as an amateur in 1930. He made his debut on April 25, 1932, though spent much of the early and mid-1930s as a reserve player. He featured regularly for the Gunners in unofficial matches during the Second World War, once scoring ten times against Leyton Orient - a remarkable feat considering his usual position was as centre half.

After the war had ended, he became a mainstay in the Arsenal side, winning the First Division title in 1948, and the FA Cup in 1950 (having scored a last-gasp equaliser in the semi-finals against Chelsea). Compton made his debut for England in 1950 against Wales, making him the oldest ever England debutant at 38 years and 64 days, a record that still stands (and is unlikely to be broken).

Compton retired from playing football in 1953, having played 273 matches and having scored 6 goals. He stayed on at Arsenal for another three years as a coach and scout.

Compton also played cricket for Middlesex, playing as wicket-keeper from 1938 to 1956. He appeared 272 times, scoring 5,814 runs (an average of 16.75), and taking 468 catches and 131 stumpings.

He died in Hendon from complications of diabetes, aged 72. His younger brother Denis also played for Arsenal and Middlesex.

Edward Joseph "Ted" Drake (August 16, 1912 - May 30, 1995)

Born in Southampton, Drake started playing at Winchester City, before turning professional and joining Southampton, in

1931. A prolific centre-forward, he hit a hat-trick on his Saints debut and scored (in total) 48 goals in 72 league games. He also appeared for Hampshire County Cricket Club in county cricket

Drake moved to Arsenal in March 1934 for £6,500, and scored on his league debut against Wolves. Although he joined too late to qualify for a League Championship medal in 1934, Drake would win one the following season, after scoring a spectacular 42 goals in 41 league games. With two more goals in the FA Cup and Charity Shield, Drake scored 44 in all that season, a club record that holds to this day.

The following season, Drake scored seven in a single match against Aston Villa at Villa Park on December 14, 1935, a club record that also still stands. Drake would go on to win the FA Cup in 1936 and the League again in 1938. The Second World War curtailed Drake's career somewhat, although he served in the Royal Air Force as well as turning out for Arsenal in wartime games. However, Drake's career would not last long into peacetime; a spinal injury in 1945 forced him to retire from playing. With 139 goals in 184 games, he is the joint-fifth (along with Jimmy Brain) all-time scorer for Arsenal, as of 2005. He also won five England caps, scoring six times, and was one of seven Arsenal players who played for England in the "Battle of Highbury" against Italy in November 1934.

After retiring as a player, Drake managed Hendon in 1946, and then Reading from 1947 until 1952, when he moved to Chelsea. He proceeded to modernise the club and helped to rid the club of its old nickname, 'the Pensioners', removing the image of a Chelsea pensioner from the match programme in the process. The team were affectionately christened 'Drake's Ducklings'. He led Chelsea to their only Division One title of the 20th century in 1954-55; Drake became the first person to win a Championship title both as player and manager. After leaving Chelsea in 1962, he became reserve team manager at Fulham (where his son, Bobby, played), later becoming a director and then life president of the Cottagers.

Ted Drake died in 1995, at the age of 82.

George Hedley Swindin (December 4, 1914 – October 27, 2005)

A goalkeeper, Swindin was born in Campsall, Yorkshire. He played as an amateur for various local clubs, including

Rotherham United, before turning professional in 1934 with Bradford City. He played twenty-six times for Bradford, before being signed by Arsenal in 1936 for £4,000. He made his debut against Brentford on September 3, 1936, and played nineteen games in his first season. To begin with, his time at Arsenal was characterised by nervous and erratic displays, and he was made to share the goalkeeping spot with Alex Wilson and Frank Boulton. However, he played seventeen games in 1937-38, the most of Arsenal's three keepers, and won a First Division medal.

The Second World War interrupted his career somewhat, but Swindin continued to play through the war for Arsenal, whilst acting as a PT instructor for the Army. By the time first-class football had resumed after the war, he became Arsenal's undisputed No. 1, and stayed there for the next six seasons. By now, he had put his erracticness behind him, and he was a commanding keeper who was especially known for his aerial ability and assured handling of crosses, as well as his strong physical resilience. He won his second League title in 1948, and despite the arrival of Ted Platt in 1950, Swindin kept his place to play in the 1950 and 1952 FA Cup finals; Arsenal won the former against Liverpool, but lost to Newcastle United in the latter.

By 1952-53, Swindin was beginning to show his age, and another talented keeper, the Welshman Jack Kelsey had taken his first-team place. Nevertheless, Swindin played 14 matches that season as Arsenal won the title again, giving him his third Championship winner's medal. Despite his excellent form for Arsenal, he was never capped by England at senior level, with Sir Walter Winterbottom preferring Frank Swift and Bert Williams between the sticks. In all, he played 297 first-class matches (not including wartime games) for the Gunners.

Swindin moved to Midland League side Peterborough United as player-manager in 1954, and took his team to several famous FA Cup runs (which included getting to the Fourth Round in 1956-57 and three consecutive Midland League titles between 1956 and 1958. Peterborough would go on to win the title twice more after Swindin left, enough to win election to the Football League in 1960.

In the meantime, Swindin had returned to Arsenal in 1958 as manager, and his side initially started strongly, finishing third in 1958-59. However, the team soon flagged and spent the next three seasons in mid-table. Despite signing players such as George Eastham and Tommy Docherty, Swindin was unable to bring any silverware to the club, whilst up the road the club's rivals Tottenham Hotspur won the Double in 1961.

He resigned in May 1962, and then became manager of Norwich City for five months, and then Cardiff City from late 1962 to 1964. At Cardiff, he signed John Charles from Roma, but after a bright start Cardiff soon faded and he resigned after the club were relegated to the Second Division. After that, he had spells as manager of Kettering Town and Corby Town before leaving the game for good.

After retiring from football, Swindin first owned a garage in Corby, before emigrating to Spain, where he spent his retirement. In the later years of his life he suffered from Alzheimer's disease. He died in Kettering in 2005, aged 90.

Lawrence "Laurie" Scott (April 23, 1917 – July 7, 1999)

Born in Sheffield, Scott joined Bradford City as a youth player, and played 39 times for the Bantams, mostly as a winger. In February 1937 he was signed by Arsenal, though he only played as a reserve for the first two years at the club. At the start of World War Two, Scott joined the Royal Air Force as a PT instructor, but still guested as a player for the RAF, Arsenal and England in wartime matches.

By the time peace broke out, Scott had grown into being one of the country's most assured full backs, known for his pace and composure on the ball. He made his official first-team debut for Arsenal against West Ham United in the FA Cup in 1946, and his League debut on the first day of the 1946-47 season; he also made his official England debut against Northern Ireland in September of that year. Arsenal won the First Division title in 1947-48, but after that Scott was blighted by injury; he suffered from appendicitis in 1948, and then injured his knee whilst playing in an international for England.

Scott's appearances for Arsenal were limited for the next few seasons, but he still figured in Arsenal's 1950 FA Cup-winning side. He was picked for England's squad for the 1950 World Cup, but by now, he was 33, and had not played for his country for two years. England's first choice right-back for the entire tournament was Alf Ramsey, and Scott did not play a single minute. In 1950-51 Scott played 17 matches for Arsenal, but by now he was no longer automatic first-team choice. In all he played for Arsenal in 127 official matches (and 191 unofficial wartime matches), and 17 times for England (plus 16 wartime caps).

He joined Crystal Palace as player-manager in October 1951. He managed the Eagles for three years, but with little success; the club had to apply for re-admission to the Football League at the end of the 1953-54 season. He later had stints with non-league Hendon and Hitchin Town, reaching the semi-finals of the FA Amateur Cup twice with the latter. He died at the age of 84, after a long illness.

James Tullis "Jimmy" Logie (November 23, 1919 – April 1984)

Born in Edinburgh, Logie first played for Scottish junior side Lochore Welfare, before being signed by London giants Arsenal in the summer of 1939. Soon after World War II broke out, and Logie was called up; he served in the Royal Navy for the entire duration of the conflict.

After being demobbed he rejoined Arsenal, playing several wartime matches, before making his full first-team debut against Wolves on August 31, 1946. Logie was a talented and creative player (many observers likened him to his fellow countryman Alex James, who had played for Arsenal in the 1930s), and for the next eight seasons he was a regular in the Arsenal side, playing at inside forward. He took part in all of Arsenal's early post-war successes. Arsenal won two First Division titles in 1947-48 and 1952-53, and the 1949-50 FA Cup – Logie set up both goals in a 2-0 win over Liverpool in the final. In the latter stages of his career he also served as Arsenal vice-captain, behind Joe Mercer.

Despite his success at Arsenal, Logie only ever won a single a cap for Scotland, playing against Northern Ireland on November 5, 1952. In all he played 328 matches for Arsenal, scoring 76 goals. He left the Gunners in February 1955, joining non-league Gravesend & Northfleet, whom he played for until 1960.

After retirement Logie fell on hard times; football was not the lucrative profession it is currently, and Logie was a keen gambler. He eventually ended up working in a newsagents. He died aged in 1984, aged 64.

Wallace "Walley" Barnes (January 16, 1920 – September 4, 1975)

Born in Brecon to English parents (his father, a soldier, was stationed there at the time), Barnes initially played as an inside-forward for Southampton in wartime games, where he was spotted and duly signed by Arsenal. He played in virtually every position on the pitch for Arsenal in wartime matches (including a match as goalkeeper), and despite a serious knee injury incurred in 1944, he recovered to make his League debut for the Gunners against Preston North End on November 9, 1946.

Barnes soon found a regular place in the Arsenal side, at left back, and was part of their First Division Championship-winning side of 1947-48. By then he had also become a regular for Wales, winning his first cap against England on October 18, 1947, where he was given the uneviable task of having to mark Stanley Matthews. Barnes went on to win 22 caps, and became captain of his country.

Barnes switched to right back following an injury to Laurie Scott, and won an FA Cup winners' medal in 1950 after Arsenal beat Liverpool. Two years later, Arsenal got to the Cup final again, this time against Newcastle United, but Barnes twisted his knee badly and had to come off the pitch; with no substitutes permitted, Arsenal were down to 10 men, and went on to lose 1-0.

As a result of his Cup final injury, Barnes was out for the entire 1952-53 season (in which Arsenal won the League), although he was back in the side for the next two seasons. With age as well as past injury now counting against him, he retired from playing in the summer of 1956. In all he played 294 matches and scored 12 goals (he was often the club's designated penalty taker).

After retiring from playing, Barnes entered the world of broadcasting, joining the BBC. He presented coverage of FA Cup finals and, with Kenneth Wolstenholme, was one of the commentators for the very first edition of *Match of the Day* in 1964. He continued to serve the BBC in various capacities, until his early death, at the age of 55, in 1975.

Denis Charles Scott Compton CBE (23 May 1918 - 23 April 1997)

He was born in Hendon, Middlesex. By the late 1930s he was a leading England batsman and remained at the top of his profession for almost three decades. His dashing approach to batting and the sheer enjoyment he exuded endeared him to a generation of cricket lovers. As an all-rounder Compton was a right hand bat and a slow left arm Chinaman bowler.

One of the few people to be both a cricket and a football international, he, together with his brother Leslie, also enjoys the remarkable distinction of being the only individual to be a member of both the champion county side - Middlesex CCC - and the Cup-winning club - Arsenal FC in a single calendar year - 1950.

In 1947 he thrilled a war weary English public by breaking record after record in scoring 3816 runs; he scored 18 centuries. 753 of those runs came against the touring South Africans. This season was the summit of a glittering career that began on the ground staff at Lord's; selection for Middlesex followed in 1936 and England the following year.

He scored his first Test century as a precocious 19 year old in 1938 against Don Bradman's touring Australians. Later in the same series he scored a match saving 76 not out at Lord's; this innings was scored on a rain affected pitch and greatly impressed Don Bradman. In 1939 he scored 2468 runs for the season, including 120 against the West Indies at Lord's.

As with many other sportsman of his generation he lost some of his best years to the Second World War, during which he served in the army in India. It was in India, however, that he began his close friendship with his Australian counterpart as test cricketer, footballer and national hero, Keith Miller, who was in the RAAF and flying out of Calcutta. They faced each other several times on the cricket pitch, including during the famously high-scoring 1944 Ranji Trophy final between Holkar, Compton's team, and Bombay; and Miller was in the slips during the match at Calcutta beween the Australian Services and East Zone that was interrupted by rioting when Compton was on 94. One of the rioters who had invaded the pitch ran up to Compton and said "Mr Compton, you very good player, but the match must stop now", which Miller gleefully repeated whenever Compton came to the crease subsequently. In recognition of their friendship and rivalry, the player adjudged the best of the series in the Ashes wins the Miller-Compton Trophy.

1946 saw England touring Australia, and although beaten by the powerful Australian team, Compton distinguished himself by scoring a century in each innings at the Adelaide Test.

Back in England in 1947 he had his glorious season, thereafter he remained a wonderful adornment to the game of cricket until his retirement in 1956/1957. He finished his cricket career after playing 78 Test matches with 17 centuries at an average of 50.06. In all first-class cricket he scored 123 centuries.

Compton, spent his entire career at Arsenal. A winger, he made his debut in 1936, and won the League in 1948 and the FA Cup in 1950. However, the latter part of his sporting career was dogged by knee trouble, the knee had been damaged in a collision with the Charlton goalkeeper; he was limited to 60 official (i.e. non-wartime) appearances and 16 goals. He represented England in wartime 12 times, but never in a full official match.

Compton jointly captained Middlesex CCC between 1951 and 1952, with W.J.Edrich. They were honoured with the creation of the Edrich and Compton stands at the Nursery End in Lord's Cricket Ground.

Compton's absent-mindedness was legendary. Colin Cowdrey writes that Compton turned up for the Old Trafford Test of 1955 against South Africa without his kitbag. Undaunted, he sauntered into the museum and borrowing an antique bat off the display, went on to score 155 and 79 not out. This absent-mindedness was particularly obvious in his tendency to run out his partners at the crease; Trevor Bailey declared that 'a call for a run from Compton should be treated as no more than a basis for negotiation.' Typically, at his brother Leslie's benefit match in 1955, he managed to run him out before he had faced a single ball.

Peter Parfitt, the Middlesex and England batsman, was a speaker at a major celebration in London for Compton's 70th birthday. He claims that the chief guest was called to the telephone by a lady who had heard about the dinner: eventually, he agreed to take the call. "Denis," she said, "it's me, your mother. You're not 70, you're only 69."

After retiring from sport, Denis Compton became a journalist and later a commentator for BBC Television. He was made a CBE in 1958. He became the first former professional cricketer to be elected President of Middlesex CCC in 1991. He served two terms, until a week before his death in Windsor, Berkshire aged 78.

Denis was my school boy hero.

David Lloyd "Dave" Bowen (June 7, 1928 – September 25, 1995)

Born in Maesteg, Bowen first played for Northampton Town, before joining Arsenal in the summer of 1950. He made his debut against Wolves on March 24, 1951, but it wasn't until 1954-55 that he was a regular in the Arsenal side, playing as a useful central midfielder.

In the meantime, Bowen had also made his debut for Wales, in a friendly against Yugoslavia in September 1954. Bowen went on to win 18 caps for Wales, and was the team's captain for their 1958 World Cup campaign; Wales drew all three of their group matches and qualified for the quarter-finals, where they were beaten 1-0 by Brazil, the goalscorer being a 17-year-old Pelé. Along with goalkeeper Jack Kelsey, Bowen was the first Arsenal player to play in a World Cup.

Bowen's spell at Arsenal coincided with a lack of success at the club, so he didn't win any domestic honours. However, he did play for a London XI in the 1958 final of the Inter-Cities Fairs Cup (as the UEFA Cup was originally known), losing 8-2 on aggregate to FC Barcelona, and was Arsenal captain in his final two seasons. In all he played 162 matches for the club, scoring twice.

In 1959, Bowen returned to Northampton Town as player-manager. Bowen would manage the Cobblers for eight years, and became known as a canny manager who signed quality players despite a tight budget. He steered Northampton from the Fourth Division to the First in just five seasons. However, the club spent only one season (1965-66) at the top, before being relegated.

Bowen left Northampton in 1967, after a second successive relegation, though he rejoined the club for a second stint as manager between 1969 and 1972, by which time they had returned to the Fourth Division. He presided over the club's famous 8-2 FA Cup defeat at the hands of Manchester United, in which George Best scored six times.

In the meantime, he had also been manager of Wales between 1964 and 1974, although the side never did reach the heights it had when he was a player.

After stepping down as Wales manager, Bowen moved into journalism. He died in 1995, at the age of 67. The north stand of Northampton's Sixfields Stadium is named in his honour.

David Herd (born April 15, 1934 in Hamilton)

Herd started his career at Stockport County, for whom he played up front alongside his father, though Herd junior's appearances were limited by his national service duties. Nevertheless, he did well enough to attract the attention of Arsenal, who signed him for £10,000 in 1954. Herd made his Arsenal debut the following year against Leicester City, and soon became a regular goalscorer for the club. In 1960-61, Herd hit 29 goals, the most by an Arsenal player since Ronnie Rooke, but Arsenal's poor form meant they were nowhere near winning a trophy. Herd moved to Manchester United in the summer of 1961. In all he scored 107 goals for Arsenal, making him the club's 15th highest goalscorer.

His first game for United would come against West Ham United on August 19, 1961. Herd would help the club to the 1963 FA Cup and the 1965 and 1967 league championships. He left the club in 1967 with 144 career goals, good for 9th on the all-time club list. He also won five caps for Scotland.

George Edward Eastham OBE (born September 23, 1936)

Eastham was born in Blackpool, Lancashire, but first played for Northern Irish club Ards under his father George R. Eastham, before being signed by Newcastle United in 1956. A skilful midfielder/inside forward, he spent four seasons with the Magpies, but looking to go elsewhere, in December 1959 he refused to sign a new contract. Newcastle refused to let Eastham go, retaining his player registration. Eastham took the club to the High Court, arguing that it was an unfair restraint of trade; the judge ruled in Eastham's favour, and as a result the British transfer market underwent significant reform.

In the meantime, Eastham had joined Arsenal, making his debut against Bolton Wanderers in December 1960, scoring twice. Eastham joined the England squad for the 1962 World

Cup as an uncapped player, but did not play in the tournament; his England debut finally came in May 1963, against Brazil. Eastham was also part of the 1966 World Cup squad, but did not play a single minute of England's win in the tournament. In all he won 19 caps for his country, scoring twice.

By 1966 he had become Arsenal captain, but Arsenal's declining form under Billy Wright (the club finished 14th in 1965-66) had left Eastham unhappy; he joined Stoke City in August 1966, having scored 41 goals in 223 matches for the Gunners. Eastham spent the next eight seasons at Stoke, and won the League Cup in 1972, scoring the winning goal in the final against Chelsea. He was awarded the OBE in 1973.

After retiring as a player, he returned to manage Stoke for ten months between 1977 and 1978. After that he left football completely, and later emigrated to South Africa.

Joe Baker (August 17, 1940 – October 6, 2003)

A centre forward, Baker was born in Liverpool but grew up in Motherwell, Scotland. He began his career with Hibernian, scoring 102 goals in 117 games. He made his England debut against Northern Ireland in 1959, which made the first player to be given his debut having never played in England; Baker was famous for his heavy Scottish accent, and was labelled "England's Scottish player". In all he won eight caps for the senior England side.

In 1961 Baker moved to Torino, joining other British players such as Jimmy Greaves and Denis Law. However, despite scoring in a derby match against Juventus, his time at the Italian club was short and almost ended in tragedy; Baker was involved in a serious car crash on February 7, 1962, which nearly killed him and injured Denis Law, who was a passenger.

In July 1962 Baker returned to the UK, joining Billy Wright's Arsenal, where he spent four seasons. In each of those seasons he was the club's top scorer, in all scoring 101 goals in 156 games, making him one of the club's most prolific goalscorers of all time. However, the team's poor form throughout meant Arsenal were unable to challenge for silverware, and Baker left the club in March 1966 for Nottingham Forest.

Despite earning a brief recall to the England side in 1965, scoring in a 2-0 win over Spain, Baker didn't make the squad for the 1966 World Cup. After three years at Forest he moved to Sunderland, then returned to Hibernian for a second time, before seeing out his career at Raith Rovers. He retired in 1974, having in all scored 294 league goals in less than 500 games.

Baker later became Albion Rovers manager on two occasions, but never pursued a full coaching career, instead running a pub and working for Hibernian's hospitality service. He died at the age of 63, after suffering a heart attack during a charity golf tournament.

John Radford (born 22 February 1947 in Hemsworth, Yorkshire)

Playing as a centre forward or right-winger, Radford spent most of his career at Arsenal, making 482 appearances and scoring 149 goals. After joining the club as an apprentice, he made his debut in 1963 and became Arsenal's youngest ever hat-trick scorer (against Wolves on January 2, 1965), at the age of 17 years and 315 days, a record that holds to this day.

Radford helped Arsenal win the 1970 Inter-Cities Fairs Cup and the FA Cup and League double in 1971. He continued to play for the club through the 1970s, although injury and the emergence of Frank Stapleton meant he was no longer a regular by the time he left Arsenal for West Ham United in 1976. After two seasons at the Hammers, Radford joined Blackburn Rovers, and then played for non-league Bishop's Stortford before retiring.

He won two England caps but did not score in either match. As of 2005, he is Arsenal's fourth all-time top scorer.

After retiring, he became a pub landlord, and enjoyed several spells as manager of Bishop's Stortford in the late 1980s and early 1990s.

Peter Edwin Storey (born September 7, 1945)

Storey spent most of his career at Arsenal, joining the club as an apprentice in 1961 and turning professional the following year. A tough, hard-tackling player, he started his career at right back, making his debut for Arsenal against Leicester City in October 1965, and immediately secured a regular place in the Arsenal side.

As his career progressed, Storey switched positions, moving forward to become a defensive midfielder. He lost two consecutive League Cup finals with Arsenal in 1968 and 1969, before winning the Inter-Cities Fairs Cup in 1970 and a First Division and FA Cup Double a year later. Storey played a vital part in the Gunners' winning Cup run, scoring twice in the semi-finals against Stoke City to help the Gunners draw 2-2 after being 2-0 down. Arsenal won the replay 2-0 and went on to beat Liverpool in the final.

Storey made his England debut in 1971 against Greece (in his old position of right back), and went on to win 18 caps during the early 1970s, filling the midfield role vacated by the retiring Nobby Stiles. England's dismal form at the time meant he never played in a tournament finals.

After losing his place in the 1976-77 season, Storey moved to Fulham for £10,000, but retired from the game after one season at Craven Cottage. He played 501 times in all for Arsenal, making him one of the club's leading players in terms of appearances.

Frank McLintock MBE (born December 28, 1939)

Born in Glasgow and brought up in the Gorbals, McLintock started his career as a midfielder at Leicester City, making his debut in 1959. He spent seven seasons at Filbert Street, reaching two FA Cup finals (1961 and 1963) and one League Cup final (1964), but was on the losing side on all three occasions. He was signed by Arsenal in October 1964 and went straight into the first team.

McLintock spent the next nine seasons with the Gunners, moving from midfield to centre half. He became the club's captain in 1967. He reached another two League Cup finals (losing both, again), and became so disillusioned he handed in a transfer request. He was persuaded to stay by manager Bertie Mee, and his change of heart was rewarded, as McLintock captained Arsenal to a Inter-Cities Fairs Cup win in 1970 and then the club's first League and Cup Double in 1971; that year he also won the Football Writers' Association Footballer of the Year award.

McLintock led Arsenal to their sixth Wembley final in 1972 (which they lost to Leeds), and second place in the First Division the year after, before being sold to QPR in June 1973. He spent four seasons with the Hoops, and was part of the side that qualified for the UEFA Cup after finishing a close second to Liverpool in 1976, finally retiring in 1977. In all, he played over 700 times, including 403 matches for Arsenal; he also won nine caps for Scotland. He was made an MBE in 1972.

After retiring from playing, he had an unsuccessful stint as manager of his old club Leicester, then manager of Brentford, and later was a coach at Millwall, helping the club gain promotion to Division One. He has also eked out a successful career as an after dinner speaker, and as a pundit for first BBC Radio, and more recently Sky Sports.

Frederick Charles "Charlie" George (born October 10, 1950)

Born in Islington, London, George supported Arsenal as a boy, and joined his favourite club in May 1966. He made his debut for the Gunners in August 1969, and quickly became a regular in the side, playing in both legs of Arsenal's 1970 Fairs Cup final win over RSC Anderlecht.

Despite breaking his ankle at the start of the following season, George quickly recovered, and played a significant part in Arsenal's run-in to the 1971 Division One title. However, his greatest moment for the club came in the FA Cup final against Liverpool that year; Charlie George scored a spectacular 20-yard winner in extra time to make the score 2-1, famously celebrating by lying flat on his back with arms aloft. With that Cup win Arsenal completed their first "Double".

George played four more seasons at Highbury, but his career was hampered with injuries and loss of form, and he gradually fell out with the club and the manager, Bertie Mee. In 1975 he moved to Derby County, where he memorably scored a hat-trick against Real Madrid in a European Cup match. He would later play for Southampton, Nottingham Forest, before trying his luck in Australia, the United States and Hong Kong.

In all he played 179 matches for Arsenal, scoring 49 goals. He won a solitary cap for England, playing for 60 minutes against the Republic of Ireland in 1976.

Ray Kennedy (born Northumberland, England, 28 July 1951)

Kennedy trained as an apprentice with Port Vale but was told by manager Stanley Matthews at the age of 16 that he wasn't good enough to be a professional footballer. Accepting that a man who had once been England's greatest player was probably speaking the truth, Kennedy returned to his native north-east and started playing as an amateur and working in a sweet factory.

He was then spotted by a scout for Arsenal, who signed him in 1968. Two years later he made his first team debut as Arsenal progressed to the Fairs Cup final. As a substitute in the first leg, Kennedy scored a crucial goal which reduced a heavy deficit inflicted by opponents Anderlecht, and Arsenal completed the comeback in the second leg and won the competition.

The following year Kennedy was a regular fixture (he only missed one game in all competitions) in the Arsenal side which became only the second in the 20th century to win the coveted "double" of League championship and FA Cup. A tight, dramatic finale to the title race saw Kennedy score the only goal of the game against Arsenal's fiercest rivals Tottenham Hotspur to secure the title for the first time since 1948. Three days later, Arsenal beat Liverpool 2-1 to win the FA Cup. Kennedy didn't score in the final, but did end the season with an impressive 36 goals.

Arsenal returned to Wembley to defend the FA Cup the following season but lost 1-0 to Leeds United. Kennedy had scored 26 goals during the season but was only named as a substitute for this final. For the next two seasons he played and scored consistently but Arsenal did not win a trophy.

After the 1974 season ended, Kennedy was sold to Liverpool for 180,000 pounds. He turned out to be the last signing made by legendary Anfield manager Bill Shankly, who announced his retirement on the same day.

Despite his ability as a striker, Kennedy's chances to play in his favoured centre forward role at Liverpool were restricted due to the presence of the prolific Kevin Keegan and John Toshack. Shankly's successor Bob Paisley, however, had other plans for Kennedy. Giving him the Number 5 shirt, Paisley converted the burly striker into a cultured attacking midfield player, based on the left flank, and Kennedy flourished in this role for the rest of the decade, also winning his first of 17 caps for England in this position. He never played as an orthodox centre forward again.

With Liverpool, Kennedy won the League title and UEFA Cup in 1976, scoring in the final of the latter, and came close to equalling his "double" achievements with Arsenal when in 1977 Liverpool ventured to Wembley for the FA Cup final having already regained their title. Victory over Manchester United would have enabled Kennedy to become the first player to win the "double" with two different clubs, but Liverpool lost the game 2-1. Kennedy nearly forced extra-time in the last minute when his long-range shot hit the crossbar.

With dreams of the traditional "double" gone, Liverpool went to Rome to contest their first European Cup final against Borussia Monchengladbach and won the game 3-1, earning Kennedy his third European honour. Kennedy and Liverpool retained the trophy the following year and again in 1981, while also winning the League twice more and their first League Cup.

After the emergence of young midfielder Ronnie Whelan in 1982, Kennedy left Liverpool (having played enough games to guarantee a final title medal) to join the renaissance of Swansea City under his former team-mate Toshack, who had previously recruited fellow Liverpool legends Tommy Smith and Ian Callaghan.

Kennedy's spell at Swansea ended acrimoniously, with Toshack accusing Kennedy publicly of not trying, when the truth was that Parkinson's Disease was setting in. Kennedy tried to resume his career in his native north-east at Hartlepool United but his condition worsened and he was forced to retire in 1984 just before his 33rd birthday. His condition was finally confirmed by a specialist when he was 35.

Kennedy's only work in football after he finished playing was a brief spell at Sunderland as a coach. He has spent the majority of life since retirement and diagnosis working towards publicising and raising funds for the research and treatment of Parkinson's. Arsenal and Liverpool played each other in a testimonial game in 1991 to raise money for the cause.

Appendix

∞

B

30th March, venue, at home versus Dallas, result loss for Vancouver 1-2 after a penalty shootout. Kevin Hector scoring only goal. Attendance 24,850.

Teams.
Vancouver:-
Parkes, Bolitho, Craven, Kenyon, McNab, Lenarduzzi R, Sammels, Lewington, Hector, Whymark, Johnston, Valentine (sub).

Dallas:-
Manager Al Miller(USA). Scorer Zequinha.
Stepney (England), Gano (Argentina), Pecher (USA), Myernick (USA), Ley (England), Ryan (Scotland), Simoes (Portugal) Kewley (England), Zequinha (Brazil), Milton (Brazil), Milton (Brazil), Wilson (USA) (sub), Secchi (Brazil) (sub), Gomez (Argentina).

6th April, venue at home versus Edmonton, result win for Vancouver 2-0. Craven and Hector scorers. Attendance 18,097.

Teams.
Vancouver:-
Parkes, Bolitho, Craven, McNab, Lenarduzzi R, Sammels, Lewington, Hector, Whymark, Johnston, Daniel, Valentine (sub).

Edmonton:-
Manager Hans Kraay (Holland)
Endeman (Holland), Manzini (Canada), Lodeweges (Canada/Holland), Klinkenberg (Holland) Atuegbu (Nigeria), Kraay (jnr) (Holland), Leifsson (Iceland), Ban (Yugoslavia), Atack (Enland/USA) (sub), Turudija (Yugoslavia), Goossens (Holland).

Arsenal to Armenia

14th April venue away versus Chicago at Wrigley/Soldier Fields, result won 3-2 after penalty shoot out. Scorers Sammels, Hector. Attendance 10,130.

Teams
Vancouver.
Parkes, Bolitho, Craven, Kenyon, Lenarduzzi. R.(sub), Sammels, Lewington, Hector, Whymark, Johnston, Valentine (sub), Daniel, Lenarduzzi.D,(sub), Parsons.

Chicago.
Manager Willy Roy (W. Germany/USA). Scorers Crantiza, Van Hanegem.
Mahoney(England), Spalding (Scotland), Long(Zaire/USA) (sub), Griffiths (Wales), Skala (W. Germany), Wilson (Canada), Strenicer (Hungary/Canada),Grantiza (W. Germany), Kristensen (Denmark), Acocatt (Holland), Van Hanegem (Holland), Ressel (Holland).

21st April, venue at home versus Portland, result won 2-1, scorers Whymark 2. Attendance 23,137.

Teams
Vancouver.
Parkes, Bolitho, Lenarduzzi.R, Sammels, Lewington, Hector, Whymark, Johnston, Daniels, Parsons, Valentine.

Portland.
Manger Don Megson (England). Scorer Bain
Poole (England), Day (England), Toomey (USA) (sub), Stanley (Canada), Bain (Scotland) Scullion (Scotland), Conway (Ireland), Best (Bermuda), Grant (Canada), Seale (Barbados), Charles (England), Thompson (England), Butler (England) (sub).

27th April, venue away versus San Diego, at San Diego Stadium, result lost 0-1. Attendance 10,514.

Teams
Vancouver.
Parkes, Bolitho, Lenarduzzi.R, Sammels, Lewington, Hector, Whymark, Johnston, Valentine ,Daniels, Lenarduzzi.D, (sub), Parsons, Possee (sub)

San Diego

Dennis Loze

Manager Hurbert Vogelsinger (Austria/USA), Scorer Nover. Mayer (Scotland), Wieczorkowski (W. Germany), Veee (Hungary/USA), McCall (Scotland), Willrich (W. Germany), Heck (W.Germany), Liotart (USA), Cuellar (Mexico).

2nd May, venue home versus San Diego, result won 3-1, scorers Hector 2, Whymark. Attendance 16,985.
Teams
Vancouver
Parkes, Bolitho, Craven, Lenarduzzi.R, Sammels, Lewington, Hector, Whymark, Johnston, Valentine, Daniels.

San Diego
Scorer Nover.
Mayer, Nover, Donnelly, Dogancic (Yugoslavia), Wieczopkowski, Veee, Orthan (Cyprus), Armstrong (Northern Ireland) (sub), Willrich, Heck, Liotart (sub), Cuellar.

5th May venue away to San Jose at Spartan Stadium result won 2-1, scorers Hector, Daniels. Attendance 14,107.
Teams
Vancouver.
Parkes, Bolitho, Craven, Lenarduzzi, R.Sammels, Lewington, Hector, Whymark, Johnston, Valentine, Daniels.

San Jose
Manager Terry Fisher (USA). Scorer Gersdorff.
Hewitt (Scotland), Cryns (W. Germany), Bick (USA), Versen (W. Germany), Etterich (W. Germany) (sub)Gersdorff (W.Germany), Ryan (USA), Jensen (Denmark) (sub), Lawson (Liberia/USA), Webers (W.Germany)

11th May venue home to Rochester, result won 1-0 in over time, scorer Valentine. Attendance 22,078.
Teams
Vancouver.
Parkes, Bolitho, Kenyon, Lenarduzzi.R, Sammels, Lewington, Hector Whymark, Johnston, Valentine, Daniel.

Rochester
Manager Dragan Popovic (Yugoslavia)

Arsenal to Armenia

Messing (USA), D'Errico (USA), Fazlic (Yugoslavia), Reynolds(USA) (sub), Mijatovic (Yugoslavia), Cila (Brazil), Sutevski (Yugoslavia), Ercoli (Canada), Stojanovic (Yugoslavia), Pollihan (USA), Silva (Portugal) Grgurek(Yugoslavia/USA).

18th May venue at home versus Philadelphia, result won 2-0, scorers Hector, Whymark. Attendance 18,293.
Teams
Vancouver.
Parkes, Bolitho, Kenyon, Lenarduzzi.R, Sammels, Lewington, Hector, Whymark, Johnston, Valentine, Daniel, Posse (sub).

Philadelphia
Manager Marko Valok (Yugoslavia)
Van Eron (USA), Cyrder (USA), Nikolic (Yugoslavia), Dempsey (England/Ireland), Martinovic (Yugoslavia), Glavin (Scotland), Lukic (Yugoslavia, Djordjevic (Yugoslavia) (sub), Robb (Scotland), Redfern (England), O'Brian (Ireland), Ball (England), Worthington (England).

30th May venue away versus Edmonton, at Commonwealth Stadium. Result won 3-1 scorers Hector 3. Attendance 10,529.
Teams
Vancouver
Parkes, Bolitho, Kenyon, Lenarduzzi. R, Sammels, Lewington, Hector, Whymark, Johnston, Valentine, Daniel, Parsons (sub)

Edmonton   Scorer Kraay (Jnr)
Endeman (Holland), Lodeweges (Canada/Holland), Atugbu (Nigeria), Legfsson (Iceland), Atack (England/USA), Turudija (Yugoslavia), Goossens (Holland), Evans (Guyana/USA), Anton (USA), Hikes (Holland/W.Germany) (sub), Schoemaker (Holland), Ouwehand (Holland).

2nd June venue home versus Houston, result lost 0-1. Attendance 26,013.
Teams
Vancouver
Parkes, Bolitho, Kenyon, Lenarduzzi R, Sammels, Lewington, Hector, Whymark, Johnston, Valentine, Daniel, Parsons (sub)

Houston

Dennis Loze

Manager Timo Liekoski (Finland). Scorer Marasco.
Hammond (England), Anderson (Scotland), Jump (England), O'Sullivan (USA), Manzo (Mexico), Schuberth (W. Germany) (sub), Charbonneau (USA), Morales (Uruguay), Marasco (Argentina).

7th **June** venue away versus Tulsa at Skelly Stadium, result won 2-1 scorers Lewington, Sammels. Attendance 10,102.
Teams
Vancouver
Parkes, Bolitho, Kenyon, Lenarduzzi R, Sammels, Lewington, Hector, Whymark, Johnston, Valentine, Daniel.

Tulsa
Manager Alan Hinton (England). Scorer Abrahams.
Boulton (England), Daracott (England), Chapman (England), Nish (England) (sub), Hughes (England), Danaiford (Iran), Earle (England), Woodward (England), Sautter ((USA), Abrahams (England), Skotarek (W.Germany/USA) (sub), Ryan (W. Germany/USA), Powell (Enland), O'Riordan (Ireland).

9th **June** venue away versus Minnesota at Metropolitan Stadium, Bloomington, result lost 0-1. Attendance 24,061.
Teams
Vancouver
Parkes, Bolitho, Kenyon, Lenarduzzi R, Sammels, Lewington, Hector, Whymark, Johnston, Valentine, Daniel, Parsons (sub), Possee (sub)

Minnesota
Manager Roy McCrohan (England) Scorer Futcher
Gross (W. Germany) Litt (England), Merrick (England), Merrick (England), Vogel (USA), Ntsoelengoe (S. Africa), Nordquest (Sweden), Willey (USA), Alonso (Argentina) (sub), Want (England), Moran (USA), Futcher (England), Morgan (Scotland), West (England).

13th **June** venue away versus California at Anaheim Stadium, result lost 3-2 penalty shootout. Scorers Hector, Possee. Attendance 7,182.
Teams
Vancouver

Arsenal to Armenia

Parkes, Bolitho, Lenarduzzi R, Sammels, Lewington, Hector, Whymark (sub), Johnston, Valentine, Daniel, Lenarduzzi D (sub), Parsons, Possee.

California
Manager John Sewell (England) scorer Ingram 2.
Mahoney (England), Jokerst (USA) (sub), Clarke (USA), Wall (England), Barrett (England), Suhnholz (W. Germany), David (Trinidad) (sub), Huson (Channel Isles), McBride (Kenya/England), Cahill (England), Lindsey (England), Cohen (S. Africa) (sub)
Ingram (England).

16th June venue home versus New York, result won 4-1, scorers Sammels, Hector, Valentine, Possee. Attendance 32,372.
Teams
Vancouver
Parkes, Craven, Lenarduzzi R, Sammels, Lewington, Hector, Whymark (sub), Johnston, Valentine, Daniel, Parsons, Possee.

New York
Manager Eddie Firmani (S. Africa/Italy) scorer Chinaglia.
Brand (W. Germany/Canada), Alberto (Brazil), Formoso (Spain/USA), Garbett (England), Davis (USA), Chinaglia (Italy), Tueart (England), Rijsbergen (Holland), Bandov (Yugoslavia) (sub), Smith (USA), Carbalani (Argentina), Etherington (England/USA), Liveric (Yugoslavia/USA), Moraic (Brazil) (sub).

24th June venue home versus California, result won 2-1 in over time, scorers Johnston, Ball. Attendance 20,814.
Ballys' first game.
Team
Vancouver
Parkes, Bolitho, Sammels, Lewington, Hector, Whymark, Johnston, Valentine (sub), Daniel, Lenarduzzi D (sub), Parsons, Possee, Ball.

California
Jokerest (USA), Clarke (USA), Barrett (England), Krauthausen (W. Germany) (sub), Sohnholz (W. Germany), Allen (Channel

Isles), David (Trinidad), Huson (Channel Isles) (sub), McBride (Kenya/England), Cahill (England), Lindsey (England), Cohen (S. Africa).

27th June venue away versus Atlanta at Fulton County Stadium, result won 3-1, scorers Hector 2, Ball. Attendance 5,152.
Teams
Vancouver
Parkes, Bolitho (sub), Lenarduzzi R, Sammels, Hector, Whymark, Valentine, Daniel, Parsons, Possee, Ball.

Atlanta
Manager Dan Woods (USA). Scorer Roberts.
Noqueira (Mozambique), Lichaba (S. Africa), McMahon (Scotland) (sub), Strong (USA), Brooks (England), Nanchoff (Yugoslavia/USA), Sono (S.Africa), Bourne (England), Roberts (England), Balson (England), Makowski (USA), Dewslip (England).

30th June venue away versus Fort Lauderdale at Lockhart Stadium, result lost 3-2 in penalty shootout. Scorers Whymark, Possee. Attendance 15,259.
Teams
Vancouver
Parkes, Bolitho (sub), Lenarduzzi R, Sammels, Lewington, Hector, Whymark, Johnston, Valentine (sub), Daniel, Parsons, Possee, Ball.

Fort Lauderdale
Manager Ron Newman England. Scorers Cubillas, Walker.
Mausser (USA), Whelan (England), Whittle (England), Hudson (England), Park (England), Germeri (Yugoslavia/Canada), Cubillas (Peru) Bodonczy (Chile/USA) (sub), Nije (USA) (sub), Fowles (Jamaica/USA)(sub) Irving (England), Muller (W. Germany), Walter (England), Stanley (England).

4th July venue away versus Toronto at Exhibition Stadium, result lost 2-1, scorer Valentine. Attendance 13,754.
Teams
Vancouver.

Parkes, Bolitho (sub), Lenarduzzi R, Sammels, Lewington, Hector, Whymark, Johnston, Valentine, Lenarduzzi D, (sub), Parsons, Possee, Ball.

Toronto.
Manager Keith Eddy (England), Scorer Lorimer, Lukacevic.
Tamindzic (Yugoslavia), Franks (England), McVie (Scotland), Mitchell (Scotland), Ferreira (Brazil), Gibbs (England), Lorimer (Scotland), Busby (Scotland), Bone (Scotland), Lukacevic (Yugoslavia) Lenarduzzi S, (Canada).

7th **July** venue home versus Seattle, result won 3-1, scorers Ball 2, Whymark. Attendance 20,041.
Teams
Vancouver.
Parkes, Bolitho (sub), Lenarduzzi R, Sammels, Lewington, Hector, Valentine, Daniel, Parsons, Possee, Ball.

Seattle
Manager Jim Gabriel (Scotland). Scorer Ryan.
Ivanow (China/USA), Webster (England), Barton (England), Hudson (England), Ryan (England), Smethurst (S.Africa), Bridge (Canada), Ord (England), Davies (Wales), Impey (England), Neighbour (England), Miller (Canada) (sub).

11th **July** venue home versus Los Angeles, result lost 1-0. Attendance 28,764.
Teams
Vancouver
Parkes, Bolitho (sub), Lenarduzzi R, Sammels, Lewington, Hector, Whymark, Johnston, Valentine (sub), Daniel, Parsons, Possee, Ball.

Los Angeles
Manager Rinus Michels (Holland), Scorer Cruyff.
Boulton (England), Keri (Yugoslavia), McGrane (Scotland/Canada), Sibbald (England), Rongen (Holland), Dangerfield (England), Wagner (W. Germany) (sub), Hulcer (USA), VanVeen (Holland), Cruyff (Holland), Galindo (Mexico), Suurbier (Holland).

15th July venue away versus New York at Giants Stadium, result won 4-2, scorers o.g., Lenarduzzi R, Sammels, Lewington, Hector,
Teams
Vancouver
Parkes, Craven (sub), Lenarduzzi R, Sammels, Lewington, Hector, Whymark, Johnston, Valentine (sub), Daniel, Parsons, Possee, Ball.

New York
Manager Ray Klivecka (Lithuania/USA), scorers Chinaglia, Neeskens.
Yasin (Turkey), Eskandarian (Iran), Alberto (Brazil), Beckebauer (W. Germany), Formoso (Spain/USA) (sub), Davis (USA), Seninho (Angola/Portugal), Chinaglia (Italy), Tueart (England), Rijsbergen (Holland), Carbognani (Argentina) (sub), Liveric (Yugoslavia/USA) (sub), Neeskens (Holland), Ryan (W. Geramany/USA).

18th July venue away versus Washington at Robert F Kennedy Stadium, result lost 2-1, scorer Ball. Attendance 12,321.
Teams
Vancouver
Parkes, Craven (sub), Lenarduzzi R, Sammels, Lewington, Hector, Whymark, Johnston, Valentine (sub), Daniel, Parsons, Possee, Ball

Washington
Manager Gordon Bradley (England) scorers Droege, Askew.
Irwin (N. Ireland), Iarusci (Canada), Droege (USA), Dillon (England), O´Hara (Scotland)
Steels (Scotland), Horvath (Hungary), Stokes (England), Askew (USA), Cannell (England, Mokgojoa (S. Africa) (sub), Marcantonio (Scotland/Canada).

21st July venue home versus Toronto result won 3-0, scorers Sammels Whymark, Ball. Attendance 21,409.
Teams
Vancouver
Parkes, Bolitho, Lenarduzzi R, Sammels, Lewington, Whymark, Johnston, Valentine, Daniel, Parsons, Ball, Nesin (sub).

Arsenal to Armenia

Manger Keith Eddy (England)
Tamindzic (Yugoslavia), Roe (England), Franks (England), McVie (Scotland), Mitchell (Scotland), Gibbs, (England), Calvert (England), Lorimer (Scotland), Busby (Scotland), Bone (Scotland), Lukacevic (Yugoslavia), Arbondanza (Italy) Sub).

25th July venue home versus Tulsa, result won 1-0 scorer Whymark. Attendance 21,196.
Teams
Vancouver
Parkes, Bolitho, Lenarduzzi R, Sammels, Lewington, Whymark, Johnston, Valentine, Daniel, Parsons, Ball.

Tulsa
Brand (W. Germany/Canada), Daracott (England), Chapman (England), Nish (England), Hughes (England), Danaiford (Iran), Earle (England), Davies (England), Skotarek (W. Germany/USA) Powell (England), O'Riordan (N. Ireland) Villa (USA) (sub).

28th July venue away versus Portland, result won 3-2 in overtime, scorers Lenarduzzi R, Whymark, Ball. Attendance 12,727.
Teams
Vancouver.
Parkes, Bolitho, craven, Lenarduzzi, Sammels, Lewington, Whymark, Johnston, Valentine, Daniel, Parsons(sub), Ball.

Portland
Manger Don Megson (England). Scorers Mitchell 2.
Poole (England), Day (England), Bain (Scotland), Conway (Ireland), Best (Bermuda), Anderson (England), Seale (Barbados) (sub), Charles (England), Thompson (England), Butler (England), Grant (Canada) (sub), Ayre (Canada), Mitchell (Canada).

1st August venue home versus Minnesota, result won 1-0, scorer Lenarduzzi R. Attendance 24,656.
Teams
Vancouver.
Parkes, Bolitho, Craven, Lenarduzzi R, Sammels, Lewington, Valentine, Daniel, Parsons, Possee, Ball.

Minnesota
Manager Roy McCrohan.
Lettieri (Italy/Canada), Litt (England), Merrick (England), Twellman (USA) (sub), Nordgvist (S. Africa), Willey (England), Want (England), McLenaghen (Canada), Moran (USA) (sub), Futcher (England), West (England).

4th August venue away versus Los Angeles at Rose Bowl, Pasadena, result lost 2-0. Attendance 11,157.
Team
Vancouver.
Grobbelaar (Zimbabwe), Bolitho, Kenyon, Lenarduzzi R, Sammels, Lewington, Valentine, Parsons, Possee, Ball.

Los Angeles
Manager Rinus Michels Scorers Cruyff, Dangerfield.
Boulton (England), Shelton (USA), Keri (Yugoslavia), McGrane (Scotland/Canada), Sibbald (England), Rongen (Holland), Smeets (Holland), Van Ween (Holland), Cruyff (Holland), Galindo (Mexico), Milander (USA) (sub).

8th August venue home versus San Jose, result won 1-0 in overtime. Scorer Whymark. Attendance 25,731.
Teams
Vancouver
Parkes, Bolitho, Craven, Kenyon, Lenarduzzi R, Sammels, Lewington, Hector, Whymark, Johnston, Parsons (sub), Possee (sub), Ball, Shearer (sub).

San Jose
Manager Peter Stubbe (W. Germany).
Hewitt (Scotland), Cryns (W. Germany), Bick (USA), Versen (W. Germany), Etterich (W. Germany), Gersdorff (W. Germany), Child (England), Rowlands (England), Wood (England), Armstrong (N. Ireland).

11th August venue away, versus Seattle at The Kingdome, result won 2-1, scorers Parsons, Ball. Attendance 24,196.
Teams
Vancouver.

Parkes, Bolitho, Craven, Lenarduzzi R, Lewington, Johnston, Valentine, Daniel, Parsons, Possee, Ball, Nesins(sub), Shearer (sub).

Seattle
Manager Jim Gabriel (Scotland).
Ivanhoe (China/USA), England (Wales), Barton (England) (sub), Ryan (England), Buttle (England), Cave (England), Smethurst (S. Africa), Bridge (Canada), Ord (England), Krueger (USA), Davies (Wales) (sub), Neighbour.

Play Offs

15th **August** venue away versus Dallas at Ownby Stadium, result won 3-2 scorers Lewington, Hector, Parsons. Attendance 8,829.
Teams
Vancouver.
Parkes, Bolitho, Craven, Lenarduzzi R, Lewington, Hector, Johnston, Valentine, Daniel, Parsons, Possee (sub), Ball, Shearer (sub)

Dallas
Manger Al Miller (USA) Scorers Zewley, Zequinha.
Stepney (England), Gano (Argentina), Pecher (USA), Ley (England), Ryan (Scotland) (sub), Kewley (England) (sub), Zequinha (Brazil), Gomez (Argentina), Lippins (W. Germany) Trinklen (W. Germany), Billinger (USA), Rausch (W. Germany), Lund (Denmark).

18th **August** venue home versus Dallas, won 2-1, scorer Craven 2. Attendance 30,328.
Teams
Vancouver.
Parkes, Bolitho, Craven, Kenyon, Lenarduzzi R, Lewington, Hector, Whymark, Johnston, Daniel (sub), Ball, Nesins (sub)

Dallas.
Stepney, Gano, Ryan, Kewley (sub), Zequinha, Gomez, Lippins, Trinklen, Bellinger, Rausch, Lund.

22th **August** venue away versus Los Angeles, result lost 3-2 after penalty shootout. Scorers Valentine 2. Attendance 21,231
Teams
Vancouver.
Parkes, Bolitho, Craven, Kenyon, Lenarduzzi R, Lewington, Hector, Whymark, Johnston, Valentine, Daniel (sub), Ball.

Los Angeles
Scorer Sibbald, Smeets.
Boulton (England), Shelton (USA), Keri (Yugoslavia), McGrane (Scotland/Canada), Sibbald (England), Dangerfield (England), Smeets (Holland) (sub), Wagner (W. Germany), Hulcer (USA), Van Veen (Holland), Cruyff (Holland), Galindo (Mexico), Morrison (USA), Suurbier (Holland).

25th **August** venue home versus Los Angeles, result won 1-0, scorer o.g. Mini game won 1-0 scorer Hector. Attendance 32, 375.
Team
Vancouver.
Parkes, Craven, Kenyon, Lenarduzzi R, Lewington, Hector, Johnston, Valentine, Whymark, Parsons, Ball.

Los Angeles.
Boulton, Shelton, Keri, McGrane, Sibbald, Dangerfield, Smeets Hulcer, Suurbier, Cruyff, Galindo, Wagner (sub).

29th **August** venue home, versus New York, result won 2-0, scorers Whymark, Johnston. Attendance 32, 875.
Team
Vancouver.
Parkes, Bolitho (sub), Craven, Kenyon, Lennarduzzi R, Lewington, Hector Whymark, Johnston, Valentine, Parsons, Ball

New York
Birkenmeier (W. Germany), Eskandarian (Iran), Alberto (Brazil), Beck (W. Germany), Marinho (Brazil), Bogicevic (Yugoslavia), Davis (USA), Seninho (Angola/Portugal), Chinaglia (Italy), Tueart (England) Liveric (Yugoslavia) (sub), Morais (Brazil), Ryan (W. Germany/USA)

Arsenal to Armenia

1st September venue away, versus New York at Giants Stadium, result lost 3-2 in penalty shootout. Won 1-0 in penalty shootout. Scorers (1st game) Craven, Johnston. (2nd game) Shoot out. Attendance 44,109.

Teams
Vancouver
1st Game
Parkes, Bolitho (sub),Craven, Kenyon, Lennarduzzi R, Sammels (sub), Lewington, Whymark, Valentine, Parsons, Possee (sub), Ball.
2nd Game
Parkes, Bolitho, Craven, Kenyon, Lenarduzzi R, Sammels, Hector, Johnston, Valentine, Possee, Ball

---

New York
Scorer 1st Game Chinaglia 2.
1st Game
Birkenmeier, Beck, Garbett (sub), Marinho, Bogicevic, Davis, Seninho, Chinaglia, Tueart, Rijsbergen, Bandov (sub) Liveric (sub), Morais, Neeskens.
2nd Game
Same line up.

Final

8th September venue New York, versus Tampa Bay, result won 2-1 scorer Whymark Attendance 50,699

Teams
Vancouver.
Parkes, Bolitho (sub), Craven, Kenyon, Lenarduzzi R, Hector Lewington, Whymark, Johnston, Valentine, Parsons, Ball.

Tamba Bay
Manager Gordon Jago (England). Scorer Van der Veen.

Bilecki (Yugoslavia/Canada), Gorman (Scotland), Connell (S. Africa), McLeod (Canada), Van der Veen (Holland), Baralic (Yugoslavia) (sub), Wegerle (S. Africa), Marsh (England), Fabbiani (Argentina/Chile), Andruzewski (England), Crnja (Yugoslavia) (sub), Anderson (England).

BIBLIOGRAPHY AND RESEARCH

Playing Extra Time
  Alan Ball
The Working Man's Ballet
  Alan Hudson
Boots Balls and Haircuts
  Hunter Davies
The Official Illustrated History of Arsenal
  Phil Soar and Martin Tyler
Super Mac
  Malcolm MacDonald
Proud Preston
  Ian Rigby and Mike Payne
NASL. A Complete Record of the North American League
  Colin Jose
Game of Two Halves
  Tim Glynne – Jones
Fever Pitch
  Nick Hornby
England Number Ones
  Dean Hayes
Arsenal – Rough Guide
  Roughguides.com
1979 Official North American Soccer League Guide
  NASL
The Argyle Book
  Tony Guswell and Chris Robinson
The Crossing Place A journey among the Armenians
  Philip Marsden
Armenia and Armenians in the World
  Grigor Avagian
The Armenian Genocide
  Nikolay Hovhannisyan
Western Morning News
Leatherhead Advertiser
Vancouver Sun

Evening Herald
Sunday Independent
Lancashire Evening Post
FA Review
Athletics Weekly
Football Programmes
DVD's Whitecaps games
Athletics Weekly

ISBN 1425170765

9 781425 170769

Dennis Loze

Manager Timo Liekoski (Finland). Scorer Marasco.
Hammond (England), Anderson (Scotland), Jump (England), O'Sullivan (USA), Manzo (Mexico), Schuberth (W. Germany) (sub), Charbonneau (USA), Morales (Uruguay), Marasco (Argentina).

7th **June** venue away versus Tulsa at Skelly Stadium, result won 2-1 scorers Lewington, Sammels. Attendance 10,102.
Teams
Vancouver
Parkes, Bolitho, Kenyon, Lenarduzzi R, Sammels, Lewington, Hector, Whymark, Johnston, Valentine, Daniel.

Tulsa
Manager Alan Hinton (England). Scorer Abrahams.
Boulton (England), Daracott (England), Chapman (England),Nish (England) (sub), Hughes (England), Danaiford (Iran), Earle (England), Woodward (England), Sautter ((USA), Abrahams (England), Skotarek (W.Germany/USA) (sub), Ryan (W. Germany/USA), Powell (Enland), O'Riordan (Ireland).

9th **June** venue away versus Minnesota at Metropolitan Stadium, Bloomington, result lost 0-1. Attendance 24,061.
Teams
Vancouver
Parkes, Bolitho, Kenyon, Lenarduzzi R, Sammels, Lewington, Hector, Whymark, Johnston, Valentine, Daniel, Parsons (sub), Possee (sub)

Minnesota
Manager Roy McCrohan (England) Scorer Futcher
Gross (W. Germany) Litt (England), Merrick (England), Merrick (England), Vogel (USA), Ntsoelengoe (S. Africa), Nordquest (Sweden), Willey (USA), Alonso (Argentina) (sub), Want (England), Moran (USA), Futcher (England), Morgan (Scotland), West (England).

13th **June** venue away versus California at Anaheim Stadium, result lost 3-2 penalty shootout. Scorers Hector, Possee. Attendance 7,182.
Teams
Vancouver

Messing (USA), D'Errico (USA), Fazlic (Yugoslavia), Reynolds(USA) (sub), Mijatovic (Yugoslavia), Cila (Brazil), Sutevski (Yugoslavia), Ercoli (Canada), Stojanovic (Yugoslavia), Pollihan (USA), Silva (Portugal) Grgurek(Yugoslavia/USA).

18th May venue at home versus Philadelphia, result won 2-0, scorers Hector, Whymark. Attendance 18,293.
Teams
Vancouver.
Parkes, Bolitho, Kenyon, Lenarduzzi.R, Sammels, Lewington, Hector, Whymark, Johnston, Valentine, Daniel, Posse (sub).

Philadelphia
Manager Marko Valok (Yugoslavia)
Van Eron (USA), Cyrder (USA), Nikolic (Yugoslavia), Dempsey (England/Ireland), Martinovic (Yugoslavia), Glavin (Scotland), Lukic (Yugoslavia, Djordjevic (Yugoslavia) (sub), Robb (Scotland), Redfern (England), O'Brian (Ireland), Ball (England), Worthington (England).

30th May venue away versus Edmonton, at Commonwealth Stadium. Result won 3-1 scorers Hector 3. Attendance 10,529.
Teams
Vancouver
Parkes, Bolitho, Kenyon, Lenarduzzi. R, Sammels, Lewington, Hector, Whymark, Johnston, Valentine, Daniel, Parsons (sub)

Edmonton   Scorer Kraay (Jnr)
Endeman (Holland), Lodeweges (Canada/Holland), Atugbu (Nigeria), Legfsson (Iceland), Atack (England/USA), Turudija (Yugoslavia), Goossens (Holland), Evans (Guyana/USA), Anton (USA), Hikes (Holland/W.Germany) (sub), Schoemaker (Holland), Ouwehand (Holland).

2nd June venue home versus Houston, result lost 0-1. Attendance 26,013.
Teams
Vancouver
Parkes, Bolitho, Kenyon, Lenarduzzi R, Sammels, Lewington, Hector, Whymark, Johnston, Valentine, Daniel, Parsons (sub)

Houston